JUSTICE, RIGHTS, AND TORT LAW

# JUSTICE, RIGHTS, AND TORT LAW

Edited by

MICHAEL D. BAYLES

and

BRUCE CHAPMAN

*Westminster Institute for Ethics and Human Values*
*London, Canada*

Reprinted from
*Law and Philosophy*, Vol. 1 No. 3 and Vol. 2 No. 1

D. REIDEL PUBLISHING COMPANY

DORDRECHT / BOSTON

ISBN 90–277–1639–0



Printed in The Netherlands

## TABLE OF CONTENTS

# PREFACE

The essays in this volume are the result of a project on Values in Tort Law directed by the Westminster Institute for Ethics and Human Values. We are indebted to the Board of Westminster College for its financial support.

The project involved two meetings of a mixed group of lawyers and philosophers to discuss drafts of papers and general issues in tort law. Beyond the principal researchers, whose papers appear here, we are grateful to John Borgo, Dick Bronaugh, Craig Brown, Earl Cherniak, Bruce Feldthusen, Barry Hoffmaster and Steve Sharzer for their helpful discussion, and to Nancy Margolis for copy editing.

All of these papers except one have appeared before in the journal *Law and Philosophy* (Vol. 1 No. 3, December 1982 and Vol. 2 No. 1, April 1983). Chapman's paper which was previously published in *The University of Western Ontario Law Review* (Vol. 20 No. 1, 1982) appears here with permission.

*Westminster Institute for Ethics and Human Values,* M. D. B.
*Westminster College, London, Canada* B. C.

# INTRODUCTION

The law of torts is society's primary mechanism for resolving disputes arising from personal injury and property damage. Although most disputes, such as those from automobile accidents, do not involve litigation and are settled out of court, the principles underlying such settlements rest upon tort law. During the last decade or two, tort law has been subject to significant criticism and analysis by legal philosophers and scholars. No-fault automobile insurance developed as a response to dissatisfaction with the tort law mechanism for handling compensation. However, legal scholars have not had much success in developing a coherent and comprehensive moral theory to justify the extant common law tort system.

To understand the difficulties in developing a moral justification of tort law, one needs an overall view of that complex system. All successful tort actions involve the four following general elements.

1. The defendant had a duty to the plaintiff.
2. The defendant violated that duty.
3. The defendant's violation causally affected the plaintiff.
4. As a result, the plaintiff suffered damages.

The explanation and justification of these elements, both separately and together, across the broad spectrum of tort law creates the difficulties in developing a comprehensive moral theory of tort law.

Traditionally, torts are divided into three categories, primarily depending upon what is necessary for a defendant to violate a duty. One category comprises intentional torts such as assault, battery, false imprisonment, infliction of mental suffering, trespass, and conversion of property. This category is called intentional torts because the defendant must have intended to perform a prohibited act, usually including the harm involved, such as imprisonment or conversion of property. Intentional torts have not generated the major problems for theorists.

The second category of torts is negligence. In negligence, the defendant need not have intended the harm but only have been careless as to its occurrence or failed to take adequate precautions to prevent it. This category is perhaps the largest, including as it does all forms of negligently caused accidents, whether automobile collisions, falls on icy sidewalks, fires, or others. A major problem confronting moral theorists trying to justify tort law is the objective standard of negligence. That standard is what a reasonably prudent person would have done to avoid the accident. It does not ask whether the defendant was mentally capable of complying with that standard. Defendants cannot succesfully argue that they did the best of which they were capable if that was less than what reasonably prudent persons would have done. Consequently, defendants need not be morally culpable. Morally, it is generally held that 'ought' implies 'can', that if persons cannot perform acts, they have no duty to perform them and are not responsible for failing to do so.

The third category of torts, that of strict liability, goes even further than the objective standard of negligence in denying moral culpability. In strict liability, to violate a duty a person need only have acted voluntarily, as opposed to have behaved by mere reflex. Even the reasonably prudent person may be strictly liable despite having taken all reasonable precautions. Strict liability torts pertain to abnormally dangerous things and activities, such as blasting, and to commercial products, such as contaminated food, exploding pop bottles, and defective lawn mowers.

The three categories of torts thus set different standards for a defendant having violated a duty to a plaintiff. In intentional torts, a defendant must have intended the consequence. In negligence, a defendant need only have been objectively careless as to its occurrence. And in strict liability, a defendant need only have committed a voluntary act that caused the damage. Due to this variety of standards for violating a duty, it is difficult to develop a moral theory to justify all torts.

## JUSTIFYING AIMS AND DISTRIBUTION OF LOSSES

The justification of tort law involves answering several questions, not a single one; although the answer to one may have implications for answers to the others, it need not imply a full answer.[1] The first question is: What is the general justifying aim of tort law? Three classical answers have been given to this question: retribution, compensation, and deterrence. The retributive view is that the tort law system is to make people pay for culpable wrongdoing. The compensation view is that tort law is to compensate innocent persons for damages caused by others. The deterrence view is that the justifying aim is to deter people from conduct causing accidents and damage. (These aims are discussed in more detail below.)

Three other questions are concerned with the distribution of losses. First, who pays? The answer to this question primarily depends upon the first two or perhaps three elements of a tort action. Who pays depends upon what duties there are, what constitutes a violation of those duties, and what constitutes causing damage. The people subject to tort law duties comprise a class of potential payers. The requirements for a violation of duties pick out a sub-class, namely, those who violate duties. Finally, the causal requirement picks out of the duty violators only those whose conduct results in damage. Second, who receives benefits (compensation)? The members of this class depend upon the scope of persons to whom duties are owed, whether a violation of a duty is a legal cause of damage, and what damages are compensable. Third, how much is paid or received? The answer here largely depends upon the interpretation of legal causation and damage, although it can also depend upon the scope of the duty. For example, a defendant can have a duty to a plaintiff, but that duty not extend to the damage or loss the plaintiff in fact incurs.

Each of the classical justifying aims of tort law takes an answer

---

1 Cf. H. L. A. Hart, *Punishment and Responsibility* (Oxford: Clarendon Press, 1968), pp. 4–13, for a similar analysis of criminal law.

to one of these questions of distribution as central. Retribution as a justifying aim emphasizes an answer to who should pay – culpable wrongdoers. Its answers to the other questions primarily follow from its answer to that question. Only victims of culpable wrongdoing receive payment, and only for damages for which defendants were culpably responsible. Obviously, retribution has difficulty justifying strict liability torts, for as noted above, in them defendants need not be morally culpable. It also has difficulty with the objective standard of negligence. Due to the objective standard, some negligence defendants are not morally culpable, because they have a moral excuse.

Compensation as a justifying aim emphasizes who should benefit, namely, innocent victims. It appears to be more plausible than retribution. After all, even in strict liability, the plaintiff has innocently suffered damage. However, strict liability torts present a problem with compensation as the justifying aim of tort law. In a strict liability case, the defendant has to pay regardless of fault. But then why should compensation be limited in other cases by the requirements of intent or negligence? If the aim is to compensate innocent plaintiffs, why should not all innocent plaintiffs be compensated whether or not their injurers acted negligently or intentionally? Indeed, if the aim is to compensate innocent persons for losses, why should one restrict compensation to losses caused by others? Society often compensates individuals for losses not caused by others, as in disaster relief programs for victims of floods and storms. The tort system seems a very imperfect method of compensating innocent persons for losses. A system of national accident insurance, much as New Zealand has and has been proposed in Australia, would better achieve compensation for all innocent victims.

The deterrence view emphasizes an answer to how much should be paid, namely, as little as possible to deter accidents while permitting beneficial activities. It appears to best explain the existing tort law system. Making people pay for damage they intentionally or negligently cause will deter them from activities or make them be more careful. It might appear that to adequately deter future violations, all persons who violate duties should pay regardless of whether they cause actual damage. The difficulty is that such a system might make people pay too much and thus overdeter. For example, if each violator were to pay the cost of the damages that usually followed the violation, then violators would pay for more than the actual cost of their beneficial activity. They would thus be deterred from beneficial activity with a net loss to society. One might develop a system whereby each violator paid only a proportionate share of the total damages caused by such violations, but it would be quite different from the extant tort system. Also, as Bruce Chapman argues in this volume, potential victims might not have appropriate incentives to avoid accidents. The deterrence view might appear to have difficulty justifying strict liability torts, but one can plausibly argue that it will deter some people from engaging in activities, and everyone from engaging in activities whose cost is greater than their benefit.

Nevertheless, the deterrence view seems to imply that people should not be allowed to insure against negligently caused damage, for that might decrease their incentive to be careful. Moreover, it cannot explain some of the defences in negligence law, such as contributory negligence being a bar to recovery or even comparative negligence, for with either the incentives to avoid accidents might not be the most efficient.[2] Moreover, in its currently popular economic interpretation, the deterrence view is subject to a number of other criticisms, some of which are brought out in the papers by George Fletcher and Ernest Weinrib in this volume.

In tort law, as in criminal law, it is perhaps unrealistic to expect that one justifying aim can explain and justify all of the features of the system. No one aim or value has such absolute priority as to justify its singleminded pursuit. The law of torts has developed via court decisions over centuries and reflects varying emphases and aims as people's conceptions of justice have changed. Although legal philosophers will no doubt continue to search for a single jus-

---

[2] Richard A. Posner, *Economic Analysis of Law,* 2d ed. (Boston: Little, Brown and Company, 1977), pp. 123–24.

tifying aim, such as corrective justice (discussed in the papers by Jules Coleman and Ernest Weinrib), the actual achievement of that goal does not appear likely. Nevertheless, the pursuit of a single justifying aim or theory can still be of considerable value, for it helps to bring system and coherence as well as to suggest possible directions for change and reform. The papers in this volume contribute to that exploration of the system as a whole and to analyses of particular aspects of it. The rest of this introduction attempts to locate the papers in this volume on the conceptual map of tort law and the endeavour to justify it.

## CHALLENGES TO A UNIFIED THEORY

Several papers develop difficulties confronted by any attempt to provide a unified theory of tort law. In his paper, Bruce Chapman examines difficulties with the retributive, compensatory, and deterrence views over a broader range of problems than those discussed above. He emphasizes difficulties in one theory alone accounting for the relevance of the causal condition as well as the defenses of contributory negligence and assumption of risk. In the end, he suggests that a retributive element may be necessary to justify a system allowing injured persons to hold specific individuals liable.

Several recent theories of tort law are criticized by Jules Coleman in the first part of his two part article. He rejects the retributive view for the sorts of reasons given above. As against the responsibility or strict liability theory recently espoused by Richard Epstein,[3] he argues that it is both too strong, including cases where one justifiably harms another, and too weak, excluding some cases of omissions – failures to act. He also rejects George Fletcher's theory of liability for nonreciprocal risk taking, because it does not adequately account for the causal element and does not provide an adequate moral basis.

---

[3] Richard A. Epstein, *A Theory of Strict Liability* (San Francisco, Calif.: Cato Institute, 1980).

In the second part of his article, Coleman puts forth his view of corrective justice as the annulment of unjust gains and losses. As far as a tort system does this, it corrects unjust departures from a given system of holdings. Coleman emphasizes the difference between the grounds or foundation of claims and the mode of rectification, that is, how unjust gains and losses are to be remedied. Tort law is merely one system for rectifying unjust gains and losses, one in which the party causing a loss or receiving a gain pays. A system of comprehensive accident insurance, as in New Zealand, is an alternative mode of rectification, at least for annulling wrongful losses. Moreover, the tort law method does not always involve a defendant who has an unjust gain with which to compensate the plaintiff. Consequently, as Coleman recognizes, this theory of corrective justice does not justify all the elements of tort law. Some elements may not be morally required but may be justifiable on other grounds, such as efficiency.

George Fletcher is also concerned with the possibility of synthesizing the various parts of tort law into one system. He emphasizes the differences between an *ex ante* and an *ex post* analysis of liability. An *ex ante* analysis considers the risks of injury at the time of the defendant's conduct, while an *ex post* analysis starts from the occurrence of damage and works back to the cause. Fletcher applies these two approaches to both negligence and strict liability tort law. Generally, *ex post* analysis has dominated negligence law, and *ex ante* analysis has dominated strict liability law. Fletcher notes that a uniform *ex ante* analysis would go a considerable way towards uniting the two parts, but in the end an *ex ante* analysis cannot account for the defenses of contributory and comparative negligence. This consequence might be expected, as an *ex ante* analysis is largely one of deterrence, and deterrence cannot justify these two defenses.

Both Coleman and Fletcher devote considerable attention to the case of *Vincent* v. *Lake Erie Transportation Co.*[4] In the case,

---

4 109 Minn. 456, 124 N.W. 221 (1910).

the plaintiff dock owner sued the owner of a freighter for damages resulting to his dock when the ship remained moored to it during a storm. As interpreted by Coleman and Fletcher, this case strikes at the very heart of tort law. They both consider the conduct of the ship captain to have been not merely excused, but justified. In the circumstances, the defendant had no duty not to moor at the dock. That is, the captain's conduct did not violate any duty; indeed, it would have been wrong for the dock owner to force the ship to sea. Even though the defendant did not violate any duty to the plaintiff, the court held the ship owner liable for the damage. This seems contrary to the first two elements of a tort case as elucidated. Coleman and Fletcher both propose possible solutions to this case.

An alternative is to hold that the case was wrongly decided. Some support for this view can be found in a similar Canadian case in which the plaintiff was denied recovery,[5] but in that case damages were claimed only on the grounds of negligence. Thus, it does not stand for the proposition that damages could not have been recovered on any grounds. Moreover, most people's basic feelings are that the defendant should have paid damages. Consequently, *Vincent* remains a central challenge to a unitifed theory of tort law.

## MORALITY AND NEGLIGENCE

If it is difficult to provide a comprehensive justifying theory of tort law, it might be easier to provide a theory for one branch, such as negligence law, and perhaps for other branches by assimilating them to negligence law. In his paper, Ernest Weinrib undertakes the former task. He reject's Coleman's account precisely because it does not justify the connection between plaintiff and defendant (mode of rectification) found in extant tort law. Weinrib takes that as a given to be justified. He contends that any account

---

[5] *Manor & Co. Ltd.* v. *M.V. 'Sir John Crosbie,'* 52 D.L.R.2d 48 (Nfld. 1965), affd. [1967] 1 Ex. 94.

of tort law must use an Aristotelian corrective justice framework of argument, one of restoring pre-existing equality between plaintiff and defendant. On this basis, he rejects the different views of Richard Posner and Charles Fried as both based on a distributive justice argument framework. But an Aristotelian corrective justice framework does not provide the principles of negligence law. For that, Weinrib turns to Kantian moral theory. The two central elements to be justified, he claims, are the use of the objective standard of negligence and the criterion of duty. The objective standard, he contends, can be justified by appeal to the Kantian argument that one could not conceive of a system of rights that depended upon the subjective conditions of others, yet that is precisely what would result were the objective standard of negligence not used. One's rights to property and so forth would vary with the mental capabilities of others. To determine the duty of care owed, Weinrib claims, one should consider whether one could will the action were the risks to others risks to oneself. Would one have placed one's hayrick, with its risk of catching fire and the fire spreading, so close to a neighbour's cottage were the cottage one's own?

In their paper, Robert Prichard and Alan Brudner are concerned with a particular aspect of determining tort duties not to be negligent. They examine a moral theory as to when, in the absence of specific wording in the statutes allowing or forbidding them, statutory duties provide a basis for negligence actions. As they indicate, courts usually decide such matters by appeals to the intent of the legislature, although these are precisely the cases in which the legislature has not made its intent known or clear. On an Hegelian natural rights theory, they suggest, a tort action should lie if, and only if, a statute protects natural rights to autonomy. If a statute does so, then the usual negligence standards should apply. Violation of such a statute would create a presumption of negligence.

Joseph Steiner is concerned to assimilate strict liability for defective products to negligence. In his paper, he primarily takes an *ex ante* approach to liability. He concludes that people should be held liable when their conduct is (a) intended to create peril, (b) substantially certain to cause harm, or (c) such that the harm is reasonably foreseeable. He argues that in products liability, *ex ante* a manufacturer can reasonably foresee that harm will result from manufacturing the product, for example, due to the inability of quality control to prevent all defective products reaching the market.

Steiner's assimilation of strict liability to negligence does not appear to be justifiable by Weinrib's theory. A manufacturer might well be willing to assume a low risk of purchasing a defective product were he or she a consumer. Consequently, on Weinrib's theory of negligence, the duty of care has been fulfilled. Here one finds a difference between a low risk of accidents in individual cases and a high risk of accidents over a large number of such cases. In effect, Steiner appears to have adopted a form of economic deterrence theory for strict liability, making manufacturers pay for the foreseeable costs of their activities, whether or not these costs result from carelessness in particular cases.

## SPECIAL PROBLEMS

The final two papers in this volume consider issues somewhat different from the rest. Theodore Benditt is concerned with whether people should be liable in tort for failing to perform an easy rescue of a stranger. Generally, common law jurisdisctions have held that one does not have a legal duty to perform even easy rescues of strangers, although one does have a duty to rescue persons with whom one has a special relationship, such as employees. However, in recent years several authors have argued that the law ought to recognize such a duty, and most European countries recognize such a duty in criminal law.

Benditt specifically argues against a tort duty to perform an easy rescue of a stranger, although he does think the criminal law might do so. Primarily, he contends that such a tort action would be inappropriate because it would not meet either the causal or damage conditions. The failure to rescue a person, he argues, is not the cause of that person's injury. Rather, the injury is brought about by some other set of events which a would-be rescuer fails to prevent causing injury. However, Benditt claims that there is a moral duty to rescue, and that persons in peril may even have a moral right to be rescued. Even so, he does not believe victims have a basis for compensation in tort law. Such compensation is due only (1) as a return or paying back, as in unjust enrichtment or reparations, or (2) as making good a guarantee when there is some relationship prior to the event and the event is connected to that relationship, for example, when employers fail to rescue employees imperiled on the job.

Finally, S. C. Coval and J. C. Smith are concerned with how courts can choose between plaintiff and defendant in hard cases. For example, in negligence law, a defendant will not be liable if the risk was a reasonable one, and that is usually taken to mean comparing possible benefits to the defendant with risks to the plaintiff. Coval and Smith, however, do not see the issue as balancing the interests of the two parties. Rather, they contend, court decisions must be based on the rights of the parties. Rights, they hold, are indefeasible, that is, incapable of being overridden by utilitarian considerations, policies, goals, or interests of others. Nonetheless, rights are not absolute. Consequently, they want to provide a conceptual mechanism for determining the extent of rights. Instead of saying a right has been outweighed by some other consideration, they wish to delimit the right so that it does not apply to the situation. Thus, the right remains indefeasible but not absolute.

Their proposed solution is to look to the goals underlying rules establishing rights. Each rule prescribes or proscribes specific conduct in order to achieve some goal. If in a particular case that conduct will not achieve the goal, or although it will achieve it, it will also produce a greater harm or prevent a greater benefit, then the conduct is not required, that is, the rule has an exception. In hard cases, courts should look to the ordering of goals in previous or analogous cases to determine what rule applies to the instant case. Coval and Smith elucidate this approach by considering several actual and hypothetical cases.

## CONCLUSION

The papers in this volume do not begin to address all the moral and philosophical issues in tort law. They do, however, discuss the major views of the justification of tort law and address a number of more specific issues. Even though no consensus is reached and some of the differences are very fundamental, as over the concept of corrective justice (Coleman and Weinrib), they do shed light on a number of matters. They also indicate how central the concepts of justice and rights are in thinking about tort law. Indeed, in the attempt to understand tort law, perhaps as much is learned about justice and rights as about tort law.

MICHAEL D. BAYLES
BRUCE CHAPMAN

BRUCE CHAPMAN

# ETHICAL ISSUES IN THE LAW OF TORT

ABSTRACT. This paper surveys some leading issues in the extant law of tort with a view to exposing some of its assumed values. Three different ethical theories provide the basis for discussion, namely the theories of compensation, retribution and deterrence. While no one of these three theories can fully explain or justify existing tort law, it is suggested that the deterrence theorist provides the best rationale of the three for the harm requirement and for certain doctrines of proximate cause. On the other hand, the compensation theorist, once he is supported with retribution-like concerns for the relative innocence of the affected parties, does better in explaining the legal approach to problems of multiple causation. Finally, it is suggested that the difficulty with all three of the theories is that, unlike a theory of corrective justice, they encourage us to give separate consideration to the fortunes of plaintiff and defendant.

## INTRODUCTION

Like so many other social institutions, the law of tort has recently come under a great deal of popular and academic scrutiny. One author, in a recent survey of the relevant literature, goes so far as to refer to "the crisis of tort law" and argues that "[d]issatisfaction with existing tort law is a universal phenomenon."[1] Observations such as these suggest that there are social values which the law of tort ought to promote and that if it is not up to doing this adequately, alternative institutions and rules of law, better able to serve those values, should be devised. Too often, however, the values in question are either never made explicit or are simply assumed without argument. For example, the fact that about half of every insurance premium dollar is eaten up by adminis-

[1] Izhak Englard, 'The System Builders: A Critical Appraisal of Modern Tort Theory,' *Journal of Legal Studies* 9 (1980): 27.



*From University of Western Ontario Law Review* 20 (1982), 1–21.

trative and legal costs in a fault system is usually thought to provide fairly conclusive evidence that the fault system should be replaced with some kind of system of no fault.[2] Implicit in this recommendation, of course, is an emphasis on the compensatory role of tort law, since the possible negative implications of any kind of insurance, economic or otherwise, for the other possible goals of tort law such as deterrence or retributive justice, are simply not discussed. In this paper, I shall survey some leading issues in the extant law of tort with a view to exposing some of its assumed values. Only if we are familiar with the relevant value issues in the traditional law of tort will we be able to assess the current proposals for reform or design the appropriate empirical tests for changes already being made.

Three different kinds of ethical theory will provide the basis for my discussion, namely, the compensation theory, the retributive theory, and the deterrence theory. The first two of these have the feature in common that they are backward-looking theories of justice. By this I mean that they look to what actually happened in any given tort case, not to what might happen in the future, and that they are concerned somehow with setting things right. Where they differ is in their particular focus of concern. The compensation theorist looks to the plight of the tort victim and wonders how those losses might be alleviated. He will ask questions about who is in the best position to bear the losses without hardship, or how the losses might be widely distributed so that no particular individual bears any great burden. The retributive theorist, on the other hand, shifts his gaze to the alleged tortfeasor and asks whether this person is somehow culpable and should pay for what he has done. Questions of voluntariness, fault, or intention will obviously be important here.

The third kind of theory, which I have termed the deterrence

[2] See, for example, *Royal Commission on Civil Liability and Compensation for Personal Injury* (The Pearson Report) (London: HMSO 1978), Vol. 1, pp. 211–12; and P. S. Atiyah, *Accidents, Compensation and the Law* (London: Weidenfeld & Nicholson, 2nd ed., 1975), pp. 456–57.

theory, is different from the first two in that it is a forward- not backward-looking theory of justice. That is, it is not so much concerned with what has happened in any given tort case, but rather with how we might avoid these happenings again in the future. The issue for the deterrence theorist then is loss, or cost, avoidance. More specifically, the deterrence theorist is concerned with avoiding future costs without imposing even greater costs of avoidance. If some future losses are simply too costly to avoid, the deterrence theorist will treat these losses as more or less inevitable and turn his attention to losses which are more easily controlled. Thus, we might more accurately term this third kind of theory one of optimal, or efficient, deterrence, but for ease of exposition I shall use the shorter term "deterrence" throughout my discussion.[3]

None of these three ethical theories operates totally untainted by the other two, of course. For example, it seems as reasonable to speak of efficient compensation or efficient retribution as efficient deterrence. One might choose to compensate in money rather then in kind on efficiency grounds, or demand retributive payments through fines rather than injunctions for similar reasons. And a deterrence theorist, of course, will not be able to ignore the instant case even if he is only concerned about future costs; after all, the instant case provides him with "the example" he needs "pour encourager les autres." More important, however, is the fact that the compensation theorist must smuggle in some kind of concern for culpability, or the relative innocence of the various parties to a tort action. Without some such concern he will find it difficult to explain why compensation for losses which some individual suffers at the hands of another by way of legitimate punishment are not an issue for tort. It seems that the compensation theorist, therefore, is really only concerned with the losses of an individual

---

[3] Economic analysis of tort law is the most obvious example of optimal deterrence theory. See Richard Posner, 'A Theory of Negligence,' *Journal of Legal Studies* 1 (1972): 29, and *Economic Analysis of Law* (Boston: Little Brown, 2nd ed., 1977), Chapter 6.

who is innocent in some sense. This realization will prove important for our later discussion.

Despite these obvious impurities in the three theories, the fact remains that each kind of theory suggests a quite different kind of moral concern. The purpose of the following discussion is to trace aspects of the three theories through various areas of tort law.

## THE IMPORTANCE OF HARM

The first thing to notice about the law of tort from a moral point of view is the fact that actual occurrence of harm generally seems to be required for liability.[4] This is noteworthy since it is not obvious why actual injury is in itself morally significant. Consider the following two cases:

(1) The defendant A, without considering the possible consequences, tosses a bottle from a fast-moving train. The bottle hits plaintiff B who happens to be out for a hike.

(2) A, again without consideration of the possible consequences, tosses a bottle from the train, only this time the bottle lands safely in a ditch.

From a moral point of view, A's callous disregard for the safety of others seems equally culpable in the two cases. It might well be asked why the fortuitous event of B's being out on a hike, which (improbably) put him in the wrong place at the wrong time, should be allowed to distinguish morally A's conduct in case (1). If liability in tort is thought to track culpability of conduct on the part of the defendent, as the retributive theory seems to require, then A should be subject to liability as much in (2) as in (1).[5]

---

[4] Strictly speaking, this is not true, for example, in the case of trespass; it is more obviously a requirement for tortious liability in negligence. See Allen Linden, *Canadian Tort Law* (Toronto: Butterworths 1977), p. 123. However, if harm is thought of as a violation of a legally protected interest, and in trespass as a deprivation of exclusive use and enjoyment of land, then harm is necessary in the sense that mere intention to trespass will not do.

[5] For philosophical discussion, see Thomas Nagel, 'Moral Luck' in his book *Mortal Questions* (Cambridge: Cambridge University Press, 1979), pp. 24–

Of course, the fact that B suffers actual injury in case (1) is not without some significance. Results do matter after all; one has only to ask B. But if the conduct in (1) and (2) is equally culpable from the defendant's viewpoint, does the actual loss in (1) add anything of *moral* significance? Certainly it is an unfortunate or bad result for B, but is it more so than the loss B would have suffered had a branch fallen from a tree (a natural event) causing him a like injury? Or if the same branch had fallen because of vibrations from the passing train (possibly a non-natural event, but one which was unforeseeable either by A, B, or the train engineer)? Indeed, put case (2) together with either of the latter two events to make the following case (3):

(3) A, without considering the possible consequences, tosses a bottle from a fast-moving train. The bottle lands safely in a ditch, but at the same time B is hit by a branch falling from a tree.

Here we have culpable behaviour on the part of A in combination with an injury to B without a causal link between the two as in case (1). Is this causal link morally significant? For whom?

---

38. A study by the World Health Organization in 1962 found that a good driver makes a mistake every two miles and an American study in 1964 suggested that on average a good driver makes nine mistakes every five minutes. See *Royal Commission*, p. 210. Needless to say, bad luck only converts some of these mistakes into accidents. In the *Laws* (Bk. IX: 887 trans. Jowett), Plato argues that he who fails to cause actual harm is luckier than he who causes it and that we should respect (not alter) this show of luck. The difficulty is that the argument is circular. The ineffective defendant is only luckier if we fail to hold him liable; he cannot be liable, therefore, on the basis of his luck. See J. Halberstam, 'Criminal Attempt and Moral Judgment,' in J. B. Wilbur (ed.), *Values in the Law* (Geneseo, NY: SUNY 1980), p. 59.

For a legal opinion that supports culpability without damage, see Andrews J. (dissenting) in *Palsgraf v. Long Island Railroad Co.* (1928) 162 N.E. 99, at 102: "Where there is the unreasonable act, and some right that may be affected there is negligence whether damage does or does not result. That is immaterial. Should we drive down Broadway at a reckless speed, we are negligent whether we strike an approaching car or miss it by an inch. The act itself is wrongful not only to those who happen to be within the radius of danger but to all who might have been there – a wrong to the public at large."

Not for A's culpability or B's injury apparently. And who else should be concerned?[6]

Here the deterrence theorist would appear to have the answer. Unlike the theorist of retributive justice who seems to demand a like penalty for A's culpable conduct in all three of the above cases, or the compensation theorist who should be as much moved by innocent B's injury in (3) as in (1), the deterrence theorist looks forward to how different liability rules might affect the future behaviour of others. For him what is important is the resultant losses and how they might cheaply be avoided. It is essential, therefore, that the typical tort case have the characteristics of case (1), i.e., that B suffer actual injury and that A (or someone else) was in a position to act otherwise so that the injury would not have occurred. To be concerned about actual losses where there is no causal link to alterable human behaviour is to be concerned about the inevitable, akin to worrying about "spilt milk." Hence, the deterence theorist can explain the concern of tort law for case (1) rather than case (3). Moreover the deterrence theorist would argue that to penalize culpable behaviour in all those cases in which there might have been losses but where in fact there were none is to impose a burden on that behaviour in excess of its true costs, something to be avoided not because it is unjust, but because it is inefficient.[7] Thus, the deterrence theorist seems

---

[6] For some argument that harm, as opposed to injury, only involves coming to grief at someone else's hands, see John Kleinig, 'Crime and the Concept of Harm,' *American Philosophical Quarterly* 15 (1978): 27.

[7] One must be careful here. The mere threat of harm, without full compensation, may impose costs (eg. investment in care, apprehension, etc.) on the possible tort victim. Thus, one might want to deter even the threat of harm. However, even here a defendant who is unlucky enough to cause actual damage will pay more than a defendant who does not, a result difficult to explain on retributive grounds. On the deterrence theory, one might think that we could get the same amount of deterrence if liability attached to every negligent act (whether or not it caused actual damage) but where the amount of liability in each case was smaller, since the expected costs of being negligent would be the same. The difficulty here is that potential tort victims may be less careful, since if the liability payment goes to a plaintiff who has

to be able to explain why case (1) might lie within tort law unlike case (2).

However, there is an obvious criticism of the deterrence view in that it fails to explain the causal link between defendant's conduct and plaintiff's loss as the law actually sees it. Consider the following case:

(4) X negligently blocks the sidewalk forcing Y to step into the street where he is hit by a passing motorist. Z, who is nearby and sees what is about to happen, fails to warn Y of the impending danger.

From a deterrence point of view X and Z seem to be equally responsible for Y's actual injury. Had either acted otherwise than he did, the injury need not have occurred. Yet, it seems well established in common law that Y only has a cause of action against X, not Z, since Z has not actually acted so as to harm Y, but only omitted to confer an equivalent benefit (i.e., to save Y).[8] Thus, the particular causal link to which the law responds in tort is not so easily explained by the deterrence theorist.[9] Whether theories of retributive or compensatory justice fare any better in this respect requires us to look more closely at the issue of causation.

---

only been endangered but not injured, then that plaintiff enjoys a net gain. For similar argument see the text accompanying footnote 24, below.

[8] Linden, *Canadian Tort Law*, p. 271.

[9] Some deterrence theorists have attempted to respond to this problem. See, eg., William Landes and Richard Posner, 'Salvors, Finders, Good Samaritans and Other Rescuers: An Economic Study of Law and Altruism,' *Journal of Legal Studies* 7 (1978): 83. The argument depends on substitution effects (viz. that if there was an obligation to perform a costly rescue, potential rescuers would avoid getting into rescue situations, for example, by avoiding crowded shipping routes, and this would be inefficient.) However, it seems possible to think of situations where substitution effects would not be possible (eg. where someone has the requisite kind of bone marrow for a marrow transplant), yet where the law has not required the person to come to the aid of someone in distress. For discussion of the bone marrow case, see Eric Mack, 'Bad Samaritanism and the Causation of Harm,' *Philosophy and Public Affairs* 9 (1980): 230.

## CAUSE-IN-FACT

Case (4) is usefully dissected into the following sequence:

(4) (a) X negligently blocks the sidewalk forcing Y into the street.

(b) At the same time a motorist is about to pass by that spot.

(c) Z observes the motorist on a collision path with Y but fails to give any warning.

(d) Y is hit by the motorist.

Without the chance occurrence of (b) – and hence (c) and (d) – X's culpable behaviour in (4) provides no ground for tortious action since there is no actual damage, much like case (2) above. Without (d) there is also no ground for a tortious action, although now Z's behaviour is relevant and does seem to be culpable. However, is it as morally culpable as X's negligent behaviour?

The answer seems to be that although Z's inaction may be culpable, it is less so than the action of X. To think otherwise is to ignore the fact that X is actually responsible for creating the risk to Y (in addition to failing to alleviate it) and why should we do that?[10] The law's requirement that the defendant be, at a minimum, a "but for" cause of Y's actual injury would seem to be the method by which it accommodates this additional aspect of culpability. Thus, aspects of the retributive theory seem to loom large in explaining the legal concern for cause-in-fact.

However, there are at least two difficulties with the retributive view. First, one might wonder whether "but for" causation can really sustain the distinction the law draws between X and Z. But for 4(a) it does seem true that 4(d) would not have occurred. Yet, this seems to be equally true of 4(c), i.e., but for Z's failure to warn Y, Y would not have been hit. So Z's inaction would appear to be as necessary a causal condition for Y's injury as X's action. But if the two conditions are equally necessary then perhaps X

---

[10] See Judith Thomson, 'Rights and Deaths,' in M. Cohen, T. Nagel and T. Scanlon (eds.), *The Rights and Wrongs of Abortion*, (Princeton: Princeton University Press 1974), p. 127.

and Z are equally culpable after all, and so the retributive theorist's explanation for the law's particular interpretation of cause-in-fact seems to fail. However, something has clearly gone wrong in this argument against the retributive theorist. Consider what would have happened had Z not existed at all or even been absent from the scene. Then conditions 4(a) and 4(b) would have been jointly sufficient for 4(d) to occur. To argue that Z's inaction is a "but for" (i.e., necessary) cause of Y's demise is to suggest that the conditions which were once jointly sufficient for the occurrence of an event suddenly become insufficient for its occurrence once the *non*-occurrence of another condition (e.g., Z's calling out a warning to Y) is recognized.[11] Needless to say such a conception of factual causation is terribly indiscriminate (since anyone's absence from the scene and consequent failure to warn seems to be a cause). I conclude, therefore, that the first objection to the retributive theorist's explanation for factual causation in tort law cannot be sustained.

However, there is a second objection to the retributive theorist's account of factual causation which has more force. Although we must concede that the law is sensitive to how X, unlike Z, is causally responsible for Y's originally being in danger, it is not the case that the law requires that X's creation of the risk to Y be negligent (and thus culpable) in any way.[12] For example, if X had, through no fault of his own, forced Y into the street, and was in the same position as Z to give a warning, then X would, unlike Z, be under a duty to do so. Thus, where 4(a) alone may not amount to culpable behaviour if it is non-negligent, and where 4(c) alone, though culpable, will not give of a cause for action for liability, if the *same* individual is in the position of both X and Z in 4(a) and 4(c), then the same amount of culpability as 4(c) alone gives grounds for actual liability in the latter case. Those who think

---

[11] Mack, 'Bad Samaritanism,' p. 255.

[12] See, eg., *Fagan* v. *Commissioner of Metropolitan Police*, [1969] 1 Q.B. 439 and the discussion in Ernest Weinrib, 'The Case for a Duty to Rescue,' *Yale Law Journal* 90 (1980): 255–57.

equal liability should track equal culpability, especially if actual injury does take place, might be hard pressed to explain some of these fine legal distinctions. In the end, mere causation, without culpability, may be the most important determinant of liability, as recently argued with some force by Richard Epstein.[13] However, as the foregoing has shown, that seems to be a view hard to reconcile with any of the usual theories of deterrence or retributive justice.

The absence of a legal duty to rescue, even though it does not seem to follow culpability, does seem to turn on some kind of necessary "but for" causal link between plaintiff's loss and defendant's conduct. However, in other cause-in-fact problems, and in particular in the cases of concurrent tortfeasors, it might nevertheless seem that culpability (and hence retributive justice) and not causation actually grounds liability. If both A and B negligently light fires at different places and the fires spread to engulf the plaintiff's house, each defendant might argue that his own fire is not a "but for" cause of plaintiff's damage since the fire of the other alone would have been sufficient.[14] Similar arguments might be used in pollution cases where many defendants pollute a given stream. Rather than allow all defendants to use this argument to escape liability, however, the usual legal solution has been to apportion the costs of damage between the equally culpable tortfeasors.[15] Although this seems to be the just solution on any kind of retributive view, complications arise if the behaviour of only one of the two defendants, say A, is culpable. Then it seems possible for A to argue that plaintiff's loss would, at least within a fault system, lie where it falls and that A's action adds nothing to

---

[13] Richard Epstein, 'A Theory of Strict Liability,' *Journal of Legal Studies* 2 (1973): 151.

[14] Linden, *Canadian Tort Law*, p. 129.

[15] Apportionment may come through a second action for contribution by the defendant initially held liable for the full damage against the other contributing defendant. See the discussion of multiple causation in Linden, *Canadian Tort Law*, pp. 129–30 and G. Williams, 'The Aims of the Law of Tort,' *Current Legal Problems* 4 (1951): 169–70.

plaintiff's misfortune. Indeed, this would appear to be the sort ot reasoning used in the case of *Dillon* v. *Twin States Gas and Electric Co.*[16] in which the plaintiff's deceased, while apparently falling to his death from a bridge, grabbed on to some electrical wires which were negligently maintained by the defendant so as to be a hazard, and was electrocuted. The judgment of the court was that the defendant's conduct, though culpable, did not deprive the plaintiff at that moment of any real prospect of life. Here "but for" causation again seems to raise its ugly head against the retributive rationale for tort liability, although on the deterrence view it might seem likely that little is to be gained by imposing liability in this case.[17]

One is tempted to ask whether a more sophisticated interpretation of the compensation theory might do better than either the deterrence or retributive views to explain at least part of the legal approach to factual causation. Consider an interesting variant on the problem of concurrent tortfeasors in which one of two persons has caused actual harm but it is not certain which one. The leading cases are *Summers* v. *Tice*[13] and *Cook* v. *Lewis*,[19] cases in which two hunters negligently fired their guns simultaneously. One of the shots hit the plaintiff but it could not be determined from which gun it came. Note, therefore, that in this case, of the three parties concerned (the two hunters and the plaintiff), two are innocent of causing actual harm. Yet the courts have seemed to do justice of

---

[16] 1932, 163 A. III (N.H.S.C.). Joel Feinberg discusses this case in 'Problematic Responsibility in Law and Morals' in his book *Doing and Deserving* (Princeton: Princeton University Press 1970), p. 29.

[17] On the retributive theory, if someone should be liable for his culpable behaviour whether or not actual harm happens to result (case (2) in the text), then that person should also be held liable even if his culpable behaviour only causes (the same kind of) harm which in the instant case could not have been avoided. On the deterrence view, of course, to hold someone liable in such cases might be to hold the person liable for more losses than he can efficiently avoid, something which would have little point within the theory.

[18] (1948), 33 Cal. App. 2d 80, 199 P. 2d. 1.

[19] [1951] S.C.R. 830.

some kind by allowing the plaintiff to sue either defendant for the whole of his losses and then allow the defendant so sued to sue the other defendant for contribution. The rationale for this solution might be found within compensation theory: although in such a decision some *share* of the damages will fall to one of the hunters innocent of causing actual harm, this seems to be better, at least within a compensation theory, than having the *whole* loss borne by the equally innocent plaintiff.[20] Moreover, the same rationale might argue for the same solution in the case where only one of the hunters is found guilty of faulty conduct in firing his gun. However, there may be an argument here for holding the one culpable hunter liable for the whole of plaintiff's loss. In such a solution there is a 50 per cent *chance* that the full loss will fall on a hunter innocent of actual harm; again, however, this would appear to be better than imposing the full loss on a plaintiff who is certainly innocent. Note that in none of the above solutions do the justifications have to turn on the idea of penalizing culpable behaviour independent of its causing actual harm (a retributive view); that kind of behaviour can be thought "innocent." Rather, they turn on the quite different kind of argument which comes from compensation theory that it is better that smaller losses be borne by the innocent than larger losses, or that the same loss ought to be borne by that party who is more likely to be at fault in some respect. However, the precise meaning of fault or innocence in these cases may depend on how we treat the issue of "proximate cause." To this topic we now turn.

## PROXIMATE CAUSE

Although tort law seems to require that the defendant's conduct is probably one of the many possible "but for" causes of plaintiff's injury, such a finding is only necessary, not sufficient. Attaching actual liability to that conduct usually falls to the more value-

---

[20] See Williams, 'Aims of the Law of Tort,' p. 170.

laden notion of "proximate cause."[21] The most important constituent element of proximate cause would seem to be the issue of "foreseeability" or "remoteness" of damage.

Under a negligence rule, it is sometimes thought reasonable that the concept of foresight must serve to limit liability as well as to create it.[22] That is, if a defendant is to be held liable because he should have foreseen that this conduct was likely to cause a given type of damage to a foreseeable plaintiff, then it seems equally true that he should not be held liable for that conduct if either the *category* of plaintiff was not foreseeable, or if the *type* of damage to a foreseeable plaintiff was not itself foreseeable, or if the *extent* of a foreseeable type of damage to a foreseeable plaintiff was not actually foreseeable.

However reasonable these limitations of liability might appear to be, it is not clear that the common law always observes them, nor is it evident that they are all so very reasonable on either a deterrence, retributive, or compensation view of the law of tort. Taking the latter kind of theory first, the fact remains that however unforeseeable either the actual plaintiff or the type and extent of his damages were, he is innocent and has suffered injury. Quite possibly, therefore, the same kind of reasoning that imposed liability on the culpable one of two "concurrent tortfeasors," even though a causal link to the harm could not be proved with certainty, may be sufficient to impose liability on a negligent defendant even if the harm which was actally fore-

---

21 That proximate cause is essentially a policy concept rather than a matter of fact seems to be a widely held view. See, eg., Guido Calabresi, 'Concerning Cause and the Law of Torts,' *University of Chicago Law Review* 43 (1975): 90; and Allen Linden, 'Foreseeability in Negligence Law' in his casebook *Canadian Tort Law* (Toronto: Butterworths 1980), pp. 9–43. For a view that even factual causation involves policy considerations, see Ernest J. Weinrib, 'A Step Forward in Factual Causation,' *Modern Law Review* 38 (1975): 529–33.

22 W. Seavy, 'Mr. Justice Cardozo and the Law of Torts,' in *Selected Essays on the Law of Torts* (Cambridge, Mass: Harvard Law Review Association 1959).

seeable did not arise. After all, the loss must be borne by someone, and under a compensation theory it is the worst result that someone who is certainly and totally innocent should bear all of the loss.[23]

Richard Posner has argued that it makes little sense on a deterrence view to hold a defendant liable in negligence for damage to unforeseeable (unlikely) plaintiffs (although it may not affect deterrence behaviour to hold him liable either), but has also argued that there is a good economic reason for holding a defendant liable to a foreseeable plaintiff for damage which is unforeseeable in its extent. To optimally deter, the total liability of negligent injurers should equal the total cost of their accidents. If instead of attempting to determine damages in each case on an individual basis, an average figure was used, then there would be overcompensation of some plaintiffs and undercompensation of others. But overcompensation may encourage those potential plaintiffs to have "accidents," something a law of negligence can only avoid by making liability equal to actual damages. However, lest the total liability of negligent injurers fall short of the total cost of their behaviour, those who would be undercompensated under an "average rule" must now be compensated to the full extent of their actual injuries.[24] Hence, the "thin skull" rule.[25]

---

[23] See, for example, J. Fleming, 'The Passing of Polemis,' *Canadian Bar Review* 39 (1961): 501: "... as between one who unjustifiably created an unreasonable risk and his innocent victim, the balance of equities should favour the latter rather than him who by his own negligence has set the whole thing in motion, even if it means that the sanction may sometimes be incommensurate with his original fault."

[24] See Posner, 'A Theory of Negligence,' pp. 47–48. An example should help to illustrate the point. Suppose a common carrier handles packages and every so often negligently drops one. In a given package there may be either a Ming vase or a piece of cheap china. If the courts awarded average damages to each plaintiff, there would be appropriate incentives for the carrier (who will treat every package with unknown contents as an average package anyway), but the owners of the cheap china would have incentives to encourage 'accidents' (eg. they would wrap the china poorly, use weak string, etc.). The

This argument seems to assume (as a deterrence theory must) that the defendant is able to calculate (and hence foresee) the *range* of possible injuries and their likelihood, although not the particular damage a plaintiff might suffer in a given case. Otherwise, the "thin skull" plaintiff with extensive damage begins to look very much like the one who is totally unforeseeable. If that is true, then Posner's argument should equally apply to the case of a foreseeable plaintiff who may not actually suffer a particular type of damage, so long as the range of possible types is predictable in the same way.[26]

On a culpability or retributive justice theory it has already been noted that a defendant should be liable for his culpable behaviour whether or not harm actually occurs. Thus, it would appear to be equally true that the defendant should be liable for and to the extent of the usual consequences of that behaviour even if harm in the instant case happens to be to an unforeseeable plaintiff or if it is of a kind or an extent that was not foreseeable. Whether or not this liability based on culpability should actually be paid to the plaintiff might depend on a compensation theory or, at least in the cases of extent or type of damage, on whether one finds Posner's deterrence argument at all convincing.

---

problem is the one familiarly known in the insurance literature as 'moral hazard'. But see below footnote 28.

[25] For legal discussion of the 'thin skull' rule, see Linden, *Canadian Tort Law*, p. 322.

[26] It might be thought that on a deterrence view it is not actually necessary that compensation be paid *to* the plaintiff and, therefore, that Posner's argument turns on something other than a pure deterrence theory. However, this is not the case. If the plaintiff is not fully compensated for accident costs, he will have an incentive to avoid those costs himself. At first glance, this may appear to be a good thing (and should even operate under the 'average rule' for undercompensated plaintiffs). However, if the defendant is the cheapest cost avoider and plaintiff's behaviour induces defendant to invest less in accident avoidance, then deterrence is being bought at too high a price. It is worth noting, however, that this argument turns as much on the plaintiff's ability to foresee accidents as the defendant's.

Table I indicating defendant's liablity, summarizes the recommendations of the three kinds of theory, deterrence, compensation, and retributive justice, for the three kinds of unforeseeability or remoteness:

TABLE I

Liability of Defendant for the Unforeseeable:

| *Theory* | *Plaintiff* | *Type of Damage* | *Extent of Damage* |
|---|---|---|---|
| Compensation | fully liable | fully liable | fully liable |
| Retribution | fully liable | not fully liable (liable for usual damages only) | not fully liable (liable for usual damages only) |
| Deterrence | not liable at all | fully liable | fully liable |

How does the positive law of tort measure up to the recommendations of the various theories in these categories of remoteness? The law on unforeseeable extent of damages seems to be the most settled of the three categories: the tortfeasor must take his victim as he finds him.[27] However, in this respect the law would appear to be more sensitive to unforeseeable but extensive damages which follow from bodily injury than those which flow from injury to property. Thus, where the deterrence and compensation theorists do well to explain the paradigm "thin skull" cases, they are less able than the retributive justice theorist to explain the law's retreat from *Re Polemis.*[28] As for the unforeseeable plaintiff, the retributive justice view appears to be the one espoused by Mr. Justice Andrews' dissenting opinion in *Palsgraf*,[29] although that case is complicated in that it seems to involve both an unforeseeable plaintiff and a remote kind of damage. Mr. Justice Cardozo's

---

[27] *Dulieu* v. *White and sons* [1901] 2 K.B. 669, p. 679.

[28] [1921] 3 K.B. 560. Oddly enough, Posner's optimal deterrence explanation for the 'thin skull' rule seems to be most convincing as a matter of theory in the property cases, as exemplified in footnote 24. Yet the rule holds best as a matter of law for cases of personal injury.

[29] See above, footnote 5.

majority opinion, which was for no liability at all, is only consistent with a deterrence view. *Wagon Mound (No. 1)*[30] seems to turn on the unforeseeability of type of damage since, although it was negligent to spill bunker oil into the harbour given the damage it might cause by fouling the slipways of the various dockowners, the actual damage complained of was caused by fire and was unforeseeable. Viscount Simonds' majority judgment in this case that defendants should not be held liable seems inconsistent with a deterrence view if one takes the facts of *Wagon Mound (No. 2)*[31] which were that some "possibility" of this kind of damage was foreseeable and that the category of plaintiff was plainly foreseeable. Taken together those findings appear to supply the raw data for Posner's deterrence argument, not surprising perhaps since it will often be difficult to distinguish "kind" from "extent" of damage.[32] *Wagon Mound (No. 1)* is plainly inconsistent with a compensation theory, although later cases such as *Hughes* v. *Lord Advocate*[33] may be based on a concern for the losses of an innocent victim. On a retributive view, the defendants in *Wagon Mound* should have been held liable only for the damages normally foreseeable whether or not they actually occurred.

## DEFENCES

### 1. *Contributory Negligence*

In his discussion of the "thin skull" rule, which argued on deterrence grounds that the defendant must take his victim as he finds

---

[30] [1961] A.C. 388 (P.C.).

[31] [1967] A.C. 617 (P.C.).

[32] The courts have shown some reluctance to distinguish different cases of burning as different kinds of injury (*Hughes* v. *Lord Advocate* [1963] A.C. 837). Likewise, they have refused to distinguish unlikely frostbite from more likely illness due to cold (*Bradford* v. *Robinson Rentals* [1967] 1 All E.R. 267). Yet, they have shown some ingenuity in distuinguishing between types of diseases caused by rats (*Tremain* v. *Pike* [1969] 3 All E.R. 1303).

[33] See above, footnote 32.

him, Richard Posner also considers the possibility that the thin skulled plaintiff may be in a position to take cost-justified precautions (i.e. less costly precautions than those of the defendant) to prevent his particular injury. If this is true, then Posner suggests that some kind of contributory negligence rule may be necessary to give the plaintiff the appropriate incentive.[34] Such a suggestion follows quite naturally from a deterrence rationale for tort and stands in stark contrast to Richard Epstein's view that the particularly sensitive plaintiff is under no obligation to protect himself so as to reduce the damages to be paid by those who might harm him. "Where the plaintiff is in a weakened condition, he has not caused the harm, ... even if he had the opportunity to prevent them [sic] from occurring. As in the case of the Good Samaritan, one man is not under a common law duty to take steps to aid a stranger."[35]

Epstein's arguments, unlike Posner's, take seriously the idea that one man's activity *causes* harm to another. Posner, on the other hand, is much influenced by Ronald Coase's classic article "The Problem of Social Cost,"[36] which argues that avoidable accidents are simply the result of at least two individuals wanting to make inconsistent use of a scarce resource. In such cases, *both* the individuals cause the harm in the sense that were either to withdraw there would be no problem. From this position of "reciprocal cause" it is an easy step to conclude that both individuals *contribute* to the harm and to ignore what is important for Epstein, namely the important fact that before the law steps in all the costs of the "reciprocal harm" are borne by the victim. In this sense, Epstein argues, the defendant's activity causes injury to the victim which is not reciprocated by the activities of the victim on the defendant.[37]

---

34 Posner, *Economic Analysis of Law*, p. 131.

35 Epstein, 'A Theory of Strict Liability,' pp. 164–5.

36 Ronald Coase, 'The Problem of Social Cost,' *Journal of Law and Economics* 3 (1960): 1.

37 Epstein, 'A Theory of Strict Liability,' pp. 164–5.

The question is how important all this is morally. A undertakes an activity which exposes B to danger. With damage heading his way B undertakes no precautionary measures and simply carries on with his usual business. Where Posner and Coase would argue that B then contributes to any harm that results, Epstein would support B's claim that he has done nothing to A and so shouldn't have to burden himself with costly precautions so that A's damaging behaviour (for which he will be held liable) will be the less so. While we might agree that a man should not be allowed to create extra obligations in another by what he does unilaterally, it does seem likely that we have certain duties to look out for our own safety, at least if we are going to complain about the damage that might result. If a man walks perilously close to a cliff's edge and the soft ground gives way beneath him (a natural event), we nevertheless feel his own foolish behaviour is at least partially responsible. (This might continue to be true even if a stranger is in a better [least cost] position to warn [and so deter] him. Thus, cheap deterrence may not be the basis for our concern here.) Moreover, if the man is an invitee to the premises, Epstein argues that the defendant owner-occupier is only under an obligation to warn about those dangers which the defendant might *reasonably* foresee.[38] Clearly, this is *not* to take one's victim as one finds him, since the plaintiff, who might be of a foolish or gambling disposition, will not be compensated for any unreasonable risks he might take. It is difficult to see exactly why a plaintiff is under a duty to look out for himself when an owner-occupier has acted upon him by inviting him to the premises, but is not so obligated when the defendant acts upon him as a stranger by creating dangerous conditions. Nor can the invitee's consent to enter at his own risk explain the difference here, since under the usual circumstances of contributory negligence the plaintiff has also agreed not to undertake precautions for his own safety.

Thus, where on a deterrence view the argument for a defence

[38] Richard Epstein, 'Defenses and Subsequent Pleas in a System of Strict Liability,' *Journal of Legal Studies* 3 (1974): 211–12.

of contributory negligence seems clear, on a retributive theory much will depend upon whether one agrees with Coase that defendant and plaintiff are to be likened to joint tortfeasors, each contributing to the harmful result, or whether one is moved by Epstein's claim that a man need not look out for himself simply because another threatens him with harm. Of course, if plaintiff acts so foolishly as to behave unforeseeably, then defendant cannot be faulted and perhaps should not be held liable according to the retributive view. Epstein's willingness to shift the loss even in this case is based on the heavy moral weight he attaches to mere causation independent of culpability.[39] A compensation theorist might equitably divide the loss between two innocents, defendant and victim,[40] although it is possible that Epstein's argument might convince that theorist to shift the full cost to the defendant if he is at all culpable in the creation of risk to the plaintiff and even if the plaintiff could have undertaken precautions to reduce that risk or the damages which flow from it.

### 2. *Assumption of the Risk*

Another defence to a tort action, and one which is sometimes difficult to keep separate from contributory negligence, is voluntary assumption of the risk. No injury, apparently, is done to one who consents to run the risk of it.[41] Consent either can be given by express agreement or may be implied by the conduct of the

---

39 Compare John Fleming, *The Law of Torts* (Sydney: Law Book Co., 5th edition 1977), p. 7: "The ... [interest in security] ... requires that a person who has been harmed in consequence of another's action should be compensated by the other, regardless of the latter's motivation and purpose; the ... [interest in freedom of action] ... requires that a person who harms another should be held responsible only when his activity was intentionally wrongful or indicated an undue lack of consideration for the interest of others. The former is content with imposing liability for faultless causation; the latter insists on 'fault' or 'culpability' as a prerequisite for legal responsibility."

40 Williams, 'Aims of the Law of Tort,' p. 162n.

41 For discussion, see Linden, *Canadian Tort Law*, p. 424.

parties.[42] However, it seems important that the plaintiff voluntarily and knowingly *act* to assume the risk; mere knowledge will not do.[43] This feature, arguably, distinguishes this defence from contributory negligence, a distinction hard to maintain as important under a deterrence theory. Suppose, for example, that plaintiff accepts a ride in defendant's car. At that time defendant is perfectly sober. Once under way, however, defendant begins to drink excessively and becomes intoxicated. If plaintiff becomes aware of defendant's condition and fails to get out of the car, for example, at the next traffic light, then plaintiff may be contributorily negligent but has actually done nothing new to assume the extra risk.[44] Getting out of the car at this point may efficiently avoid future injury, but to make a duty of it is to fall prey to Epstein's concern that defendant should not be allowed to unilaterally (as opposed to contractually) create obligations in plaintiff by his own dangerous behaviour. Indeed, if one were to refer to plaintiff's continued presence in the car as contractual, or as voluntary assumption of the risk, then one might be tempted to speak of a coercive contract or consent obtained under threat of

---

[42] *Ibid.*, p. 425.

[43] *City of Sarnia* v. *Shepley et al.* (1969) 4 D.L.R. (3d) 315, p. 319: "*Volenti non fit injuria* is not the equivalent of *scienti non fit injuria.*"

[44] See, for example, *Lehnert* v. *Stein* (1962), 36 D.L.R. (2d) 159. "...the time to determine *volens* was when the plaintiff got into the defendant's car.... At that time the plaintiff did not know how much drinking the defendant had done and did not assume any risk of drunkenness because there was then no risk. [Later], even though the defendant was noticeably drunk, this did not make the plaintiff *volens*, but only contributorily negligent." But consider the following case: Knowing of the possibility of 'whiplash' as a kind of injury, Jones nevertheless fails to install headrests in his car. Out driving one day, he is hit from behind by Green who is following too closely. Jones suffers whiplash. Is this voluntary assumption of risk or contributory negligence? Does it matter? For Epstein it should matter since *volenti* is merely an exercise of contractual autonomy whereas contributory negligence, he argues, should not even be a defence. See Epstein, 'Defences and Subsequent Pleas', p. 185 and the text accompanying footnote 35 above.

harm.[45] The harm threatened, of course, is not injury through negligent or reckless driving (that is what is consented to), but the inconvenience or possible danger associated with leaving the car ("Carry on with me or else I'll leave you here").

This should not suggest that mere conduct, in combination with knowledge of the risk, is enough to make up a defence of voluntary assumption of the risk. There must be reasonable alternatives from which to choose, even if none of those alternatives actually makes plaintiff worse off. Something of this probably underlies the law's reluctance to continue the use of the defence in the case of industrial accidents (lack of employment is too stark an alternative for a potential worker), but it is also suggested when the law refuses to recognize that coming to the nuisance is a defence.[46] If A sets up his smoky factory in the wilderness and homeowner B moves in next door, it is no defence to an action in nuisance for A to argue that B assumed the risk of damage from A's activity by locating there. Theories of deterrence, compensation and retribution might all be reluctant to hold A completely liable since B could easily have avoided the resultant harm, a harm which was not unilaterally imposed by A since he had decided to locate away from B. However, it seems true that there must be some kind of limit to our concerns for A in this respect. If A had bought land in the wilderness to start a firing range, and had announced well in advance to all comers that he was a careless sort of fellow inclined to let bullets go astray, then, even if B were to move in next door fully aware of this, we would still feel inclined to think that A was under a duty to buy land large enough to contain his activity and so not harm B. Whether or not the smoky factory is to be likened to a firing range seems to require a substantive theory of justice on harmful or perhaps even undesirable activities. Epstein's predictable claim that what is important is the fact that A's activity

---

[45] For good discussion on this see Robert Nozick, 'Coercion,' in S. Morgenbesser et al. (eds.), *Philosophy, Science and Method* (New York: St. Martin's Press 1969), pp. 440–72.

[46] *Sturges* v. *Bridgman* (1879) 11 Ch. D. 852.

"invades" B's property (and not vice versa) doesn't seem to be convincing.[47] If P moves in beside Q, the notorious busybody, it still seems true that P has grounds for complaint against Q if Q uses an extrasensitive listening device to "invade" P's privacy. This seems to be true despite that fact that there is no actual invasion of P's property (if anything, the reverse is true) and that P moved in next to Q fully aware of the possibilities. Our intuitions may or may not be the same if Q had an obscene billboard on his property in full view of P, but it does seem clear that there are some substantive protections which one need not bargain for. Perhaps it is the case that certain exercises of contractual autonomy are so irresponsible or disrespectful of one's own self that they are inconsistent with the individual integrity which underlies contract as a value.[48]

## STRICT LIABILITY AND THE REASONABLE MAN

It is generally accepted in ethical theory that "ought" implies "can." That is, if an individual, for some reason, is unable to perform an act X it cannot be true that he ought to perform that act.[49] However, if we think that one's legal obligations ought to be coincidental with one's moral obligations, this basic proposition appears to be inconsistent with the law's objective standard of the

---

[47] Richard Epstein, 'Nuisance Law: Corrective Justice and Its Utilitarian Constraints,' *Journal of Legal Studies* 8 (1979): 72–73.

[48] For some discussion of contract values and the moral foundations of bargaining, see Charles Fried, *Right and Wrong* (Cambridge, Mass: Harvard University Press, 1978), pp. 100–104, Weinrib, 'The Case for a Duty to Rescue,' pp. 268–79 and John Kleinig, 'The Ethics of Consent,' *Canadian Journal of Philosophy* **11** (1983). Kleinig argues that "when X consents, X does not generally consent to anything at all, but to some determinate act, *a*, and to what is normally associated with *a*. This should not surprise us since consent implies responsibility, and it is irresponsible to accept unlimited responsibility."

[49] For an interesting dissenting view, at least within the context of tragic dilemmas, see Bernard Williams, 'Ethical Consistency' in his *Problems of the Self* (Cambridge: Cambridge University Press 1973), pp. 166–86.

reasonable man. For it is no defence to a plaintiff's action in tort law that the defendant has done his personal best to avoid causing injury and that any more was beyond his particular competence. Rather, what is required is that the defendant live up to the objective standard of the reasonable man; if he falls below that he acts at his peril.[50]

Although on a culpability theory we might believe initially that no one has done anything wrong if he could not have done otherwise, we are moved, I think, by Holmes's response in *The Common Law* that if a man "is born hasty and awkward, is always having accidents and hurting himself or his neighbours, no doubt his congenital defects will be allowed for in the courts of Heaven, but his slips are no less troublesome to his neighbours than if they sprang from guilty neglect."[51] Holmes's point seems to be wholly based on the importance of a compensation theory, since on a deterrence view there seems to be little point in holding to a subjectively unattainable standard.[52] However, even on the compensation view Holmes's argument comes close to Epstein's that causation, without actual fault, is enough to impute some guilt to the defendant and so shift the entire loss from a wholly innocent plaintiff. We might question whether mere causation is up to bearing that kind of moral burden. A doctrine of equitable liability, such as has been adopted in Hungary, might be more attractive in distributing the costs more equally.[53]

---

[50] For discussion, see Linden, *Canadian Tort Law*, p. 82.

[51] O. W. Holmes, *The Common Law* (Cambridge, Mass: Belknap Press 1963), p. 86.

[52] There may be some arguments from optimal deterrence if it is recognized that a subjective standard is costly to administer. See Posner, *Economic Analysis of Law*, p. 125. Also, there may be a deterrence argument for using an objective standard if an individual incapable of meeting that standard can nevertheless choose not to participate in the relevant activity. On this, see Steven Shavell, 'Strict Liability versus Negligence,' *Journal of Legal Studies* 9 (1980): 1. Thus, the point in the text may have to be restricted to activities which an individual cannot reasonably choose to avoid.

[53] See Williams, 'Aims of the Law of Tort,' p. 162n.

If negligence in tort is not a form of moral fault, we seem to end up with the result, paradoxical to the lawyer, that liability for negligence is a form of strict liability. Or, at least, so argues Glanville Williams. Williams presses the argument even further, however:

> All this is simply part of the general argument for the determinist view. If inadvertent negligence is not a form of moral fault, advertent negligence and intentional wrongdoing are not either, for in each case a person simply behaves as he is made or conditioned to behave. Thus, liability for intentional wrongdoing also becomes strict liability![54]

Thomas Nagel has drawn a like conclusion in his discussion of "moral luck."[55] Sometimes we are simply unlucky that someone gets in the way of the bottle that we negligently throw from a fast-moving train; but we are not responsible for that person being there at that time and so we might wonder, as argued above, why the resultant harm is so significant for a moral assessment of our action. Similarly, however, we are not actually responsible for our innate abilities and temperaments, or our inclinations to develop them, and so does this not also mean that there is little moral difference to be found between an act which is performed unavoidably and one which is performed negligently or even intentionally? Isn't it *all* just a matter of bad luck that we are what we are and nothing more? Moral condemnation implies that one should not be like that, but if ought implies can and we cannot be other than what we are, then it may make more sense to restrict our judgments to the evaluation of unfortunate *results* rather than to condemn a person for his culpable *actions.*

This argument, which considerably shrinks the domain of individual responsibility, points us in two quite different directions, however, when we turn back to the implications for tort law. We may accept that a person is not responsible for what he is, and consequently, what he does or is inclined to do, but we need not end up with the conclusion, which now seems to be implied

---

54 *Ibid.*, p. 160.

55 See Nagel, 'Moral Luck,' pp. 24–38.

by a retributive or culpability theory, that, for example, all accident costs should lie where they fall. For if a man is not responsible for his vices or natural weaknesses, he is not responsible for his virtues or natural assets either.[56] Thus, we do him no injustice if, on policy grounds or any other, we appropriate some of the wealth he enjoys as a consequence of his possessing those assets. Therefore, there seems to be nothing unreasonable in holding to one's concerns for the deterrence of avoidable harms and in restricting the imposition of tort liabilities to those who cause actual harm. If the latter kind of tortfeasor complains that he has been unjustly singled out because in his case some plaintiff just happened to be in the wrong place at the wrong time (a morally insignificant event), then we can respond that it is equally true that his own claim (i.e. his claim to the money which goes to compensate the plaintiff) is a claim to the fruits of his morally undeserved assets and so has no basis in justice. With arguments of justice so neatly put aside, arguments of policy, or deterrence, can easily carry the day. One might wonder, however, if any notion of self really survives this idea of shrinking individual responsibility, and question whether it provides a sufficiently meaningful locus for the greater happiness that should follow from a policy of cheap deterrence.[57]

While the above argument lumps together as equally culpable acts of inadvertent negligence, advertent negligence, and intentional wrongdoing, another argument, common in the area of strict products liability, is the one which collapses forms of negligence into intention as the probability of a foreseeable injury

---

[56] Whether or not it is unjust to appropriate the fruits of undeserved natural assets is an important issue dividing John Rawls, *A Theory of Justice* (Cambridge: Harvard University Press 1971) from Robert Nozick, *Anarchy, State, and Utopia* (Oxford: Blackwell 1974). See in particular Nozick's discussion at pp. 213f. For more discussion of the issue in a policy contenxt (reverse discrimination), see T. Nagel 'Equal Treatment and Compensatory Discrimination' in M. Cohen, T. Nagel and T. Scanlon, (eds.), *Equality and Preferential Treatment* (Princeton: Princeton University Press 1977), pp. 3–18.

[57] For good discussion of this issue, see Fried, *Right and Wrong*, pp. 7–29.

approaches one, or a certainty that the injury will occur. Richard Posner, for example, has made the point:

> The distinction between intentional and unintentional torts – thought by most tort lawyers to be fundamental – is both confusing and unnecessary. Most accidental injuries are intentional in the sense that the injurer knew that he could have reduced the probability of the accident by taking additional precautions. The element of intention is unmistakable when the tortfeasor is an enterprise that can predict from past experience that it will inflict a certain number of accidental injuries every year.[58]

Posner's argument is like the one discussed above in the sense that it collapses human agency into mere certainty of result. Yet the Roman Catholic doctrine of "double effect" would be careful to distinguish morally between, on the one hand, choosing an evil (e.g., the death or injury of another) either as one's ultimate end or as the means to one's end and, on the other hand, choosing in such a way that the same evil is a foreseeable and certain side effect, so long as the good of the ultimate end outweighs the evil of the *unintended* concomitant. Where the former is prohibited absolutely, the latter is at least permissible.[59] Now "double effect" seems based on a spurious distinction if it is used to make out a moral difference, for example, between saving a mother by performing a craniotomy on the fetus (where the fetus's death is the means) and realizing the same end by removing the mother's cancerous womb (where the fetus's death is only a certain side effect). On the other hand, it does seem true that we would want to distinguish morally between marketing a cheaper product with the foreseeable side effect that (at least) one third party will certainly be killed over a sufficiently long run of production, and the same firm actively sending that person a letter-bomb so that his estate will pass to a worthy charity. Nor should the fact that in the latter

---

58 Posner, *Economic Analysis of Law*, p. 119.

59 For good discussion of 'double effect', see Charles Fried, 'Right and Wrong – Preliminary Considerations,' *Journal of Legal Studies* 5 (1976): 184–86, and Joseph M. Boyle, 'Toward Understanding the Principle of Double Effect,' *Ethics* 90 (1980): 527.

case the addressee is named and known in advance make any difference; our moral outrage in this case would also hold for the situation in which the addressee is an unknown whose name is chosen at random from a directory of wealthy philanthropists. There is a clear need, therefore, for some kind of explanation as to why our intuitions might pull in opposite directions in these different kinds of cases.[60]

A possible consideration is the following.[61] Suppose a firm is marketing a drug which saves lives, but which is also in danger of causing the occasional death. However, suppose that the expected benefits greatly outweigh the expected costs. Now so long as this net benefit includes the idea that there is some *possibility* that the firm can save lives without causing any death *at all*, we might feel that the drug should be marketed. After all, that would be a benefit without a cost. However, if over a sufficiently long production run the possibility of death becomes a certainty, then the actual cost of saving the lives of many individuals is the life which another individual actually loses. We might continue to feel that the benefits of marketing the drug are still worth this cost, but we should at least pause to ask the following question: "Worth it for whom?" Since any individual can only live one life, more lives, as such, are not worth more to him. Thus, the benefit to be had in marketing the drug and saving more lives is no greater, at least for any individual so saved, than the cost of losing his life is to the

---

60 The doctrine of 'double effect' may be useful in explaining the law on economic torts. Where one cannot use certain means to put someone out of business (*Tarleton* v. *McGawley* (1793), 170 E.R. 153 (K.B.)), nor maliciously intend that someone go out of business even though one uses conventional means (*Tuttle* v. *Buck* (1909), 119 N.W. 946), one can nevertheless use legitimate means for one's own ends even when it is certain that someone will go out of business as a result (*Mogul* v. *McGregor* [1892] A.C. 25).

61 The following discussion is inspired by John Taurek, 'Should the Numbers Count?' *Philosophy and Public Affairs* 6 (1977): 293. For critical discussion of Taurek, see Gregory Kavka, 'The Numbers Should Count,' *Philosophical Studies* 36 (1979): 285, and Derek Parfit, 'Innumerate Ethics,' *Philosophy and Public Affairs* 7 (1978): 285.

individual who dies. And where else can the benefit be enjoyed except in the minds of individuals? To whom can it be relevant that some number of lives greater than one is saved?[62] A moral theory which takes seriously the separation between individuals may have to be indifferent between, on the one hand, saving many lives and causing the death of one and, on the other hand, not causing the death of one but failing to save many lives. Note too that none of this turns on a denial of the possible moral distinction between (actively) causing death and (passively) letting die where these are different kinds of actions. All that is at issue here is what should comprise a meaningful evaluation of the results of an action.

## CONCLUDING COMMENTS

The purpose of this paper is not to draw any firm conclusions on what kind of values should be promoted in the traditional law of tort or its proposed substitutes. Rather, its more limited aim has been to expose some of the values and value issues that might be found within the extant law.

The focus has been on three kinds of ethical theory, viz., retribution, deterrence, and compensation. This particular taxonomy of theories tends to lead us to consider separately the

---

[62] I do not want to deny that someone might actually feel better, all other things equal, if more rather than fewer people are saved. Indeed, I am sure that most of us actually have such feelings. However, one might still want to ask *why* we actually have such feelings (or whether we *should* have them), since one doesn't actually secure any greater happiness for any one individual if one saves the many rather than the few. Moreover, even if one were to admit that the happiness of each and every individual includes a component of consideration for the happiness of others (as one surely must), the general question remains as to why one would want to save many such individuals rather than a few, since that kind of happiness, like life, can only be enjoyed within the consciousness of a single individual. Can we not do as much by saving the one as the many?

fortunes of the defendant and plaintiff.[63] For example, on a retributive theory it is important that the negligent tortfeasor pay a penalty whether or not he causes actual harm; on a deterrence view the same tortfeasor should only pay for actual losses. However, with some possible reservations in the case of deterrence, that the penalty is actually paid *to* the plaintiff does not seem to be required. That requirement is part of a compensation theory, but the compensation theorist would appear to be as much moved by the losses of a victim when he suffers them at the hands of a negligent or non-negligent defendant or even when they are the result of purely natural event.

Clearly there are some difficulties here if we want to satisfy all the theories all of the time. But suppose we take the simplest case of a culpable tortfeasor who causes foreseeable harm to a plaintiff. On both a deterrence and retributive view of tort the tortfeasor should pay his due and on a compensation theory that payment should go to the plaintiff. In this case we seem to be able to satisfy the requirements of all of the theories. But is it all that is required? Would it be enough, for example, for the plaintiff to simply receive his social insurance cheque for compensation in the mail, never actually knowing who injured him and/or whether he had been found at fault? Does retributive justice not require more and in particular that each man should have his day in court in full view of the other? Should this not be at least an ultimate background possibility for the bargaining even if most cases are settled

---

[63] A theory which begins with a discussion of the relationship between defendant and plaintiff, and which focusses not just on the conduct of the defendant (because it is not at all concerned with culpability), nor on the plight of the plaintiff (because it is concerned with how an interpersonal relationship comes to be upset) is the theory of corrective justice. The classic source for the theory, of course, is Aristotle, *Nichomachean Ethics*, Book V. For recent discussion see Jules Coleman, 'Corrective Justice and Wrongful Gain,' *Journal of Legal Studies* **11** (1982): 421; Richard Posner, 'The Concept of Corrective Justice in Recent Theories of Tort Law,' *Journal of Legal Studies* **10** (1981): 187, and Ernest J. Weinrib, 'Toward A Moral Theory of Negligence Law,' this volume.

out of court? One can imagine in some cases, such as defamation, that this vengeful motive, directed by one man knowingly against another who has harmed him, will be more important, but one wonders if it is not a fairly general human need, and one which the private action in tort goes some way towards satisfying. Walter Berns has recently argued that the ability to "bear a grudge" is a mark of our humanity, the particular awareness which we have as a species of our continuing selves and the continuing selves of others over time.[64] We might well question whether it is an aspect of our humanity which we want to encourage, but that it is important for at least some aspects of the private tort action seems difficult to deny.

*Westminster Institute, London, Canada*

64 Walter Berns, *For Capital Punishment* (New York: Basic Books, 1979), especially pp. 151–52 and Chapter V.

JULES L. COLEMAN

# MORAL THEORIES OF TORTS: THEIR SCOPE AND LIMITS: PART I

ABSTRACT. One approach to legal theory is to provide some sort of rational reconstruction of all or of a large body of the common law. For philosophers of law this has usually meant trying to rationalize a body of law under one or another principle of justice. This paper explores the efforts of the leading tort theorists to provide a moral basis – in the sense of rational reconstruction based on alleged moral principles – for the law of torts. The paper is divided into two parts. In the first part I consider and reject the view that tort law is best understood as falling either within the ambit of the principle of retributive justice, a comprehensive theory of moral responsibility, or an ideal of fairness inherent in the idea that one should impose on others only those risks others impose on one. The second part of the paper distinguishes among various conceptions of corrective or compensatory justice and considers arguments – including previous arguments by the author himself – to the effect that tort law is best understood as rooted in principles of corrective justice. This paper argues that although the use of principles of justice may render defensible many (but by no means all) of the claims to repair and to liability recognized in torts, it cannot explain why we have adopted a tort system as the approach to vindicating those claims. Some other principle – probably not one of justice – is needed to explain why it is that the victims claim to repair is satisfied by having his losses shifted to his injurer – rather than through some other means of doing so. The paper concludes that the law of torts cannot be understood – in the sense of being given a rational reconstruction – under any one principle of morality.

Tort law distinguishes between those cases in which a plaintiff's case for recovery requires that he show that the defendant was at fault in causing him harm and those which permit the plaintiff to recover even if the defendant was not at fault. The first sort of cases are said to be governed by principles of fault liability; the second by principles of strict liability.[1] The question for the legal

[1] In addition to fault and strict liability, there are cases resolved under a principle of absolute liability. Strict liability can be defeated by a defence of plaintiff negligence; absolute liability cannot. This paper does not discuss either absolute liability or the moral basis of the various defenses to liability.

philosopher is whether any moral principle or consistent set of such principles can adequately explain and (because they are moral principles) justify both fault and strict liability.

In this essay, which is to appear in two parts in consecutive issues of this journal, I consider four arguments from moral principles that have been offered as explanatory or justificatory of either fault or strict liability (or both). I argue that none of these arguments is fully capable of performing the ambitious explanatory and justificatory tasks their advocates have set for them, that in spite of their shortcomings several of these arguments are insightful and will play a role in any full theory of torts, but that in the end no single moral principle or consistent set of moral principles requires the *tort system*. The arguments I consider are: (1) The Retributive Argument; (2) The Argument from A Theory of Responsibility; (3) The Argument from Reciprocity of Risk; and (4) The Argument from Corrective Justice.[2]

## 1. TORT LIABILITY AND RETRIBUTIVE JUSTICE

The Retributive Argument is suggested by the view taken by tort scholars towards the introduction of the fault principle as a condition of liability. Originally, under the Writ of Trespass an individual could recover for his losses only if he was *directly* injured by another's conduct. An injurer would be liable only if his conduct directly caused another's injury. Direct hits were distinguishable from indirect ones in terms of whether the force set in motion by the agent had come to rest prior to the injury's occurrence. Under Trespass, Arthur would be liable to Richard if, for example, he mashed his head with a two-by-four. If, however, Arthur left the two-by-four about in a place where Richard was very likely to fall over it unwittingly, Arthur would not be liable to make repair to Richard. The directness of the hit, so understood, rather than the character of either the actor or his conduct, was the operative

---

[2] Two other "moral" arguments for a theory of strict liability are discussed briefly in section 3 below.

notion in determining liability under Trespass. Consequently, individuals who were injured indirectly would not recover – even if their injury was the fault of another. Eventually, a new writ, Trespass on the Case, or simply Case, was issued, which allowed recovery for indirect harms. Under Case a victim could recover for an indirect injury provided he could establish that the injurer was at fault in causing the harm. The fault requirement under Case was necessary, otherwise *all* injuries would have been compensable provided there existed a causal connection between the action and the harm. In that case, there would have been no meaningful distinction between Trespass and Case.

The difference between Trespass and Case was this. In order for a victim under Trespass to recover against his injurer he would have had to show that:

(1) He was harmed;
(2) The injurer acted; and
(3) His injury was the direct causal consequence of the injurer's action.

Under Case, the same victim would have had to show that:

(1) He was harmed;
(2) The injurer acted;
(3) His injury was an indirect causal consequence of the injurer's action; and
(4) The injurer's conduct was at fault or negligent.

The obvious problem with the Writs of Trespass and Case was that a defendant (injurer) acting without fault would be liable to those of his victims who suffered injury before the force he put in motion had come to rest, while those who might have been injured at a later stage in the causal sequence were without recourse. This was unfair both to possible injurers and victims: to possible injurers because the absence of culpability would not free them from responsibility for all harms resulting from the same conduct; to possible victims because, in the absence of injurer fault, their expectations for recovery would depend entirely on their place in the causal sequence.

This unfairness was rectified by the mid-nineteenth century cases in which the courts announced that fault was to be a condition of liability in cases involving both direct and indirect hits.[3] Commentators rejoiced over the movement away from concern for the directness of the hit in favor of considerations involving the character of the agent and his actions. In the received view, the substitution of fault for causation marked an abandonment of the immoral standard of strict liability under Trespass (which, after all, imposed liability without regard to fault) in favor of a moral foundation for tort liability based on the fault principle.

The question is what makes the fault principle a moral basis upon which to ground liability and recovery? There are really two questions here: (1) Is the criterion of fault employed in torts rooted in a moral conception of fault? and (2) What is the moral principle that requires imposing liability on the basis of moral fault?

The Retributive Argument purports to give an adequate answer to both questions. (1) Fault in torts marks a moral defect in an actor for his conduct. (2) Liability is justly imposed upon a faulty actor in order to penalize, punish, or nullify his moral fault. Put systematically, the argument is this:

(1) In fault liability a victim cannot recover against his injurer unless his injurer is at fault.
(2) To be at fault is to fail to measure up to a standard of due care.
(3) Failure to satisfy the standard of due care constitutes a moral shortcoming.
(4) Therefore, individuals at fault in causing others harm are morally culpable in having done so.
(5) Therefore, liability is rightly imposed upon them in order to nullify their moral fault.

The first thing to notice about the argument from retributive justice is that it does *not* attempt to provide a moral basis for

[3] Brown v. Kendall, (1850), 60 Mass. 292.

*strict liability*. If any of torts is to be defended on grounds of justice, it will be fault liability only. Consequently, strict liability is to be viewed either as morally unjustified – if the domain of justice is coextensive with the domain of right conduct – or as a justifiable departure from principles of justice – if it is not. How far does the argument go in defending fault liability?[4]

The argument from retributive justice relies on the claims both that to be at fault in torts is to act in a morally culpable fashion, and that tort liability is imposed on individuals in order to justly punish or penalize their moral fault. Neither of these claims can be sustained, however.

An individual may be at fault in torts without his being morally culpable. The divergence of moral from legal (tort) fault is the result of the objective (or external) standard of fault articulated in *Vaughan* v. *Menlove*.[5] According to the objective test, a defendant is at fault whenever he fails to exercise the care of a reasonable man of ordinary prudence – whether or not the defendant himself is capable of compliance. Lack of capacity to comply with the standard of due care may free an individual from moral sanction; normally it will not suffice, however, to free him from tort liability should his failure result in harm to another.

Secondly, we can penalize an individual's fault – moral or other – without the penalty taking the form of his being held liable for the costs of harms his fault occasions. In other words, even if the notions of moral fault and fault in torts converge so that every person who is at fault in torts is morally culpable, the retributive argument could not adequately explain why it is that the victim is compensated by his injurer. Indeed, the retributive argument suggests a very different sort of means for allocating costs: namely, the "at fault pool."

---

[4] The Retributive Thesis is discussed in more detail in J. Coleman, 'On the Moral Argument for the Fault System' *Journal of Philosophy* **81** (1974): 473–90. That argument is criticized in R. Pilon, 'Justice and No-Fault Insurance,' *The Personalist* 57 (1976): 82–92.

[5] Vaughan v. Menlove 3 Bing. NC 468.

Retribution presumably requires penalizing fault whether or not the fault leads on a particular occasion to another person's loss. From the retributive point of view there is no moral difference between wrongful "attempts" and "successes." Faulty motorists, for example, are presumably equally culpable whether or not the fault in their motoring happens to cause harm. The tort system, however, imposes "penalties" only on those whose fault occasions another's loss. Thus, were we to try seriously to do retributive justice in the distribution of accident costs, we would abandon the tort system as we know it. Instead we would first sum the costs of accidents as they accumulate over a specifiable period of time and then identify all faulty conduct – regardless of its having caused any of these losses – and categorize the conduct by the degree of culpability involved in each kind of fault. Once having done this we would then assign points for each fault and arrive at a dollar value for each by dividing the sum of accident costs by the number of points, then multiplying the dollar value of each point by the number of points assigned to each fault. Each wrongdoer would then pay into the pool according to the dollar value of his fault; and each victim would be compensated for the damage suffered.[6] In sum: the central claims of the retributive argument are false; and even if they were true they would lead to a system quite different from the tort system.

## 2. TWO SENSES OF STRICT LIABILITY

There are two elements in any fault judgment: the act and actor-regarding components. The first concerns the relationship between conduct and a standard or norm of evaluation. An *action* is at fault in this sense whenever it fails to measure up to a given standard of evaluation. Before we charge an actor for this failure of compliance, however, we often ask whether the failure in his

---

[6] The "at fault pool" as an alternative to the fault system is discussed in Guido Calabresi, *The Costs of Accidents*, (New Haven: Yale University Press, 1970).

conduct is *his fault*: whether, in other words, the failure in his conduct marks a *failure in his character*. An individual charged with being at fault in his doings might attempt to defeat such an allegation in either of two ways. First, he might try to show that all things considered, his action measures up to the appropriate standard, or that in the circumstances his conduct is a justifiable departure from the appropriate standard: i.e. that his act is not at fault. In contrast, he might admit that the act is at fault, but deny that this failure should be charged against him as his fault, as owing, in other words, to a defect in character or motivation. In the first case, the actor would be offering a *justification* for what he had done; in the second an *excuse*. Justifications undermine the charge that an *act* is at fault; excuses defeat the judgment that an agent is *at fault* for his faulty actions.

We can now distinguish two senses in which liability in torts might be said to be strict, that is, imposed without regard to fault. In one sense, liability is strict if it is imposed regardless of whether the harm caused was justifiably imposed. So if *A justifiably* injures *B* in order to save *C*, but must nevertheless make good *B*'s losses, then *A* is being held strictly liable in this sense for *B*'s loss. In attempting to free himself from liability, *A* would not try to excuse himself for a failure to comply with the dictate against unjustifiably harming others. Instead, he would argue that harming *B* in order to save *C* was, in the circumstances, the *right* thing to do. If he is unable to free himself from responsibility, his liability would be strict in that it would be imposed regardless of the justifiability or reasonableness of what he had done: that is, in spite of the fact that there is no fault in his conduct. In the other sense, liability is strict if it cannot be defeated by what would ordinarily count as an adequate excuse. So if *A* harms *B* in spite of his best efforts to avoid doing so – and if this fact, while it may suffice to free him from moral sanction, fails to relieve him of the burden of compensating *B* – *A*'s liability to *B* is strict in this sense.

Because fault liability cannot normally be defeated by what would ordinarily count as a good excuse, it involves strict liability in the second sense: liability without regard to personal culpability. Fault liability, however, can be defeated by the justification of reasonableness, that is, by a demonstration that the injurer acted as would have a reasonable man of ordinary prudence. Fault liability, therefore, is not strict liability in the first sense.

All arguments to the effect that fault liability is preferable to strict liability (including, but not limited to, the Retributive Argument) because it makes liability depend on personal culpability must be abandoned. Proponents of the moral theory of torts who have relied on the connection between fault and moral culpability as the cornerstone of their efforts are faced with a choice. Either they can attempt to impart normative significance upon the fault principle by subsuming it under an alternative moral principle, or they might reexamine the role the fault principle should play in a correct moral theory of tort law. The next two arguments I consider, from Responsibility and Reciprocity of Risk, adopt the latter approach; the third, from considerations of Corrective Justice, adopts the former.

## 3. THE RESPONSIBILITY THESIS AND STRICT LIABILITY

The difference between strict and fault liability is this: according to strict liability a victim can recover from his injury provided he can establish a causal relationship between his harm and the injurer's conduct (that is not negated by an intervening causal agent). In fault liability, a victim must show that the defendant was at fault and that his fault caused the victim's harm. Richard Epstein has argued that the causal condition, which is central to both strict and fault liability, should be at the center of any moral defence of tort law.[7] The moral weight which was to have been carried by the fault principle in the ill-fated Retributive Argument is to be borne instead by the causal condition. Not only would Epstein's approach, if sound, reduce, if not eliminate entirely,

---

[7] Richard Epstein *A Theory of Strict Liability: Toward A Reformulation of Tort Law*. (San Francisco: Cato Institute, 1980).

the role of fault in a just theory of liability; it would provide a moral foundation for the much maligned rule of strict liability as well. It would do both primarily by identifying as common to strict and fault liability the fact that before the costs of a victim's injury can be shifted to his injurer, he (the victim) must establish a causal connection between the defendant's conduct and his loss.

In the Retributive View, liability is imposed justly provided the defendant is culpable for his doing; otherwise, it is not. In the Responsibility View, an agent's culpability is irrelevant to the legitimacy of his liability; for, in this view, liability is imposed justly whenever an agent is *responsible* – not culpable – for the harm's occurence. Liability follows responsibility, not culpability. The range of consequences for which an individual is responsible, in Epstein's view, is determined by the causal upshots of his volitional action. Thus, if *A* harms *B*, liability for the losses *B* incurs is rightly imposed upon *A*, not because *A* acted wrongly in injuring *B* (he may not have); rather it is because *B*'s losses are *A*'s doing. As Epstein puts it:

> Indeed for most persons, the difficult question is not whether these causal assertions create the presumption (in favor or liability), but whether there are in fact any means to distinguish between causation and responsbility, so close is the connection between what a man does and what he is answerable for.[8]

In short, just liability follows personal responsibility; and the reach of an individual's responsibility is determined by the scope of his causal agency.

The Responsibility Thesis falters because its central claim that justice in liability rests on causal responsibility is both too strong and too weak. It is too strong in that were we to impose liability upon individuals for all the untoward causal consequences of their conduct, we would often find ourselves doing so inappropriately. There are any number of ways, for example, in business and in love, in which *A* may innocently or justifiably harm *B* – where the theory of liability based on causation would have us wrongly

---

[8] *Ibid.*, p. 25.

impose *B*'s losses upon *A*. The problem is that there is no general duty not to cause harm; only a duty not to harm *unreasonably* or *unnecessarily*. Since there may be nothing objectionable in the harm done, causing harm, by itself, provides an inadequate basis for imposing liability. On the other hand, were we to reformulate the prohibition against causing harm as a restriction against causing harm without sufficient reason or justification, we would simply be reintroducing the fault requirement as a condition of liability, since to cause harm unreasonably or unjustifiably is to be at fault in doing so. In short: liability based on causal agency lacks a normative basis. Liability for the harms one causes without sufficient justification has a moral basis in the prohibition against causing unnecessary harm to others. Unfortunately *that* prohibition supports the principle of fault, not strict liability.

The Responsibility Thesis is too weak in that it limits the scope of the harms for which one is responsible to those one causes. Surely one's responsibility extends beyond the limits of one's causal agency. For example, *A* may negligently fail to take steps to prevent harm to *B*: steps which are not only within his grasp but also his duty to take. If *B* is injured, we might blame his loss on *A* on the grounds that it was *A*'s responsibility to prevent it. Still there may be no (metaphysically) acceptable sense in which *A* caused *B*'s injury – especially if we intend our causal judgment to mean something other than the claim that *B*'s loss is *A*'s responsibility. (And, of course, if we want to *justify* the claim that *B* is responsible for *A*'s loss on the grounds that *A* caused it, the claim that he caused it must be logically distinct from the judgment of his responsibility for it.)

The Responsibility Thesis fails because it misses the point of the distinction between two senses of the term "responsible." In one sense, an ascription of responsibility for an action is no more than an identification of authorship. In this sense, when we say that *A* is responsible for *B*'s loss we mean to be saying no more than that *A*, not someone else, is the author of the action that caused the loss. Responsibility in this sense crucially depends on the notion of causation. However, from the fact that *A* is responsible in this sense for *B*'s loss, nothing follows about the appropriateness of shifting *B*'s loss to him; indeed, from this fact alone we cannot determine whether *B*'s loss is one for which he should recover.

In the second sense, an ascription of responsibility amounts to the conclusory judgment that liability to penalty (or reward) is appropriate or warranted. Causal agency, and thus responsibility, in the first sense are often part of the case for grounding a judgment of responsibility in the second sense, but they are neither necessary nor sufficient to doing so. *A* may be responsible (in the second sense) for a loss that he does not cause, but which he ought to have prevented; and he may cause and thus be responsible (in the first sense) for a loss which should be someone else's (perhaps even the victim's) responsibility.

Epstein's strategy, remember, is to put aside the fault principle as central to a just theory of liability in favor of the causal condition. The normative punch of the causal condition is supposed to come from a general theory of responsibility. But causal responsibility is neither a necessary nor a sufficient condition for personal responsibility, and so an adequate account of the latter will not confer upon the former the moral foundation Epstein seeks.

There are two other related lines of argument that have been advanced to support the causal condition as the moral link in a just theory of tort liability. I want to discuss them briefly. One argument relies on the claim that there are no grounds upon which to criticize an individual for causing himself harm. On the other hand, there is injustice in causing another harm. The way to eliminate the latter injustice is to shift the loss from the party upon whom it initially falls to the party who caused it, thereby turning a loss imposed on another into a loss imposed upon oneself. Because tort liability has the effect of turning a loss one imposes on another into a loss one imposes on oneself, it is justified as involving the transformation of an unjust loss (to another) into a permissible one (to oneself.)[9]

---

[9] Certain of Epstein's remarks indicate he has held and argued for such a view. Cf. *Ibid.*, p. 12.

The problem here is that even if it is permissible to harm oneself or to cause oneself to suffer a loss, it is another question whether the *state* is justified in imposing a loss upon an individual. Tort liability, after all, is not a self-inflicted wound. Whether the state is justified through the courts in imposing a loss upon the agent whose conduct occasions another's loss depends upon whether causing another harm is necessarily unjustifiable. It begs the question to assert that a loss *A* imposes upon *B* constitutes an injustice *simply* because it is not a loss *A* imposes upon himself. What's lacking is a moral principle that makes harming another wrong; and once such a theory presents itself (which it is unlikely to do) the rest of the argument becomes excess baggage. For if it is wrong to cause another harm, the loss is rightly shifted to the defendant in order to rectify a wrongful loss, *not* because a justifiably shifted loss is exactly like a self-inflicted one.

The second argument relies on the analogy to Takings. Aspects of this argument are discussed in more detail below, but the idea is simple enough.[10] If *A* takes *B*'s property, *A* has an obligation to return it to *B*, or, if he destroys it, to replace it or to fully compensate *B*. Causing harm *via* a taking requires compensation. Causing another harm, in this view, simply consists in *taking* another's property without his or her consent, and thus requires compensation as well.

The problem here is that the justification for compensation in a Takings case is that the injurer has taken what another has a well established *right* to without securing the property right holder's consent.[11] On the other hand, in causing another harm it does not follow that one has violated another's right or taken what another has a right to. Causing harm is one of the ways in which an individual might diminish another's well being. Taking what another has a right to is another. And while it may always harm an individual to take from him what he has a right to, harming an indi-

---

[10] See Section 7 of Part 2 of this article.

[11] For an argument against the view that takings always involve the infringement of a right, see section 7 of Part II of this article.

vidual need not always consist in violating or infringing a right of his. The analogy between taking property and causing harm breaks down precisely because the former presupposes the existence of a right (whose violation calls for compensation) whereas the latter does not.

## 4. RECIPROCITY OF RISKS

The Retributive and Responsibility Theses, as well as both the analogy to Takings and the argument from self-inflicted harm, do not separate the victim's claim to recompense from the grounds for imposing liability upon his injurer. In the first case, the victim's case for recovery depends on the culpability of his injurer and thus on the appropriateness of imposing the victim's loss upon him. If it would be wrong to impose the victim's loss on his injurer, the victim ought not be compensated. In the second case the victim's claim to recompense hangs on the responsibility of his injurer for it. Absent injurer responsibility, the victim has no claim to recovery. Similar remarks can be made regarding the last two arguments.

Unlike the views we have thus far considered, the argument from the principle of nonreciprocity of risk distinguishes between the grounds of recovery and liability.[12] An argument sufficient to justify a claim for recovery need not suffice to justify imposing liability on a particular injurer. In other words, there might be reasons of one kind to support the proposition that *B* (a victim) ought not shoulder his own losses, without those reasons proving sufficient to warrant shifting *B*'s losses to *A* (his injurer).

In the Reciprocity Thesis, the distinction between justice in recovery and in liability is made out as follows. To be entitled to compensation a victim must suffer a loss due to the nonreciprocal risk taking of another. In order to be justly held liable an injurer must (1) cause another loss in virtue of his nonreciprocal risk

---

[12] The leading advocate of this view is George Fletcher, 'Fairness and Utility in Tort Theory,' *Harvard Law Review* 85 (1972): 537–38.

taking; and (2) lack an adequate excuse for his having done so. Thus, an individual who has an excuse for the harm his nonreciprocal risk taking occasions ought to be free from liability, though his victim (other things being equal) may nevertheless be entitled to repair.

Let us take a closer look at the conditions of liability and recovery under the Reciprocity model. Consider first the grounds of just liability. Because of its reliance on the absence of an excuse as a necessary condition for imposing liability justly, the Reciprocity Thesis, like the Retributive Thesis, but unlike the Responsibility Thesis, *appears* to make culpability a condition of liability (but not of recovery). The excusing conditions requirement plays a different role in the two theories, however. In the Retributive View, the very purpose of liability is to annul or penalize culpable wrongdoing. Imposing liability in the face of an excuse would defeat its very purpose. In the Reciprocity View, liability is imposed, not to penalize wrongdoing, but, as we shall see below, to promote security instead. The excusing conditions requirement therefore serves as a side constraint on the pursuit of maximum security. Liability is imposed to promote security, but the pursuit of security cannot be accomplished at all costs. To secure it consistent with considerations of justice, liability cannot be imposed on those who offer a legitimate excuse for their departures from acceptable levels of risk-creation.

One consequence of the excusing conditions requirement is that the Reciprocity Thesis appears unable to account adequately for either strict or fault liability (though it may yet account for *recovery* under each principle).

That is because while the Reciprocity View makes the absence of an excuse a condition for liability to be imposed justly under both the fault or strict liability principles, in neither case is liability in fact defeasible by a showing by the defendant of a lack of defective motivation on his part.

There are three ways of attempting to meet the objection that the excusing conditions requirement robs the Reciprocity Thesis of much of its explanatory power. The first is to accept the criticism by denying that the Thesis is intended to be explanatory. Instead we should read the Reciprocity Thesis as a *normative* theory of tort law – at least in this regard. Rather than seeking to explain existing practice, its purpose is to set forth the conditions which must be satisfied in order for tort law to be justifiable. To the extent to which existing practice converges with these conditions, it is justifiable. To the extent it does not, it is not. This is the easy way out, and, for that reason, it is not particularly interesting (or plausible).

Alternatively, we might, on behalf of the Reciprocity Theory, simply drop the excusing conditions requirement in the hopes that by doing so we would increase the theory's explanatory, if not its justificatory, strength. Such a move is at least plausible since the excusing conditions requirement and the reciprocity criterion are independent of one another in that they require independent justifications. As we shall see below the reciprocity criterion is presumably connected to the goal of increasing personal security. Pursuing that goal does not entail that individuals be excused from liability for mistaken or otherwise faultless risk creation. Because nothing in the goal of maximizing security appears to require excuses as a defence to liability, why not treat the theory as if it had no such requirement – or at least until a pursuasive argument on its behalf is advanced? The problem with this approach is that it does not take the theory seriously on its own terms.

The last approach is to develop an argument in favor of the excusing conditions requirement which will show not only that such a provision is part of a just theory of liability, but that it is part of *existing* tort practice as well: and therefore that the Reciprocity Thesis is right to insist upon it. There seems to me to be such an argument. In another essay I drew a distinction between two ways in which excuses might defeat ascriptions of fault.[13] One sort of excuse goes to the question of whether the wrongful or harmful conduct should be charged against the individual as

---

[13] 'Mental Abnormality, Personal Responsibility and Tort Liability' in *Mental Illness: Law and Public Policy* (Dordrecht: D. Reidel, 1980).

evidence of defective character or motivation; the other goes to the question of whether the individual satisfies the minimal conditions of voluntary agency. When an individual offers an excuse of the first sort he takes responsibility for the conduct (in the authorship sense) as his doing, but denies that he should be blamed for it; when he offers an excuse of the second sort he denies even that the event in question constitutes a voluntary action of his. Suppose *A* harms *B* unjustifiably. To defeat an ascription of fault (and therefore liability based on fault) *A* might contend that he injured *B* by *mistake*, or that he did so while under an *hypnotic trance*. The first sort of an excuse admits agency, but denies culpability; the second denies agency and therefore culpability. In my piece I argued that every theory of liability must be committed to the existence of excuses of the second sort; otherwise liability will be imposed in the absence of responsible *agency*. So we might understand the Reciprocity Thesis as calling attention to the importance of excusing conditions of the *second sort* as a requirement of just liability.[14] Understood in that way, its reliance upon the absence of an excuse as a condition of just liability would be different from the reliance of the Retributive View on excusing conditions, since the sort of excuses countenanced by that thesis involve those that raise doubts about the agent's culpability – not his agency.

I want to leave the discussion of the role of excuses in the Reciprocity Thesis in favor of the element common to recovery and liability in both strict and fault liability: namely, the criterion of non-reciprocity of risk. Setting aside the excusing conditions requirement for now, the general thesis is this: a victim is entitled to recompense whenever he is injured by another's non-reciprocal risk taking; and an injurer is liable for those harms caused by the non-reciprocal risks his conduct imposes. One person imposes a non-reciprocal risk on others if it differs substantially in degree or kind from those risks others impose upon him. The idea is simple enough and can be readily illustrated by example. Examples of nonreciprocal risk taking include engaging in ultrahazardous

[14] See also Weaver v. Ward, Hobart 134, 80 Eng. Reprint 284.

activities and keeping wild animals on one's property (while one's neighbors confine their affections to traditional domestic pets). The principle of nonreciprocity of risk therefore explains strict liability for harms that result from such activities. Strict liability is appropriate in those cases in which one risk taker imposes risks different from the risks others generally impose upon him.

There are other activities, however, in which individuals generally impose a certain level of risk on one another. Motoring is one example. Liability is not imposed whenever an individual motorist harms another. In the Reciprocity View, that is because activities like motoring involve a level of reciprocal risk taking. For such activities liability is not strict. In order for liability to be imposed, a motorist must negligently harm another. In other words, liability is appropriate only for risks that *exceed* the general level of shared risk. These nonreciprocal risks, those which exceed the level of common risk, are all that is meant, in this view, by negligence.

In fault as well as in strict liability, the key to recovery is nonreciprocity of risk. The difference between fault and strict liability is to be understood in terms of the level of risk that constitutes the "background" of risk against which the criterion of nonreciprocity of risk is to be applied. The fault criterion is appropriate to activities of mutual involvement, like motoring, in which there exists a shared level of background or reciprocal risk taking. A faulty or negligent risk is one that exceeds the level of common or background risk. In activities that do not by nature involve participants imposing similar risks on one another, activities like blasting, strict liability is the appropriate criterion.

The problem with the principle of nonreciprocity of risk is both that it cannot explain liability in cases where liability seems appropriate, and that it would have us impose liability in cases where doing so seems inappropriate.[15] Suppose that *A* and *B* are negligent motorists; assume, moreover that they are negligent in the same respect. With respect to non-negligent motorists, *A* and *B* impose non-reciprocal risks. However, with respect to one

[15] Similar remarks are made in J. Coleman 'Corrective Justice and Wrongful Gain,' in *Journal of Legal Studies* (forthcoming, June 1982).

another, they impose reciprocal or offsetting risks. Because the risks each imposes on the other are reciprocal, neither, in the event of an accident, should have a legitimate claim against the other. But suppose that although *A* and *B* drive negligently with respect to one another, in an accident that occurs between them, *A*'s negligence, but not *B*'s, causally contributes to its occurence. *B* would normally recover against *A* because, though negligent, his conduct did not constitute contributory negligence. *A*'s negligence, not *B*'s, *caused* the harm.[16] If Epstein's theory of torts can be legitimately faulted for overemphasizing the causal condition, Fletcher's can be rightly criticized for underestimating its importance.

Examples of non-reciprocal risk taking that do *not* warrant either liability or recovery are no more difficult to find. Suppose that a non-negligent motorist injures a negligent pedestrian whose negligence is at least partially responsible for the accident. By the very nature of the two activities, the motorist imposes nonreciprocal risks on the pedestrian. In the Reciprocity Thesis the pedestrian ought to be entitled to recover. The pedestrian, however, would not normally be entitled to recompense since his negligence is a bar to recovery.[16] Because there is no sense in which his negligence can be expressed in terms of his imposing non-reciprocal risks upon the motorist, there is no way of explaining the judgment against him in terms of reciprocity of risk. Pedestrians simply do not threaten the security of motorists in the way in which motorists threaten the security of pedestrians. On the other hand, the pedestrian's negligence confronts the motorist with behavior that he could not reasonably be expected to guard against. And it is that feature of the situation that frees the motorist from liability to the pedestrian, rather than a nonexistent reciprocity of risk between them.

Even if the principle of reciprocity could obviate these difficulties, the question remains why anyone would think that non-reciprocity of risk constitutes a *moral* basis for determining liabili-

---

[16] In some cases contributing negligence does not bar, but only diminishes the extent of recovery.

ty and recovery. What, in other words, is the moral principle that underwrites the criterion of nonreciprocity of risk?

In defence of the Reciprocity Thesis, George Fletcher cites Aristotle on corrective justice, but the argument he advances on its behalf relies on Rawls. The difference is important. Rawls is concerned with the principles of distributive justice; Aristotle on corrective justice is not – at least not directly.

Citing Rawls, Fletcher argues for nonreciprocity of risk by constructing a principle of *distributive justice* that he takes to be an analog of Rawls's first principle of justice. Fletcher contends that each individual is entitled to the maximum degree of security compatible with a like level of security for all. (The "analogy" is to Rawls's principle that each individual is entitled to the most extensive liberty compatible with a like liberty for all.) Fletcher goes on to define security as freedom from harm without compensation. So defined, everyone has a right not to be harmed without being compensated. If we take Fletcher at his word, it is the fact that one has suffered harm that entitles one to recompense, not the fact that one's harm results from another's nonreciprocal risk taking. The principle that is supposed to impart moral significance on the criterion of nonreciprocity of risk actually has the effect of eliminating it. With nonreciprocity as a condition of liability out of the way, Fletcher's view collapses into Epstein's; in fact into a less defensible version of Epstein's, since Epstein is committed to the weaker proposition that causing harm is sufficient to establish the *prima facie* case for liability only.

To maintain the centrality of nonreciprocity of risk in Fletcher's theory one must reformulate the principle that is to confer moral significance on it. This can be accomplished in a number of ways, each of which is problematic. First, one might redefine the notion of security more narrowly as freedom from exposure to nonreciprocal risk taking. An individual's right to security is then the freedom from having nonreciprocal risks imposed on him. If the right one has is to freedom from nonreciprocal risks, then the right to recover that is based upon it does not require that one actually suffer damages. Exposure to nonreciprocal risk, whether or not it results in damages, triggers the right to recompense. The effect is to eliminate as central to liability what is currently necessary in both strict and fault liability: the requirement that one who seeks relief must establish damages.

It will not do to redefine security even more narrowly as freedom from harm due to nonreciprocal risk for that would trivialize the enterprise by restating the criterion of recovery as the principle that is supposed to justify it: People are entitled to recover for harms caused by nonreciprocal taking because there is a principle that asserts that individuals have such a right.

In short, absent a convincing moral argument to the contrary, it seems implausible to contend that a person's obligation to repair depends merely on the fact that his conduct imposes risks different in degree or kind from those his victim imposes on him. More may not always be better, but surely it need not always be worse; and diversity is presumably a desirable thing – at least from time to time. In fairness to Fletcher, however, there is an insight in this view that should not be overlooked. It is that the difference between recoverable and nonrecoverable losses might best be understood in terms of the difference between background and nonbackground risks. That is, there is a level of risk that individuals are expected to bear for which they can not expect to receive recompense in the event harm occurs. Exposure to risks that exceed the level of background risk creates the legitimate expectation of recompense in the event harm occurs. The problem with Fletcher's view is just that there exists no good reason for thinking that the distinction between backgrounds and nonbackground risks – and therefore between compensable and other losses – should be put in terms of the distinction between reciprocal and non-reciprocal risk taking.

*University of Arizona*

JULES L. COLEMAN

# MORAL THEORIES OF TORTS: THEIR SCOPE AND LIMITS: PART II

ABSTRACT. One approach to legal theory is to provide some sort of rational reconstruction of all or of a large body of the common law. For philosophers of law this has usually meant trying to rationalize a body of law under one or another principle of justice. This paper explores the efforts of the leading tort theorists to provide a moral basis – in the sense of rational reconstruction based on alleged moral principles – for the law of torts. The paper is divided into two parts. In the first part I consider and reject the view that tort law is best understood as falling either within the ambit of the principle of retributive justice, a comprehensive theory of moral responsibility, or an ideal of fairness inherent in the idea that one should impose on others only those risks others impose on one. The second part of the paper distinguishes among various conceptions of corrective or compensatory justice and considers arguments – including previous ones by the author himself – to the effect that tort law is best understood as rooted in principles of corrective justice. This paper argues that although the principles of justice may render defensible many (but by no means all) of the claims to repair and to liability recognized in torts, it cannot explain why we have adopted a tort system as the approach to vindicating those claims. Some other principle – probably not one of justice – is needed to explain why it is that the victim's claim to repair is satisfied by having his losses shifted to his injurer – rather than through some other means of doing so. The paper concludes that the law of torts cannot be understood – in the sense of being given a rational reconstruction – under any one principle of morality.

In the first part of this essay[1] I considered and rejected the view that the sort of justice involved in tort law is retributive, as well as the views that tort law incorporates an ideal of personal responsibility or enforces a theory of reciprocity in the distribution of risk. I now want to consider several arguments for the claim that tort law involves corrective justice. The structure of this part of the

[1] 'Moral Theories of Torts: Their Scope and Limits, Part I,' *Law and Philosophy* 1 (1982): 371–390. Reprinted above.

essay is as follows: First, I will present a general characterization of the principle of corrective justice; then I will explore the extent to which this conception of corrective justice explains fault and strict liability. I argue that there is a significant distinction between the grounds and modes of rectification, that the principle of corrective justice applies to the former, and that tort law constitutes an instance of the latter. I claim therefore that essential elements of tort law simply cannot be explained by reference to the principle of corrective justice. Once having limited the discussion to the sources of justification for claims to recovery and liability I argue that corrective justice justifies several claims to recovery but few to liability in both fault and strict liability. The paper closes by considering alternative conceptions of corrective justice which purport to justify tort law completely. I offer several additional reasons for accepting the narrower, more modest account of the scope of corrective justice in justifying and explaining elements of tort law.

## I. CORRECTIVE JUSTICE

There are a number of statements or ways of characterizing the requirements of corrective justice. I want to begin with the following conception of corrective justice. On this view, corrective or rectificatory justice is concerned with wrongful gains and losses. Rectification is, on this view, a matter of justice when it is necessary to protect a distribution of holdings (or entitlements) from distortions which arise from unjust enrichments or wrongful losses. The principle of corrective justice requires the annulment of both wrongful gains and losses.

In order to invoke the principle of corrective justice to support eliminating or rectifying a distortion in a distribution of holdings or entitlements, the distribution need not itself be just. Corrective justice is a matter of justice on this view *not* because it promotes justice in the distribution of holdings, but rather because it remedies unjust departures from the prevailing distribution of holdings. However, following the requirements of corrective justice is necessary to maintain a just distribution of holdings. Therefore, any theory of distributive justice must make provisions for a theory of corrective justice. Corrective justice is an independent principle of justice precisely because it may be legitimately invoked to protect or reinstate distributions of holdings which would themselves fail the test of distributive justice.[2]

This conception of corrective justice puts a great burden on the concepts of wrongful gain and loss. Without yet offering a set of conditions necessary and sufficient for a loss or gain to count as wrongful, we might attempt to characterize the basic idea by examples. Within the category of wrongful losses are those one suffers through the fault or wrongful conduct of another. Within the class of unjust enrichments are those one secures through one's wrongdoing, as in many instances of fraud and theft. A compensable or undeserved loss need not, however, be the result of another's wrongdoing. Sometimes the justifiable, i.e., nonwrongful, taking of what another has a well-established right to justifies a claim to rectification. An instance of a justifiable "taking" that creates a compensable loss is given by the following example of Joel Feinberg:

> Suppose that you are on a back-packing trip in the mountain country when an unanticipated blizzard strikes the area with such ferocity that your life is imperiled. Fortunately, you stumble onto an unoccupied cabin, locked and boarded up for the winter, clearly somebody else's private property. You smash a window, enter, and huddle in a corner for three days until the storm abates. During this period you help yourself to your unknown benefactor's food supply and burn his wooden furniture in the fireplace to keep warm. Surely you are justified in doing all these things, and yet you have infringed the clear rights of another person.[3]

---

[2] This analysis of corrective justice is worked out in more detail in Jules Coleman, 'Mental Abnormality, Personal Responsibility and Tort Liability', in *Mental Illness: Law and Public Policy*, Brody and Engelhardt, eds. (Dordrecht: D. Reidel, 1980), p. 107.

[3] Joel Feinberg, 'Voluntary Euthanasia and the Inalienable Right to Life,' *Philosophy and Public Affairs* 7 (1978): 93–123.

Feinberg argues, and I concur, that in spite of the justifiability of what you have done, you owe the owner of the cabin compensation for his food and furniture. Though these examples do not define in any strict sense the operative notion of wrongfulness, they help to characterize it sufficiently to make the notion a useful one.

Given this general conception of corrective justice, the above examples of wrongful gain and loss, and the central distinction between the grounds of recovery and liability, we can begin to spell out an account of the role of corrective justice in tort theory.

## II. CORRECTIVE JUSTICE AND TORT LAW

The distinction between the grounds of recovery and liability is best understood as a difference between two propositions. The first is that the victim has a legitimate or justifiable claim to repair; the other is that there are sufficient grounds for imposing liability upon an injurer. The question is when and to what extent does the principle of corrective justice ground either or both of these claims. This question may be asked with respect to liability and recovery in both fault and strict liability.

### A. *The Fault Principle*

#### 1. *Claims to Repair in Fault*

Under the fault principle a victim has a claim to repair only if his loss results from another's fault. A loss that is the consequence of another's fault is, in the sense just characterized, a wrongful one. Since the principle of corrective justice requires annulling wrongful losses, it supports the victim's claim to recompense in fault liability. Once a plaintiff has established a claim to repair as a matter of corrective justice, the burden shifts to the defendant who may present reasons why the plaintiff's claim should not prevail. These reasons, the defendant's positive defence, usually consist in his trying to establish either that the plaintiff assumed the risk or that he contributed by his own fault to the damages for which he seeks redress. The claim here is not that a plaintiff injured by another's fault invariably has a legitimate claim to repair as a matter of corrective justice. Rather, in the absence of either wrongdoing on his part or an assumption by him of exposure to negligent risk taking, his being harmed by the fault of another gives him a claim to repair that can be grounded on the principle of corrective justice.

On the retributive model, recovery and liability depend on the injurer being morally at fault for the victim's damages. That requirement of the retributive view means it cannot account for the principle of fault liability in torts which, though it requires fault, does not require moral fault as a basis of liability. The corrective justice model does not face this problem, for though the victim's claim to repair is based on the existence of fault in his injurer's conduct, the fault in the doing need not exemplify a fault in the doer. The aim of corrective justice is to identify a class of gains and losses as warranting nullification, not to identify defective motivation as warranting penalty or punishment. Consequently, under the corrective justice model, a victim's claim to repair does not depend on whether or not his injurer has an excuse for his conduct. Corrective justice squares then with the practice in torts of not generally permitting excuses to defeat liability even in cases involving the fault principle.

2. *Corrective Justice and Liability under the Fault Principle*

The relationship between corrective justice and the proposition that an individual ought to be liable for the untoward consequences of his fault is somewhat more complex. There are two kinds of cases in which the principle of corrective justice grounds an injurer's liability under the fault principle: (1) those cases in which an individual's fault results not only in another's loss, but in his gain as well; and (2) those cases in which an individual secures a wrongful gain through his fault, though his gain is not the result of another's loss. Unjust enrichment through fraud is an example of a wrongful gain that corresponds to another's wrongful loss; non-harm-causing, but nevertheless negligent, motoring is an example of conduct that creates wrongful gain in the absence of a corresponding wrongful loss.[4]

An individual may innocently, that is, nonculpably, secure a wrongful gain: for example if he innocently takes something that belongs to another believing it to be his. The important difference is between the wrong done and the agent's culpability for having done it. If the nonculpable agent gains by taking what he has no right to, he has secured a wrongful gain through no culpable fault of his own. Nevertheless, corrective justice requires that he forfeit his gain. Because his culpability is irrelevant to determining if the gain ought to be annulled in these cases, corrective justice squares once again with tort practice in which excuses do not normally defeat liability under the fault principle.

Consider the case of negligent motoring. Negligent motoring may or may not result in an accident. Whether it does or not, individuals who drive negligently often secure a wrongful gain in doing so: namely, the "savings" from not taking adequate safety precautions – those required of the reasonable man of ordinary prudence.[4] This form of wrongful gain is not, *ex hypothesi*, the result of anyone else's wrongful loss. On the other hand, if a negligent motorist causes another harm, he normally secures no *additional* gain in virtue of his doing so. In this respect faulty motoring differs from the usual case of fraud or theft.

Because harmful, negligent motoring does not result in any wrongful gain (apart from that which is the result of negligence itself), the obligation to repair the victim's wrongful loss cannot be entirely grounded on a foundation of corrective justice. There is, in other words, no wrongful gain correlative of the wrongful loss the faulty injurer imposes upon his victim; and no reason

---

[4] It does not follow that a person who fails to comply with the standard of reasonable care secures a gain. First, avoiding a cost or a loss is not equivalent to securing a gain; moreover, a person may use more effort than others and still not satisfy the standard of reasonable care. Therefore I want to amend the position I put forth in 'Corrective Justice and Wrongful Gain,' *Journal of Legal Studies*, that negligent motorists *invariably* secure a wrongful gain.

therefore as a matter of corrective justice alone for imposing the victim's loss upon his injurer. The wrongful gain, if any, negligent motorists do secure is logically distinct from any loss they may cause others; and so the occasion of another's loss cannot be the moral basis for annulling these gains as a matter of justice.

### 3. *Grounds and Modes of Rectification*

Where liability and recovery are determined by the criterion of fault, the principle of corrective justice may be invoked to support: (1) the claim to repair of a faultless victim injured by the fault of another; and (2) the claim that an injurer who has secured gain through his fault either at the expense of another or in the absence of another's wrongful loss ought to forfeit his gain. One important claim that corrective justice cannot ground is that a faulty injurer who secures no gain through his fault ought to be held liable in damages to his victim. The reason for that is quite simple. The concern of corrective justice is wrongful gains and losses. The faulty injurer we are imagining secures no gain: no gain, no liability as a matter of corrective justice. To find the source of his liability we must look elsewhere.

In addition to recognizing the legitimacy of certain claims to repair (and to liability), the tort system constitutes a specific means of vindicating claims it recognizes as valid. In the standard case, if the victim has a valid claim to repair, his claim is satisfied by imposing liability in the form of a duty to compensate on his injurer. The principle of corrective justice goes part of the way to justifying the claims to repair and liability recognized as valid in torts under the fault principle. The question is whether the principle of corrective justice requires and therefore justifies this additional, central feature of the tort system: namely the mode of rectification according to which claims to repair are satisfied by conferring a right to repair on the plaintiff and imposing the corresponding duty of compensation on the defendant. My view is that the principle of corrective justice neither requires nor explains this central feature of tort law. Both the question and my answer to it require some further distinctions.

Whenever we ask for a justification of tort law we are really asking for a justification of at least four distinct features of tort law. These are: (1) the *foundation* of a claim that a person has suffered a compensable loss or that he has secured an undeserved gain; (2) the *mode of rectification* – that is, the manner in which unjust gains and losses are to be eliminated; (3) the *character of rectification* – that is, whether a particular form of compensation, e.g., monetary awards, is appropriate in all cases; and (4) the *extent of rectification* – that is, just how much of a person's gain or loss ought to be eliminated. Much theorizing about tort law goes astray for its failure to draw these distinctions.

I want to draw attention to the distinction between the grounds and modes of rectification. This is the difference between setting forth the criterion that makes determinate the gains and losses a body of law that seeks to do justice should remedy and developing the procedure for doing so. The central point I want to make is that while the principle of corrective justice provides a substantial, but nevertheless partial, answer to the first of these questions – which gains and losses ought to be annulled – it does not provide an answer to the second – how ought we go about annulling them.

There clearly are claims to repair which the tort system recognizes and satisfies and which are rooted in considerations other than corrective justice: for example, those involved in products liability, where the best arguments for recompense are based on considerations either of cost-avoidance, i.e. efficiency, or cost-spreading, i.e. distributive justice (and, on some views, utility). Moreover, there are claims to repair that *are* grounded in the principle of corrective justice, but which are not recognized or satisfied within torts: for example, claims to reliance or benefit damages recognized and vindicated in contracts, not torts.

The principle of corrective justice may inform us that a person injured by another's negligent motoring has a legitimate claim to repair, as does a promisee who to his detriment rightly relies upon another's promise. Similarly, it may justify the claim that a person who benefits from an agreement that he fails to execute has secured a gain which ought to be annulled. However, the principle of corrective justice does *not* tell us how we should go about making good these claims. It does not inform us which claims are most appropriately dealt with under contract and which under torts; nor does it specify a particular mode of relief within either contract or tort. The law of torts provides one set of ways of rectifying wrongful gains and losses; the law of contracts another; the law of restitution still another. All are means of satisfying claims to repair, many of which are grounded in the principle of corrective justice. It cannot possibly be the principle of corrective justice, then, that explains the difference in frameworks and in modes of rectification.

Another way of putting this point is as follows. On the one hand there is the moral theory of corrective justice which requires annulling wrongful gains and losses as a means of protecting given distributions of holdings from distortions. The central concern of the theory is to spell out in a nonquestion-begging way a criterion for determining which gains and losses are wrongful. Once this has been done, the theory can provide the foundation for specific claims to repair and to liability.

On the other hand, there is the tort system which is concerned not only with the legitimacy of certain claims to repair, but with developing a specific means of vindicating or satisfying them (as well as others not based on corrective justice). That is, the tort system, once it recognizes the legitimacy of a claim to repair, goes one step further; it satisfies that claim by conferring on the the victim a right to repair which constitutes a valid claim to compensation against his injurer.

What are the implications of the distinction between the grounds and modes of recovery for the corrective justice theory of fault liability? There is an argument from corrective justice for rectifying the losses faultless victims suffer at the hands of their faulty injurers; there is, as well, an argument for eliminating whatever gains a defendant might secure from his culpable fault, as in fraud, or from his innocent fault, as in his mistakenly taken what he is not justified in having. In contrast, there is no argument from corrective justice for imposing any sort of liability upon a faulty injurer who, though he causes another's loss, does not gain thereby. After all, he has secured no gain which it is the concern of corrective justice to nullify. This is not to say that there are *no* grounds whatsoever for imposing a liability upon an injurer (even liability for his victim's losses) – only that as a matter of logic, corrective justice cannot be among them. So far so good. But my claim goes further still. I maintain that even when an injurer *gains* through his fault in causing another harm, there is no argument from corrective justice which requires that we impose his victim's loss upon him. What corrective justice requires is that both his gain and his victim's loss be annulled. To be sure, provided the gain to him and the loss to his victim are equal (they rarely are), imposing the victim's loss upon him will have the fortuitous effect from the point of view of corrective justice of cancelling both. But this just shows that sometimes there is an argument from economy or efficiency for the tort system – not that there is an argument from corrective justice for it.

B. *Corrective Justice and Strict Liability*

1. *What Is Strict Liability?*

Strict liability is liability without regard to fault. That is, the plaintiff is not required to establish that his injurer is at fault in order to make his case for repair. There are two senses of "fault" and therefore two ways in which liability may be imposed without regard to it. An ascription of fault may be defeated either by an excuse or by a defense of reasonableness (by a justification). Liability imposed when an individual has an excuse, i.e., in the absence of culpability, is strict. Fault liability based on the objective criterion of due care is strict liability in this sense. Liability imposed for damages resulting from reasonable or justifiable risk taking is strict liability as well. Strict liability in torts involves both senses of liability without regard to fault: it can be defeated neither by an excuse nor a justification. The question then is to what extent the principle of corrective justice can ground claims to repair, and liability for damages and gains resulting from conduct that may be entirely without fault.

2. *Corrective Justice and the Defendant's Liability in Takings Cases*

I suggested at the beginning of this essay that the principle of corrective justice might ground certain claims to repair even where the victim's damages could not be traced to a fault in either his injurer or in his injurer's conduct. Feinberg's back-packing example provided one such case. *Vincent* v. *Lake Erie Transport*[5] and other "takings" cases fall into this category as well. In *Vincent* the defendant shipowner kept his vessel lashed to the plaintiff's dock during a storm when it would have been unreasonable, even foolhardy, for him to set out to sea. The storm battered the ship against the dock, causing damages assessed at five hundred dollars. Unlike the wrongful losses in fault liability, the losses that arise from such "takings" are not the result of wrongdoing in the ordinary sense. The taking may be reasonable or justifiable as it is in Feinberg's example, and as it is in *Vincent* v. *Lake Erie*. The question is whether the gains and losses involved in these cases are wrongful in the sense required by the principle of corrective justice.

In cases in which a defendant justifiably takes what another has, his *gain* is not wrongful and there is no claim as a matter of justice that he forfeit it. There is an important difference between the gains one secures from *excusable* mischief, and those one might accrue from engaging in a *justifiable* departure from the usual norm of behavior. In offering an excuse, one admits that one's doing is wrongful, but denies culpability for it. Because the act in question is wrongful, the losses that result from it are wrongful as well. Though we would be unjustified in blaming the injurer for what he had done, we would be right in barring him from enjoying his innocently secured advantage or gain. On the other hand, in offering a justification, one denies that one's conduct (all things considered) falls below the relevant standard of conduct.

---

5 109 Minn. 456, 124 N.W. 221 (1910).

Because the conduct satisfies the pertinent standard, the gains one may secure are nonwrongful ones.

Furthermore, treating the gains one secures through justifiable takings as wrongful would have the unhappy consequence of requiring as a matter of justice that the taker forfeit them. This would surely defeat the purpose of recognizing the conduct as justifiable.[6]

I am not claiming that there are no grounds for imposing on the injurer a duty to render compensation. If I justifiably take some medicine of yours in an emergency, and in doing so I save my life, the very least I owe you is the market price of the medicine. The nature, extent, and grounds of liability in these sorts of cases raise enormously interesting questions, especially regarding the interface of torts and contracts. For when we think of the sort of compensation that is appropriate in these cases, we tend to think in terms of an agreement the victim and injurer would have bargained to: an agreement which would have led to the voluntary transfer, rather than the forced exchange, of the taken resource. Similarly, the hypothetical contract as a measure of one's duty to repair is used in contracts to determine the allocation of risk on matters in which the actual contract is silent. The use of the hypothetical contract with its reliance upon the standard of reasonableness has led several commentators to fret over contracts being swallowed by tort doctrine. Indeed, in the takingslike cases we have several good examples of the merging of tort and contract doctrines. The point is that while there may be very good reasons for imposing a duty to compensate on one who justifiably takes what another has a right to, corrective justice is not among them.

### 3. *Corrective Justice and the Victim's Claim to Repair in Takings Cases*

What are the grounds, if any, for thinking of the victim's loss as

---

[6] If the gain to the ship owner is wrongful just because it involves a right and is therefore subject to anullment, he would have to forfeit the cargo, or its dollar equivalent thus eliminating the very reason for his keeping the ship docked.

wrongful, and therefore its rectification as required as a matter of corrective justice? One way of getting at an answer to this question involves looking first at cases in which the injurer *wrongly* acts contrary to the victim's property right. Suppose that instead of justifiably burning a cabin owner's furniture in order to save his own life, a mountain climber, while under no threat to his life, happens upon a cabin, enters it without the owner's permission, and goes about destroying its contents for "kicks."

On one view, the victim's claim to repair derives from the fact that the mountain climber has acted contrary to the cabin owner's right. On this view, within the bundle of rights that constitute ownership of the cabin is included the right that others not burn or otherwise destroy the cabin or its contents without first securing the owner's permission to do so. The mountain climber's wrongful conduct is contrary to this right; and for that reason, the victim has a legitimate claim to repair.

One can, however, explain the claim to repair in this case without referring to any of the victim's rights. Rights protect or guarantee interests. Whether or not the cabin owner has a right that the backpacker not destroy his furniture, he certainly has a *legitimate interest* in the hiker's not doing so. The hiker's conduct contrary to that interest wrongly harms the cabin owner because it is a harm a reasonable person of ordinary prudence would not have imposed, that is, it is not a reasonable or justifiable harm. The hiker is at fault: and at fault then in causing damage to the cabin. Those losses, on the analysis given above, are wrongful ones and warrant recompense as a matter of corrective justice. The victim's claim to repair is overdetermined by the injurer's conduct. His right to repair may be explained either by the fault in the injurer's conduct or by the invasion of his property right.

Now consider the case as Feinberg presents it, in which the injurer's conduct is *not* wrongful. The victim's claim to repair can no longer be explained as rooted in the fault of the injurer; the injurer is simply not at fault in his conduct. This suggests that the claim to repair rests on the existence of the victim's right. The cabin owner's right not to have his furniture destroyed is *not violated.* A violation is a *wrongful* act contrary to a right. Instead, in this view, the victim's right not to have his furniture destroyed is *infringed*; an infringement of a right is a *nonwrongful* act contrary to it.[7] If the claim to compensation rests on the existence of a property right in *infringement* cases, the *best* explanation of compensation in cases involving right violations depends on the existence of such a right. In short, whenever a victim has an established property right, losses that result from its invasion are wrongful and thus compensable; the argument for compensation depends on the action being contrary to an existing right, not on the wrongfulness of the action contrary to it. This suggests the general thesis that a victim is entitled to repair as a matter of corrective justice if his loss results from either the wrongful conduct of another or from an infringement of a right of his. Because violations of rights are wrongful, they can be covered under the clause that makes a loss wrongful if it results from wrongful conduct. Thus it would be redundant to provide a special clause for right violations.

This way of putting the relationship between corrective justice and the grounds of repair raises two problems. First, the claims to repair in rights-infringements cases do not rely in any way upon the injurer's conduct being wrongful. In that way they differ from the fault liability cases discussed earlier in which the injurer's conduct is at fault, even if the injurer himself is not. Here neither the doer nor the doing is wrong. What reason do we have then for thinking of the victim's losses as wrongful in the sense required by corrective justice? The answer is that there is no sense in which the losses involved here are wrongful. "Wrongful" may simply be the wrong term. I think we should find some more felicitous, less misleading alternative. Still, I have no objection to using "wrongful" in the context of the principle of corrective justice provided the reader is made aware that the term is meant to apply more broadly. Perhaps we would do well to substitute for "wrongful" the term "unjust," which is less misleading, but not an altogether happy

[7] The distinction between infringements and violations of rights is discussed in Judith Jarvis Thomson, 'Rights and Compensation,' *Nous* 14 (1980): 3–15.

alternative – if only because it makes the principle of corrective justice sound a bit redundant: i.e., corrective justice requires annulling unjust gains and losses. From here on, the view under consideration is that corrective justice requires annulling unjust gains and losses; and a gain or loss is unjust if it results either from a wrong or from the infringement of a right.

Second, one might object to distinguishing damages that result from wrongs from those that result from the invasion of a right. What else could a wrong be if not an invasion of a right? In this view, wrongs are things done to rights. If this view is correct, the principle of corrective justice – that unjust gains and losses ought to be annulled – is simply the view that all and only damages which result from the invasion, i.e., an infringement or a violation, of a right must be annulled. In this view, it is not just that in some cases – infringement cases – one has to cite a right to explain the right to repair; if one cannot cite a right in every case then there are no grounds for recognizing a right to repair. This objection raises serious questions about the analysis of corrective justice I have been developing, and I want now to turn my attention to it. I want to begin by evaluating the claim that the only way to understand the claim to repair in *Vincent* v. *Lake Erie* and in Feinberg's example is by viewing them as involving an infringement of property rights.

## 4. *Infringed Rights and Principles of Compensation*

The infringement thesis is not the only way of characterizing cases like Feinberg's and *Vincent* v. *Lake Erie*. Instead of claiming that the right not to have his furniture destroyed (or dock damaged) had been infringed by the mountain climber's (ship captain's) conduct, we might say that, in the circumstances, the right had been overridden; or we might say that the cabin (dock) owner, in fact, had no right that his furniture (dock) not be destroyed (damaged); or we might say that the cabin (dock) owner only had a right that his furniture (dock) not be destroyed (damaged) *impermissibly* or *unjustifiably*. In short, instead of characterizing the cases as involving the infringement of a right, we could explain them as involving either action more important than that required by the right, or as conduct that is *not* contrary to a right. How would we choose these alternatives? What is at stake in doing so?

Proponents of the infringement thesis argue on its behalf that characterizing these cases as involving the infringement of a right is necessary to explain the victim's claim to repair as required by justice. Because the other characterizations deny the existence of an effective or operative right in the circumstances, they cannot account either for the claim to repair or the duty to compensate.

Put another way: according to the infringement theorists, when we look at these cases we find ourselves having two intuitions. One is that the injurer acted permissibly or justifiably; the other is that the victim has a legitimate claim to repair. The only way we can do justice to both of these intuitions (i.e., render them consistent) is to characterize the cases as involving the existence of full-fledged rights permissibly invaded; that is, infringed. Otherwise there is no argument for compensation as a matter of justice.

One way of understanding the infringement theory is to view it as part of the larger theory about the relationship between rights and compensation to which we referred earlier. In this view, the right to repair and the duty to compensate simply cannot be grounded unless one can cite an existing, effective right that has been invaded. Violations are wrongful invasions of rights and therefore explain the fault liability cases; infringements are permissible or justifiable invasions and are necessary to explain the strict liability, or takings cases.

Whatever reasons there might be for characterizing takings cases as infringements, the claim that it is impossible otherwise to explain a victim's claim to repair as a matter of justice is *not* among them. Surely a victim's claim to repair can derive from a more general *principle* of justice as well as from a theory of rights. We can do a person wrong and thereby cause him to suffer a wrongful or unjust loss without violating any rights of his. For example, the losses for which individuals receive recompense under the principle of fault liability do not involve the invasion of a property right. Instead they involve wrongs which consist in the unjustifiable harming of a legitimate interest.[8] That there are no existing property rights in these cases is shown by the fact that in the absence of injurer fault, no liability or recovery is warranted. That is, in order to recover, the victim's interest must be *wrongly* interfered with; justifiable, i.e., nonwrongful interference does not trigger either recovery or liability. In contrast, if a right were involved – as the infringement theory insists it must if recompense is the victim's due – then it would not matter whether the defendant's conduct were justifiable. In fact, recovery depends crucially on the justifiability of the injurer's conduct; and because it does, the case for it depends not on rights violations or infringements, but on the existence of a general principle of corrective justice which governs which losses and gains are subject to anullment.

The infringement thesis can be treated as distinct from the more general view that wherever there is a claim to repair as a matter of justice one must be able to cite a right, the violation or infringement of which grounds the claim. Proponents of the infringement thesis could distinguish those cases in which property *interests* are involved and those in which property *rights* are involved. Where interests are involved there is no right which can be cited as a basis of one's claim to repair. However, it does not follow that there can be no legitimate claims to repair in such cases. Rather, making out one's case for repair requires establishing that one's property interests are *unjustifiably* or *wrongly* harmed. That may suffice to ground recovery without appeal to rights. The infringement theorist could be understood as recognizing all this, but as drawing our attention to those other cases, like Feinberg's, in which the relevant property right *is* present. We can understand the infringement thesis to be the claim that in these cases only, the claim to repair must cite the infringement of a right as its basis.

It is simply not true, however, that in every case in which

---

8 The classic account of harms as involving interfering with legitimate interests is developed in J. Feinberg, *Social Philosophy* (Englewood Cliffs, N.J.: Prentice Hall, 1971).

there are property rights, all claims to repair must point to these rights as their basis. In cases in which property rights are *unjustifiably* invaded – that is, violated – the victim's claim to repair can rest on the fact that his losses result from the wrongful interference with a legitimate interest of his. The violation of a right is wrongful, and losses that result from such conduct are wrongful in the sense required by the principle of corrective justice. The grounds for repair rely not on rights, but on unjustified damage having been done. Consequently, even where there are property rights, claims to repair need not point to them as their basis.

This further narrows the scope of the infringement thesis. Its claim must be that in those cases where there is an alleged property right and conduct which is both *permissible* and contrary to it, the claim to compensation can be explained as a matter of justice only if one can point to a right infringed by the injurer's conduct. It is not at all clear that even this claim can be sustained, for even in these cases, repair may derive directly from a principle of compensation, rather than from the existence of an infringed right.

Let's distinguish further between two claims the infringement thesis could be making. The first is that an infringed right is necessary to the *meaningfulness* of claims to repair. The second is that an infringed right is all that could *justify* such a claim. Surely it is not necessary to the explanation or meaningfulness of claims to repair that one be in a position to cite the existence of a right. Suppose there existed a principle of compensation that went as follows: No person can use another's property for his good and the other's detriment without permission: or in the absence of permission, without compensation for its use and for whatever damages may result. Gains and losses that result from the use of property in violation of this principle would be unjust enrichments and unfair losses and require recompense as a matter of justice. No appeal to the infringement of a right grounds the loser's claim to repair. The point is *not* that this principle states a requirement of morality – though some variation of the principle very well might. Rather, it is that reference to such a principle could make claims to repair *meaningful* in the absence of a property right – even in those cases in which the infringement theory contends a claim to repair cannot be understood unless the victim can cite a right as its basis. Presumably, Feinberg's example and *Vincent* v. *Lake Erie* involve conduct that falls within the ambit of the principle spelled out above. Consequently, in both sorts of cases the victim can claim repair by invoking the principle, rather than by citing a property right.

On behalf of the infringement thesis, one might object to this analysis on the grounds that appealing to this principle requires, at least indirectly, an appeal to the relevant property right. In other words, the principle talks about the "use of another's property." Thus, it presupposes property and ownership. Ownership is best understood as consisting in bundles of rights regarding the property: for example, its use, transfer, protection and the like. Among the rights constitutive of ownership is the right that others not destroy or damage it (or some other such right that can be invoked in the appropriate case). So the principle really does not avoid reference to rights.

Moreover, or so the argument goes, what reason could one advance in favor of the principle cited, other than that because individuals have a right not to have their property destroyed or damaged others ought not destroy or damage it without rendering compensation. Not only does this principle refer obliquely to the requisite right, the existence of the right is all that could ever justify the principle. At least with respect to these sorts of cases the infringement thesis cannot be circumvented.

However, this seems altogether too strong a claim on behalf of the infringement thesis. No doubt the alleged principle that is to justify claims to repair makes reference to the ownership of property. No doubt the concept of ownership is best understood in terms of bundles of rights concerning its use. Still, it is not at all clear that constitutive of property ownership is the right not to have one's property destroyed or damaged. It does not seem to me that an individual is caught in a contradiction in maintaining that although he owns something, he has no blanket right that others not destroy, damage or use it. He may lament the fact that his ownership fails to grant him exclusive use of his property; indeed, absent that right his ownership may mean less to him, i.e., be less valuable than it could otherwise be. Surely, however encumbered, restricted ownerhsip is ownership nonetheless.

Moreover, even if ownership entailed some or other right or rights concerning the use to which others might put one's property, a blanket prohibition against its use or destruction by others need not be included among them. Thus, my ownership of a cabin or dock may entail that I have a right that others not use or destroy it unless they are compelled to in order to save lives or avoid enormous losses, etc. Is this any less ownership than if it entailed the blanket prohibition against the use of my property by others for their advantage? Surely not. Since it is not a necessary part of ownership that there be the sort of rights infringement theorists point to as necessary to awarding compensation, the principle need not make even oblique reference to such a right.

Next, the existence of such a right does not provide the only justification for the principle we constructed. How could it, since there may exist no such right in the cases we are considering? Indeed, one could imagine a utilitarian-like argument for such a principle of compensation. For example, it would be hard to develop a set of settled expectations regarding the use of one's property unless some principle restricting the use to which others might put one's property without securing permission or providing compensation were established. Utilitarians, and I am not among them, could no doubt provide even more imaginative and convincing arguments for such a principle of compensation. That is, one could construct, even on utilitarian grounds, a principle that gives you a right to compensation when your property is used in certain ways, but which does not confer on you the right that others not use your property in the way that would require their compensating you. Thus we would have a principle of compensation that, if justified, could both justify and explain your claim to repair, without conferring upon you a right of the sort infringement theorists contend is necessary.

5. *Compensation, Infringements and Corrective Justice*

There are three ways of understanding the kind of claim an infringement theorist might be making.[9] On the one hand, he could be making the general claim that it is impossible to ground *any* claim to repair as matter of justice without citing the invasion of a right as its basis. Or he might be claiming that although compensation may be someone's due in certain cases in which no property right of his is involved, wherever there is such a property right its violation is necessary to ground any claim to repair a plaintiff might have. Or he might be making the much weaker claim that whenever an injurer acts justifiably or permissibly, damages suffered by others in virtue of the injurer's conduct are justly remedied only if the injurer's conduct, though permissible, is contrary to another's property right.

I have argued against all three of these interpretations of the infringement thesis. I want to suggest yet a fourth, weaker way of interpreting the infringement theory. That is, the infringement theory makes the claim that having the relevant property, though not necessary to ground a claim to repair, is *sufficient* to do so. If, in some cases, having property includes the right that others not take, use, damage or destroy it, then the same conduct that triggers the application of the general principle of compensation constitutes an infringement of the relevant right. Thus, the infringement of a right, though not necessary, is, when it occurs, sufficient to justify a claim to repair. This interpretation of the infringement thesis is acceptable and harmless. Understood in this way, the infringement theory provides one plausible account of why it is that the losses in takings like torts cases, such as *Vincent* v. *Lake Erie*, are rectifiable as a matter of corrective justice.

---

[9] A detailed and lucid discussion of the infringement thesis appears in T. Benditt *Rights* (Totowa, N.J.: Rowman and Littlefield, 1982). The discussion here has benefited from Benditt's insightful critique of the infringement theory.

### 6. *Extending Corrective Justice Beyond Takings under the Rule of Strict Liability*

In addition to the claims to repair and liability under the fault rule we have considered two ways in which the right to repair in takings-like strict liability cases can be grounded in the principle of corrective justice. The principle of corrective justice can be extended somewhat further, to justify both liability and recovery for other sorts of strict liability cases, in particular nuisance, blasting, and ultrahazardous activities generally. The argument requires first that we draw a distinction among three ways in which the justifiability of what an actor does figures in our assessment of the rights of his victims to recompense in the event his conduct, though permissible, results in measurable damage to others.

On the one hand, there is a class of conduct which, because it is justifiable or permissible, defeats any claim to compensation for losses which might result from it. The obvious cases of this sort involve legitimate business practice and competitions. Losses that result from others' gains lie where they fall. Cases governed by the fault principle in torts also fall into this category. Under the fault principle, if *A* injures *B* justifiably, no liability or recovery is warranted. In these cases, recovery or repair is warranted *only* if the conduct engaged in is at fault; that is, unreasonable or unjustified. Let's say that in cases of this sort, the justifiability of the injurer's conduct rules out compensation.

There are other cases where the injurer's conduct is justifiable or permissible, but the justifiability of his conduct does not make recovery impossible. Indeed, in these cases the victim has a claim to repair even though the injurer's conduct is permissible. These are the sorts of cases we have been discussing where the central question appears to be whether the claim to repair depends on the existence of an infringed right, or whether it can be explained in some other way. One important feature of these cases, other than the fact that the justifiability of the injurer's conduct does not defeat a claim to repair, is that the injurer's conduct is justifiable or permissible whether or not he compensates his victim. If he fails to compensate his victim, that may well be wrong of him, but it does not make what he has done wrong. The hiker's saving his life and the ship captain's saving his ship and its cargo are both the right things to have done.

In contrast, we recognize a third set of cases in which conduct is justifiable *only* if those who engage in it compensate others who are made worse off by it. The claim here is not that rendering compensation is sufficient to make the conduct justifiable, only that it is necessary. For example, we are often faced with a choice between prohibiting or permitting certain activities of obvious social worth, but which impose substantial risks. Rather than prohibit such activities we sometimes permit them on the condition that whatever losses they occasion shall be compensated. Examples of such activities might be blasting, polluting manufacturing, and medical experimentation. These activities are justifiable provided they shoulder their social costs. Not every piece of conduct that is justifiable only if compensation is paid is of the risky sort. On the assumption that a restaurant is not in the business of giving food away, eating a meal in a restaurant is not justified, other things being equal, unless one compensates the restaurant for it. In general, securing a service is justified provided one compensates fairly for it. Otherwise it is theft, or at least unjust enrichment. Unlike cases which fall into the second category, which are justified whether or not compensation is paid, the conduct in these cases is permissible *only* if compensation is provided.

In short, there is conduct which is justifiable and which therefore defeats recovery as a matter of justice; conduct which is justifiable, but which requires compensation; and conduct which is justifiable only if compensation is paid. In the first case, losses are unjust and compensable only if the injurer engages in the conduct unreasonably or unjustifiably; in the second, according to the infringement view, losses are unjust and compensable because they involve the infringement of a right; in the third case, losses and gains are unjust if the injurer does not compensate.

Corrective justice grounds the claim to recompense and strict liability in cases of both the second and third sort. Cases of the second sort include *Vincent* v. *Lake Erie* and the Feinberg example. Examples of the third sort include blasting and nuisance cases like *Boomer* v. *Atlantic Cement Company*.[10] In *Boomer*, property owners living adjacent to a polluting manufacturer sought an injunction directing the manufacturer to cease polluting. The court refused to issue an injunction and instead permitted Boomer to continue manufacturing and polluting *provided it paid damages*. Here is an instance of conduct that is permissible only if compensation is provided. The claim to compensation derives from the conditions placed on the permissibility of the injurer's conduct. If the injurer had failed to provide compensation, his conduct would have been wrongful: both the losses it occasioned and the gains it secured would be unjust ones in the appropriate sense. Thus, the connection to the principle of corrective justice. Precisely how much of strict liability law in torts can be rationalized on this model remains to be worked out.

It is tempting to try to place all of those strict liability cases which do not fall within the second (the takings) category into the third one (conduct that is justifiable only if compensation is paid), thereby providing a corrective justice account of all of tort law. Such a move is unwarranted, however. In some activities, like product manufacturing, liability is strict, that is, imposed even when those who engage in the activities exercise reasonable care. These activities, unlike blasting and polluting, are permissible whether or not compensation is paid. They cannot fall into the third category since the claim to recompense for losses that might result *cannot* be that those who engage in the activities are entitled to do so only if they are prepared to shoulder its accident costs. Moreover, since it is hard to see how injury by defective product invariably constitutes an infringement of a property right, these cases do not fall within the takings umbrella (second category) either. Products liability simply represents a decision to permit the shifting of losses from victims to injurers on grounds other than

---

[10] Boomer v. Atlantic Cement Co., 26 N.Y. 2d 219, 309 N.Y.S. 2d 312, 257 N.E. 2d 870 (1970).

corrective justice. There are arguments both of efficiency and distributive justice for such a decision. Although there is no argument as a matter of corrective justice for these decisions, that just means that corrective justice cannot explain all of the claims to repair recognized as legitimate under prevaling tort doctrines. I have no problem with such a conclusion.

Someone who adopts my view of corrective justice in its relationship to tort law may want to use the fact that products liability and other cases cannot be resolved on the basis of corrective justice as a reason for deciding them the other way – against the victims. But that would be a mistake. Strict liability cases often involve a decision regarding who should bear a loss when neither the victim nor the injurer is at fault. Sometimes (as in takings cases) there is an argument from corrective justice for imposing the loss on faultless injurers. That does not imply, however, that when there is no argument from corrective justice, the loss ought to fall on the victim. At this point, one is entitled to appeal to considerations both of distributive justice and efficiency to determine the incidence of the loss.[11]

## III. CORRECTIVE JUSTICE, RESPONSIBILITY AND BACKGROUND RISK

I want to turn now to alternative conceptions of corrective justice in the law of torts: specifically those advanced by George Fletcher and Richard Epstein.[12] In demonstrating what is wrong with their views I hope to lend further support for the view I have been defending as a justification for many, if not most, of the claims to repair recognized and vindicated by the tort system.

---

[11] For a more detailed discussion of this point see J. Coleman, 'On the Morality of Strict Tort Liability,' *William and Mary Law Review* 18 (1976): 259–86.

[12] For a more detailed discussion of Epstein and Fletcher, see J. Coleman 'Moral Theories of Torts: Their Scope and Limits, Part I,' *Law and Philosophy* 1 (1982): 371–390. Reprinted above.

A. *Reciprocity and Corrective Justice*

It is possible to turn Fletcher's reciprocity thesis into a version of the argument from corrective justice. To do this, one hangs on to the principle of nonreciprocity of risk as the criterion of liability and recovery, but abandons the argument in support of that criterion based on the claim that nonreciprocity of risk is morally connected to a security-related variant of Rawls's first principle. Instead of an argument for nonreciprocity of risk based on a principle of distributive justice, one advances a corrective justice defence of it. This can be done by characterizing the principle of corrective justice as requiring the rectification of unjust gains and losses, then analyzing unjust gains (and losses) as those resulting from nonreciprocal risk taking. Nonreciprocity of risk is central to liability and recovery in torts, not because individuals have a right to the maximum level of security compatible with a like security for all, but rather because individuals have a legitimate claim to repair for unjust losses, and unjust losses are those which result from nonreciprocal risk taking.

One advantage of this analysis of corrective justice is that it purports to explain *all* of tort liability and recovery, since nonreciprocity of risk as a characterization of unjustness, unlike the characterization of it that I have offered, is intended to cover all of torts. The central problem with this approach is that nonreciprocity of risk is problematic as a condition of liability and recovery. Moreover, as Professor Fletcher characterizes it, the standard of nonreciprocity is not clearly a moral one. Nonreciprocal risks differ in degree or kind from other risks. But there is no reason to suppose that differences in degree or kind are decidedly moral ones. On the other hand, in order to be annulled, corrective justice requires of a loss that it be *morally* distinguishable from noncompensable losses. The criterion of nonreciprocity of risk is incapable of marking the moral difference.

B. *Corrective Justice, Causation and Property Rights*

Though Professor Epstein has always emphasized the causal condition as central to any moral account of tort liability, his view about the principle that confers moral significance on the causal condition has undergone subtle, but significant changes.

In his early essay Epstein held the view that the best way to understand, and (where possible) justify, tort liability is by rooting it in a more comprehensive theory of personal responsibility.[13] Tort liability is justly imposed, provided the conditions of tort liability conform to the requirements of responsibility. Epstein's view is that a satisfactory account of personal responsibility must be developed in terms of an analysis of causation and volition.

Running alongside the responsibility thesis in Epstein's early work is a very undeveloped argument which relies on corrective justice as the basis of tort liability. The argument is basically this: prior to the incidence of harm, individuals are in a state of "equilibrium" or "balance." Liability in torts provides the mechanism for redressing imbalances caused by harmful conduct; liability and recovery in torts serve to reestablish the previously existing equilibria. The causal condition remains central to a just theory of liability since the principle of corrective justice requires annulling gains and losses *caused* by harmful conduct.

The problem with the theory of corrective justice that relies on the fact that *A* caused *B* harm as sufficient both for (prima facie) liability and recovery (respectively) is that not every way in which *A* harms *B* is wrongful. Not every loss *B* suffers at *A*'s hands is a wrongful one; not every gain *A* secures at *B*'s expense is an unjust one.

Epstein's most recent view emerges as a response to these criticisms. In answering the charge against the responsibility thesis that *A* may have a duty to prevent harm to *B* so that both his failure to do so may be wrongful and the resulting harm to *B* his responsibility, Epstein denies that *B* has any right to rescue against *A*. To the objection that not every harm creates a wrongful loss, Epstein's response is that only those harms that involve invasions of *proper-*

---

[13] Richard Epstein, 'A Theory of Strict Liability,' *Journal of Legal Studies* 2 (1973): 151–204.

*ty rights* are compensable. In short, the emerging Epstein view is that corrective justice requires annulling only gains and losses owing to the invasion of an individual's *rights*.[14]

This account of corrective justice maintains a commitment to the causal requirement as central to a just theory of liability not because causing harm is sufficient to trigger the principle's application, but because the concept of a "right-invasion" is to be spelled out in causal terms. Causation then is necessary to liability, but no longer sufficient to justify even the prima facie case. For it is also necessary that the injurer's conduct invade one or more of the victim's property rights.

One way of understanding this view is as follows: Epstein has adopted the general conception of corrective justice according to which unjust gains and losses are to be annulled. He then analyzes the notion of "unjustness" in terms of the more basic idea of a property-right invasion. Unjust losses are those that result from the invasion of a property right. So what a judge in a tort case is deciding upon is whether *B* has a property right against *A* which *A* has failed adequately to respect. If the claim "*A* invaded *B*'s property right" is true, then it follows in this view that *B* has a further right against *A* to recompense for whatever loss *A*'s invasion may have occasioned.

There are two central claims in Epstein's account. The first is that a compensable loss must involve the invasion of a right. The second is that the invasion of a right creates a further right to recompense for subsequent losses. The first claim is important because, if true, it supports the theory of *strict liability*. A right may be invaded either wrongfully, innocently, or justifiably. If compensation rests on the fact of invasion itself rather than on either its unjustifiability or inexcusability, then liability is strict: that is, it is justly imposed without regard for fault in either of the two senses I have discussed.

The second claim is important because if the violation of a right

---

14 Richard Epstein, 'Nuisance Law: Corrective Justice and Its Utilitarian Constraints,' *Journal of Legal Studies* 8 (1979): 49–102.

entails a further right to recompense, then Epstein's version of corrective justice explains not only which losses are compensable, but central aspects of the specific mode of rectification the tort system constitutes as well. Only losses caused by the invasion of property rights are compensable as a matter of corrective justice; because the invasion of a right creates a right to repair, the correlative of which is an obligation to repay, corrective justice explains the tort system's reliance on correlative rights and duties as the means of rectifying those losses.

The second claim cannot be sustained since it is no part of a satisfactory analysis of a right that to have a right *means* to have a right to recover for losses that might arise in the event of its being invaded. Having a right to repair is not constitutive of having a right. In short, the argument for repair must be moral, not logical.

One might reformulate the principle of corrective justice so that the relationship between the existence of property rights and rights to recover for their invasion is moral, not logical. This conception of the principle of corrective justice would hold that an individual is entitled to recover as a matter of justice if and only if he suffers a loss in virtue of another's invasion (i.e. causal trespass) of a property right of his. In this view, the right to recover follows not as a matter of logic, but as a matter of corrective justice from the invasion of a property right.

This statement of the principle of corrective justice states not only grounds in support of claims to repair, but the mode of rectification as well. But surely there are ways of rectifying wrongful gains and losses other than a system of private actions for damages by which a victim with a legitimate claim to repair is entitled to secure compensation from his or her injurer. And it seems unlikely that all such systems could be ruled out as inconsistent with the principle of corrective justice. Moreover, it is not obvious that the invasion of a right always triggers a right to compensation. In some cases it calls for an injunction against future invasions; in other cases it may at most call for an apology; and in yet other cases, it may call for nothing at all. Compensation, after all, is only one of several mechanisms for securing, guaranteeing or protecting rights. The claim that an invasion of a right necessarily gives a right to repair is true neither as a matter of logic or of morality.

Epstein's other claim is that the invasion of a right distinguishes compensable from other losses; that, in the language of corrective justice, a rights invasion is what makes a loss unjust. This claim must be true in order to generate the theory of strict liability.

As the discussion of the infringement theory shows, claims to compensation need not rest on the invasion of a right. That is, in explaining the basis of a person's claim to repair one need not point to a right the violation or infringement of which brings forth the claim; and in some cases, those involving fault liability, the right to repair rests on an unreasonably harmed *interest*, not a right.

One might attempt to defend Epstein by arguing on his behalf that his claim is not that *all* claims to repair require that a right be invaded; rather, it is that in all *torts* cases, the victim's claim to repair rests on a right invasion. After all, Epstein is not interested in making a general point about the moral grounds of compensation; his concern is the basis of claims to recompense that are brought forth and vindicated under tort doctrines.

However, this line of defence will not work. Consider two cases that would arise in torts under the fault principle. In one case *A* injures *B* unreasonably; in the second case *A* injures *B* nonnegligently. Under the fault rule, *B* will recover (other things being equal) in the first case, but not in the second. In Epstein's view this can only be explained in terms of right invasions: in the first, but not in the second case, *A* must have invaded *B*'s right. But that is the one way in which the cases *cannot* differ. For if *B* has a right against anyone (including *A*) not to be injured, then it is no part of his case against *A that A* acted negligently – since the notion of a right invasion is to be analyzed exclusively in causal terms. (If *B* has no right against *A* to be injured in this specific way, he has no claim to repair in either case). If Epstein is correct, *B* should either recover in both cases or in neither – but in fact he recovers in the first, but not in the second because the injury he suffered is one he can expect compensation for if it is *unjustifiably* (i.e., unreasonably) imposed (as in the first case), but not otherwise (as in the second). Though Epstein tries, one simply cannot avoid concern for whether or not the harm was unjustifiably or wrongly imposed; in short, in fault liability, one cannot escape the importance of fault.

## IV. CONCLUSION

A claim to repair can be based on considerations of justice or, broadly speaking, utility. Not every claim to repair in torts is best understood as required by corrective justice; and not every claim to repair that can be grounded in corrective justice is vindicated in torts.

In addition to recognizing the legitimacy of certain claims to repair, the tort system constitutes both a mode of identifying which claims are legitimate, and a means of vindicating these claims. Both of these features of the tort system have been largely overlooked, especially the first. Let us suppose that there are individuals who have legitimate claims to repair as a matter of justice. Corrective justice requires that we recognize and satisfy these claims. But first we have to be made aware of them. The tort system is only one of many ways of individuals bringing forth claims to repair, so that we might be in a position to distinguish the legitimate from the illegitimate. We could imagine other ways of individuals stating their claims: e.g., administrative tribunals; or we could mail claim forms to everyone: "In the last year have you suffered a loss (or secured a gain) which, given the above characterization of corrective justice, ought to be annulled?" Because of the costs of litigation, many legitimate claims may not be discovered, and, therefore, not satisfied. I am not suggesting that the tort system is on balance an unsatisfactory method of bringing forth such claims. My point is the more modest one that, on the face of things, there is no reason to believe that it is the most satisfactory means of bringing forth such claims, and therefore, to the extent that justice requires their recognition and enforcement, of doing justice.

Certainly the tort system is an inefficient means of bringing forth claims to forfeiture of unjust gains since an injurer's wrongful gain comes to the court's attention only if it has triggered another's wrongful loss. Only in seeking to vindicate a claim to repair does the injurer's having secured a wrongful gain present the court with an opportunity for annullment. If corrective justice involves identifying legitimate claims both to repair and forfeiture, the tort system, because of its reliance on private actions initiated by particular victims, very likely does only an adequate job with respect to claims to repair and an inadequate job with respect to recognizing rectifiable gains. To that extent tort law may not be the best way of doing justice to these claims.

Finally, the tort system constitutes a particular mode of making good certain claims to repair (and to liability for wrongful gain). Nothing in the principle of corrective justice requires the tort system as the mode of rectification. I am prepared to believe that with further analysis we will find that some claims to repair (for example, those which arise when an injurer's conduct is justifiable only if compensation is made) are most efficiently and appropriately recognized and enforced through a tortlike system; whereas other claims to repair (for example, those that arise from accidents – automobile and other) may be most efficiently and appropriately dealt with in some other way – perhaps through a no-fault system or through the general tax coffers. While legal theorists have been attempting a global characterization of tort law as rooted in some overarching principle – efficiency for economists, and corrective justice (usually) for philosophers – the fact is that no single principle is capable of explaining the full extent of tort law. More important, the interesting questions regarding tort law as a means for identifying and vindicating claims to repair and liability have gone unattended.

*Department of Philosophy, University of Arizona*

GEORGE P. FLETCHER

# THE SEARCH FOR SYNTHESIS IN TORT THEORY

For nearly two decades diverse schools of tort theory have attempted to reduce liability for personal injuries to a few basic principles.[1] Calabresi advocates the principle of minimizing the total costs of accidents and accident avoidance;[2] Posner advocates the principle of encouraging those activities whose benefits outweigh their costs.[3] Epstein endorses a system of tort law in which causing harm is a sufficient condition for liability.[4] My own work is read as advocacy of "non-reciprocal risk-taking" as a standard of liability.[5]

Most of these efforts suffer from a basic ambiguity: are these arguments about the ideal system of tort law or are they interpretive accounts of the common law of torts? All four approaches contain both normative and interpretative dimensions, though, of course, the relative weight of these dimensions varies from author to author. A pure commitment to either positive or normative theory might be ideal, but the tension between the two, particularly in legal theory, seems inescapable. Normative claims must draw on interpretations of the legal materials: interpretations trade on their normative plausibility.

---

1 For a summary and critique of these efforts, see Izhak Englard, 'The System Builders: A Critical Appraisal of Modern American Tort Theory,' *Journal of Legal Studies* 9 (1980): 27–69.

2 See generally Guido Calabresi, *The Costs of Accidents* (New Haven: Yale University Press, 1970).

3 Richard Posner, *Economic Analysis of Law*, 2nd ed. (Boston: Little Brown and Co., 1977), pp. 119–59.

4 R. Epstein, 'A Theory of Strict Liability,' *Journal of Legal Studies* (1973): 151, reprinted along with related essays in R. Epstein, *A Theory of Strict Liability* (San Francisco: Cato Institute, 1980); hereinafter "Epstein."

5 Fletcher, 'Fairness and Utility in Tort Theory,' *Harvard Law Review* 85 (1972): 537–73; hereinafter "Fletcher."

In this paper, I address some of the difficulties of reducing tort law to a few basic principles. I shall sidestep economic approaches to law and concentrate on claims of principle inspired by considerations of fairness both to the victim and to the injurying defendant. The exposition reflects the more general tension between normative and interpretative argument. At times I shall be addressing arguments for reforming the law; at times, principles and perspectives implicit in the common law. In the course of the discussion, I shall criticize both Epstein's and my own prior work and, in general, stress the impediments that mark the pursuit of order and coherence in tort theory.

## 1. THE SIMPLE CAUSATION FORMULA

We could construct the entire field of tort law on the basis of three generalized elements: (1) a concept of harm to the plaintiff; (2) a criterion for linking the defendant to the occurrence of the harm; and (3) an explanation why the defendant's link to the harm justifies transferring the loss from the plaintiff to the defendant. A simplified rule of liability meeting at least the first two desiderata would be this: Whoever causes harm to another should pay compensation.

For the sake of simplicity, we shall limit the inquiry to the infliction of the core injury in the law of torts – personal injury. The link between the harm and the defendant's conduct resides in the admittedly problematic concept of causation. Yet the problem with this "simple causation formula," inheres not so much in the analysis of "harm" and "causation" as with the third desideratum: Does causing harm give us a good reason for shifting the loss?

Epstein adopts the single causation formula as the cornerstone of his theory of strict liability.[6] He argues that the formula should have applied in *Morris* v. *Platt*,[7] where the defendant used force in justifiable self-defense and accidentally injured an innocent by-

[6] Epstein, pp. 5, 14.
[7] 32 Conn. 75 (1864).

stander. Though the defendant could rely on the traditional excuse of inevitable accident, Epstein argues that accident or not, inflicting injury on an innocent bystander should have been sufficient for liability.

Of particular interest is the more general principle that Epstein invokes on behalf of the simple causation formula. Imposing liability is required by the principle "that the defendant must bear the costs of those injuries that he inflicts upon others as though they were injuries that he suffered himself."[8] The same principle is invoked to explain why the law should not recognize infancy and insanity as excuses for causing harm to others: the person causing harm should "be required to bear those costs and to treat the harm he has inflicted upon others as though it were inflicted upon himself."[9] This passage states a principle of justice that seems so obvious to Epstein that he does not bother to support it with further argument. It is up to us to explicate the conception of society and of justice that would ensure that he who injures another is treated as though he injured himself.

Epstein apparently assumes that all humanly caused losses are of two sorts: those that people inflict on others and those that they inflict on themselves. The former are bad, for they represent the injustice of individuals treading upon each other's sovereign sphere. The latter, those losses that people inflict upon themselves, are all right, for there is no injustice in individuals hurting themselves. Therefore, if we can convert the former losses into the latter, we eliminate a problem of injustice in human affairs. Epstein's argument for the simple formula reminds us of the Kantian interpretation of capital punishment: Executing convicted murderers is not a matter of the state's killing an individual citizen; it is a matter of the citizen's bringing death upon himself by violating the law.[10]

---

[8] Epstein, p. 13.

[9] Ibid., p. 78.

[10] I. Kant, *The Metaphysical Elements of Justice*, tr. John Ladd (Indianapolis: Bobbs-Merrill, 1965), pp. 105–6. The statement in the text is only an approximation of Kant's more subtle view.

If capital punishment converts the state's killing into an act of killing oneself, the law of torts, as Epstein argues, should convert one individual's harming another into an act of harming oneself.

If Epstein's metaphor should control our perception of tort liability, we could hardly question the implicit justice of the simple causation formula. After all, there is no injustice in being allowed to inflict harm on oneself. The problem, of course, is whether the metaphor should control. Why should we regard shifting the loss from the victim to the defendant as a matter of the defendant's harming himself? Is it right and just that we camouflage the law's coercive intervention (i.e., imposing liability and forcing payment) under an image of self-regarding behavior?

To lay bare the fallacy in Epstein's argument, we have to disentangle two interwoven, rhetorical moves. The first is the assumption that all harm is either inflicted on oneself or on others. The second is the related assumption that the state's intervention does not inflict harm or incur costs: it merely converts harm to another into harm to oneself. I shall refer to the first claim as the assumption that all losses are "individual losses."

The harm is "individual" in two senses. A single individual, choosing to act, brings forth the harm, and we perceive the harm as falling exclusively on a single individual – the victim. The interaction of states in the international community serves as the model for this kind of harm. Each state can, if it chooses, remain within its borders. If it "crosses the boundary" of another and causes harm, it commits a clear wrong, requiring corrective action.

The alternative to this conception of "individual harm" comes from grasping that some harms are the product of the inevitable interaction of human beings living in the same community. These "circumstantial harms" can occur as a result of voluntary interaction in the public sphere: two skiers, two cars, two airplanes, colliding in the ordinary course of skiing, driving and flying. These harms are authored not so much by the choice to "cross the boundary" of another, as by the joint choice, both of defendant and victim, to interact in the same dangerous arena.

My critique of Epstein focuses on his ignoring a range of "circumstantial harms" that occur in excused interactions. These are cases in which the common law courts traditionally found for the defendant, but the simple causation formula points to liability for the plaintiff. Faultless accidents, such as the injury to the bystander in *Morris* v. *Platt,* represent one important strain of cases.[11] Injurying under coercion represents the other. A good example is *Cordas* v. *Peerless Transportation Company*,[12] in which an armed, escaping robber jumped on the running board of the defendant's cab, the defendant lept from his moving cab, and the cab careened into a nearby crowd, thereby injurying the plaintiff. The New York court denied liability, but Epstein would presumably maintain that the defendant driver, like the defendant defending himself in *Platt*, should be required to bear liability, the harm thus transposed into one self-inflicted.

Assuming that these defendants have good excuses – one based on unavoidable ignorance and the other on compulsion[13] – we need not conceptualize the harm as Epstein would. The harmful transaction occurs because a third party brings about the situation in which the defendant acts faultlessly. The aggressor forces Platt to defend himself; the gunman forces the cab driver to react to a sudden danger. Ideally, some legal device would generate an action against third parties who bring about harmful interaction. As between the defendant and the plaintiff, both victims of circumstance, the harm hardly fits the model of one person trespassing against the other. It is true that the defendant in both cases "acts" so as to cause harm, but if the act is excused, the harm is no more attributable to the defendant than it is to the victim. It grows out of a situation in which both the defendant and the victim

---

[11] This is the basis of the theory of reciprocal risk-taking as developed in Fletcher, pp. 544–51. Cf. Charles Fried's theory of the "risk pool" in C. Fried, *An Anatomy of Values* (Cambridge: Harvard University Press, 1970), pp. 177–93.

[12] 27 N.Y.S. 2d 929 198 (N.Y. City Ct. 1941).

[13] The classification of excuses into these two categories dates back at least to the *Nicomachean Ethics* of Aristotle, Book III, ch. 1.

happen to be caught. Excused harms are circumstantial, for they derive not from the responsible choice of the defendant, but the defendant's and plaintiff's being thrown together by circumstance.

Epstein, too, needs a residual notion of "circumstantial harm" to cover those cases in which the defendant's body is merely the instrument of harm to the plaintiff. Suppose A pushes B over a cliff and B falls upon and injures C. Epstein would be hard pressed to think of this case as one in which B "shifts the loss" from himself to C.[14] B does not do anything at all: A orchestrates the interaction. As between B and C, the harm to C must be thought of as the regrettable consequence of B and C having been both subject to an unfortunate set of circumstances.

The critical difference between Epstein's view and the common law derives from Epstein's rejection of recognized excuses, both of unavoidable accident and of compulsion. By treating any action, any choice, as equivalent to a full and voluntary choice to do harm,[15] Epstein minimizes the scope of circumstantial harm and maximizes the set of cases in which he regards it as proper to think of B's choosing to harm C. The point of the traditional excuses is precisely that in light of the circumstances, it is unfair to regard the excused infliction of harm differently from the case of irresistible force: A's pushing B onto C.

Now it should not matter in the theory of excuses whether a third party or natural forces bring about the circumstances excusing the defendant. If an earthquake causes B to fall on C, the case would be the same as if A pushed B onto C. Similarly, if the cab driver in *Cordas* lept from his cab to avoid an unexpected natural danger, his doing so would be excused precisely as it was when he sought to avoid harm from the gunman on his running board. Accident and mistake generate excuses, even if there is no third party aggressor as there was in *Platt*. It is not the third party that generates the excuse, but the circumstances that render it unfair

---

[14] See Epstein, p. 33 (conceding implicitly that where there is no "act at all" there would be no liability).

[15] Ibid.

to treat B's constricted choice as a responsible decision.

It is important to note the implications of subscribing to the view that all (or nearly all) harms are individually caused. The reasoning goes like this:

1. Individual losses that one person inflicts on another are unjust.
2. Individual losses that one suffers oneself are not unjust.
3. If the former can be converted into the latter, we eliminate a problem of injustice.

This, we have noted, is the metaphoric logic that controls Epstein's thinking. The logic of circumstantial losses is different. It is expressed in the following, more conventional mode of thinking about tort liability: [16]

1. Harms resulting from excused interactions are the product of the circumstances in which both the defendant and the plaintiff find themselves.
2. There is no good reason why either the defendant or the plaintiff should bear the loss.
3. Shifting the loss from the victim to the defendant incurs additional social costs – the costs of lawyers, courts and enforcement.
4. Therefore, the loss should remain with the victim unless there is a good reason for incurring the costs of shifting the loss.

The point of this argument is that circumstantial losses should receive the same treatment as natural losses. A compensation scheme, shifting the loss to the public at large, might absorb these losses; but there is no apparent reason for requiring a single individual, the excused defendant, to bear the entire burden.

The second premise of Epstein's thought calls into question his well-known reputation as a libertarian legal theorist. The argument

---

[16] *Cf.* O. Holmes, *The Common Law* (Boston: Little, Brown and Company, 1881), p. 15.

that harm to the victim can be converted into the defendant's own harm suppresses the reality of the state's intervention to shift the loss. Epstein sidesteps the costs of loss-shifting. His faith resides in simple, supposedly self-administering rules.[17] Yet no rules of liability, however simple, administer themselves. Rules of self-help and of self-defense may not require the state's intervention. But Epstein is not proposing that victims seize the assets of a recalcitrant defendant. There is no denying that the state forces the defendant to render compensation, and that fact alone should put libertarians on their guard.

This critique of the simple causation formula would be incomplete without reference to the famous case that Epstein regards as the best proof for his claim. In *Vincent* v. *Lake Erie Transportation Company*,[18] the defendant shipowner kept his vessel lashed to the plaintiff's dock during a two-day storm when it would have been unreasonable, indeed foolhardy, for him to set out to sea. The storm battered the ship against the dock, causing damages assessed at five hundred dollars. The Minnesota Supreme Court held that the shipowner was liable for the damage. This precedent had less impact on the law than tort teachers would like to admit.[19] Yet the resolution of this fairly simple conflict has proved to be the touchstone for far-ranging reconstructions of the theory of liability.

The most significant aspect of the case is that the court imposed liability regardless of the reasonableness of the defendant's behavior. The case seems to support the simple causation formula, for on one interpretation of the transaction, all the defendant did was cause harm to the dock. Epstein takes this interpretation of the case as the foundation for the claim that *Morris* v. *Platt* should have been decided in the same way.[20] As the shipowner caused harm

---

[17] Epstein, p. 48 ("the matter is left in private hands where it belongs... .").

[18] 109 Minn. 456, 124 N.W. 221 (1910).

[19] For a contrary result, denying liability, on almost identical facts, see Manor & Co. Ltd., v. M.V. "Sir John Crosbie" 52 D.L.R. 2d 48 (1965) (Newfoundland), aff'd/1967/1 Ex. 94.

[20] Epstein, p. 13.

and was held liable, so Platt caused harm to an innocent bystander and should have been held liable.

The reduction of the facts in *Vincent* to simply causing harm overlooks a number of critical features of the case: (1) the shipowner chose to keep his ship moored to the dock; (2) the shipowner was fully aware (or could easily have been aware) that his keeping the ship moored was causing harm to the dock; and (3) the shipowner directly benefited from harming the dock (he saved his ship). Any one of these features of *Vincent* would distinguish the case from accidentally injurying a bystander in the course of justifiably defending oneself. Platt did not choose to injure Morris; nor was he aware that shooting would injure Morris. True, he benefited himself by acting in self-defense. But his decision to defend himself did not entail harm to the bystander – at least not in the way that the decision to save the ship ineluctably caused harm to the dock. The leap from *Vincent* to *Platt* obviously suppresses too many critical facts.

The proper interpretation of *Vincent* remains controverted. It is difficult to know whether it was essential to the outcome that the shipowner was aware of what was going on or whether it was critical that the ship survived the storm. The case might well be overdetermined in the sense that many factors, some perhaps redundant, supported the court's finding of liability. Though we continue to debate the teaching of the case, we can be fairly confident that reducing the holding to the simple causation formula goes too far.

Two additional questions about *Vincent* bear mentioning. First, what is the bearing of the storm on the defendant's conduct? Secondly, what is the significance of the victim's being required passively to suffer the harm to his dock? The storm rendered the defendant's conduct reasonable. His conduct was privileged and it would have been tortious for the dockowner to unleash the vessel and force the defendant to brave the open seas.[21] Epstein reads the case differently. He sees the storm as a coercive factor, con-

[21] Ploof v. Putnam, 81 Vt. 471, 71 A. 188 (1908).

stricting the shipowner's freedom of choice.[22] Since, according to Epstein, compulsion should not be admitted as an excuse, [23] *Vincent* correctly disregards the storm as a defense against liability. My own interpretation of the case, developed elsewhere,[24] treats the storm as a basis for justifying rather than excusing the shipowner's behavior. The shipowner did not respond to a sudden emergency, as did the cab driver in *Cordas*. He had time to make a reflective decision about the benefits and burdens of setting out to sea. He weathered the storm and even replaced the cable holding the ship to the dock. Though there were coercive elements in the situation, they appear to be insufficient to classify the shipowner's behavior as the reaction to a sudden emergency.

There are good reasons for disregarding a justification based on benefiting oneself at the expense of an innocent, passive victim.[25] I would agree with Epstein that the case was correctly decided. But if we understand the shipowner's conduct as justified rather than excused, the case hardly supports Epstein's general rejection of excuses in analyzing liability.

That the victim was required by law to suffer the loss might be the most significant factor in *Vincent* v. *Lake Erie*. The analysis of this factor will receive due attention later, when I return to the teachings of *Vincent*.

## 2. CAUSATION PLUS FAULT

The simple causation formula fails, for it disregards a significant requirement of fairness. Individuals should be held accountable only for unexcused actions. Any approach that disregards excuses hardly warrants approval as a just basis for shifting losses.

The concept of "fault" came into the common law of torts as

---

22 Epstein, p. 33.

23 Ibid.

24 Fletcher, pp. 546–47.

25 My thinking on this point has not advanced beyond earlier exposition, ibid., pp. 564–68.

a way of describing this additional requirement that causing harm must be unexcused.[26] As the case law under trespass stood in the seventeenth and eighteenth centuries, a faultless, or excused, trespass was insufficient for recovery. The best explanation for this requirement is simply that as a matter of fairness to the defendant, a compromised choice should be treated as equivalent to no choice at all. Of course, the question whether a choice is sufficiently compromised by compulsion or ignorance (whether the compulsion should have been resisted or the mistake avoided) is patently a matter of judgment about the demands we choose to place on each other.

In the course of the nineteenth century, the courts began to think of this normative issue as a matter of "neglect" or "blame" to be attributed to the defendant.[27] Eventually, the requirement of blameworthy or faultful conduct became sufficiently important to displace the element of "trespass" in defining the kind of causal interference sufficient for liability. By the end of the nineteenth century, the courts and commentators began to speak of fault not as a basis for excusing a trespass, but as an essential condition for imposing liability.[28]

This transformation of the place of fault in thinking about tort liability led, in turn, to a major division in the categories of liability. Opposed to the new insistence on fault there developed a new line of cases imposing liability without proof of fault. Some of these, such as liability for grazing cattle, were of ancient vintage.[29] Others, such as the uncertain principle of *Rylands* v. *Fletcher*[30] (liability to adjacent landowner for damage done by reservoir)

---

26 The most widely discussed early case is Weaver v. Ward, 80 Eng. Rep. 284 (K.B. 1616).

27 See, e.g. Harvey v. Dunlop, Hill & Denio Supp. 193 (N.Y. 1843); Vincent v. Stinehour, 7 Vt. 62 (1835).

28 For a discussion of the critical case, Brown v. Kendall, 60 Mass. (6 Cush.) 292 (1850), see Fletcher, pp. 561–63.

29 See 72 Eng. Rep. 156 (1497).

30 159 Eng. Rep. 737 (Ex. 1865), rev'd L.R. 1 Ex. 265 (1866), aff'd L.R. 3 H.L. 330 (1868).

emerged in the nineteenth century. Still others, such as liability for the consequences of blasting, crop-dusting, fumigating and ground damage done by crashing airplanes, reflected efforts to come to grips with the technological dangers of the twentieth century.[31] These are all now called instances of "strict" liability.

Although the literature on tort law tends to assume that fault and strict liability are logically incompatible, the conflict is far from clear. Both forms of liability lend themselves to opposing interpretations. Consider a typical case of blasting, in which the defendant detonates explosives in order to clear a way for a desired, admittedly useful construction project; rocks fly and injure a bystander some distance away. Either a standard of fault or of strict liability might apply to the case. Yet because both "fault" and "strict liability" might be approached in two distinct ways, there are in fact four modes of analysis:

I. *Fault Liability*

F1. *Ex Post Analysis*

The starting point for the analysis would be the occurrence of harm. Looking backwards (ex post) toward the genesis of the harm, one would conclude that the blasting company brought about the harm and therefore committed a common law trespass. The question of liability would turn on whether in the particular act of blasting the company should have been able to avoid the harm to the victim. If not, the trespass would be regarded as an unavoidable, faultless accident.

F2. *Ex Ante Analysis*

The starting point for analysis would be the risk generated by the detonation. The question posed by the

---

[31] E.g. Exner v. Sherman Power Constr. Co., 54 F.2d 510 (2d Cir. 1931) (storing explosives); Western Geophysical Co. of America v. Mason, 240 Ark. 767, 402 S.W.2d 657 (1966) (blasting).

fault standard is whether the risk was reasonable under the circumstances. Did the benefit of blasting outweigh the probable costs to bystanders? If the risk is deemed reasonable, the blasting would not be regarded as negligent. There would be no liability for the personal injuries that ensued.

II. *Strict Liability*

SL1. *Ex Post Analysis*

The starting point would be the harm. The approach would differ from an ex post analysis of fault solely on the availability of excuses. An ex post standard of strict liability would not admit faultness accident as an excuse.

SL2. *Ex Ante Analysis*

The starting point would be the risk. As contrasted with an ex ante analysis of fault, the standard for assessing the risk would not be reasonableness, but something like "ultrahazardous risks" or "abnormal risks." These are the standards that appear, respectively, in the first[32] and second[33] Restatements of Torts for defining strict liability in cases like blasting, fumigating and crop-dusting.

Applying these four different approaches to a typical case of blasting, courts could readily conclude that the company was exempt from liability under either version of the fault standard, but liable under either version of strict liability. These conclusions conceal the different modes of reasoning called for under the con-

---

32 *Restatement of Torts* § 519 (1938).
33 *Restatement (Second) of Torts* § 519.

flicting interpretations of fault and of strict liability. This is the way the arguments might go:

> F1: no liability, for there was no way for the blasting company to avoid the harm to the innocent bystander.
> F2: no liability, for in view of the company's beneficial purpose, the benefit of the risk outweighed the cost of probable injuries to the bystanders.
> SL1: liability, for the blasting caused the harm and the excuse of faultless accident is unavailable.
> SL2: liability, for the risk is "ultrahazardous" or "abnormal" relative to the general background of risk in the community.

These four approaches to liability, all of which are well represented in Anglo-American legal thought, enable us to formulate more precisely a range of important claims about tort liability.

1. Both F1 and SL1 focus on the particular incident that issues in harm. F2 and SL2 shift the focus to risk and overall quality of the risk (unreasonable, ultrahazardous). The shift to risk analysis requires consideration of the general activity that causes harm, in this case, blasting. The very concept of risk requires abstraction from the particular case and assessment whether the risk in general is socially useful, ultrahazardous or abnormal. Risk-assessment leads invariably to thinking about a range of cases that produce a risk of particular gravity and utility.[34]

2. It follows from point 1 that ex post analyses (F1 and SL1) coincide with focusing on the particular case; ex ante analyses (F2 and SL2) entail a broader focus on the class of functionally equivalent risks.

3. The general drift in the analysis of fault has been from F1 to F2. In the traditional way of thinking about fault, F1, the defendant asserted the faultness of his conduct as a way of excusing his trespass. In the contemporary way of thinking, F2, the plaintiff

---

[34] This might not be true about ultrahazardous or abnormal risks; attending to a single incident might be sufficient to interpret these risks as excessive.

asserts the faultfulness of the risk as a way of demonstrating that the creation of the risk was socially unjustified.[35]

4. Strict liability, as formulated in the Restatements, focuses on the quality of the risk and therefore seems to fit more clearly in the theory of SL2. Also, some of the modern rationalia for strict liability, such as "enterprise liability," stress the danger of the overall activity and the ability of the entrepreneur to calculate and insure against the general risks implicit in his enterprise.[36]

These preliminary points enable us to bring into focus the nature of the tension between fault and strict liability. The conventional wisdom stresses the incompatibility of SL1 with either F1 or F2. The incompatibility derives from the rejection of excuses in SL1 and the recognition of excuses (as will be explained presently) in both F1 and F2. If SL2 is taken as the correct reading of strict liability, however, the tension with theories of fault takes a different philosophical turn.

SL2 and F1 converge in important criteria. Both impose a standard of prima facie liability based solely on intrusion against others. The standard of intrusion in F1 is trespass, in SL2, of subjecting innocent bystanders to abnormal risk. Both standards, I would argue, acknowledge the fairness of excusing intrusions on the basis of ignorance or compulsion. Excuses are explicitly required under F1. The role of excuses under SL2 requires some elaboration.

SL2 focuses on the ongoing risk-taking of especially dangerous enterprises, such as blasting, airplane overflights, and fumigating. Viewed as recurrent instances of risk-creation, these activities generate predictable harm to their surroundings. From this perspective, the harm caused by flying rocks and crashing planes is surely avoidable: the entrepreneur need not undertake the dangerous activity at all. The decision to enter upon the activity is fully voluntary: the entrepreneur knowingly exposes his surroundings

---

35 See note 28 supra.

36 See e.g., A. Ehrenzweig, 'Negligence Without Fault' (1951), reprinted in 54 *Calif. L. Rev.* 1422 (1965).

to a high degree of risk. Thus the shift in focus to the general activity undercuts the claim of accident. What appears as an unavoidable, faultless byproduct of a single incident of blasting takes on the appearance of a predictable consequence of the recurrent enterprise. Of course, if the type of harm that occurs is bizarre or, as lawyers say, "unforseeable," then even in the cases of so-called strict liability causing harm is excusable and not subject to liability.[37]

My claim is that the way we now think about strict liability, namely with emphasis on the ex ante analysis of the risk, recognizes implicitly that only voluntary, unexcused activities generate liability. With regard to the excuse of ignorance or accident, this claim is documentable.[38] With respect to compulsion, we have no case law at our disposal. Yet it is fair to assume that if the blasting company detonated an unplanned charge under compulsion, the circumstances would take the case out of the ordinary run of risk-taking and would generate a good case for denying liability.

If it is true that excuses operate under SL2 as well as under F1, then the difference between the two standards turns solely on the criteria of intrusion. The former focus on intrusive risks; the latter, on direct trespasses as compensable intrusions. The two approaches to liability turn out to be at least nominally harmonious.

We should not forget, however, that F1 and SL2 do lead to different results in the blasting case. F1 leads us to recognize an excuse of unavoidable accident; SL2 invites us to think of the risks as ultra-hazardous. Although F1 and SL2 share a recognition of excuses, the distinction between an ex post analysis of the particular trespass and an ex ante analysis of the class of similar cases leads to a different view about which accidents are excusable.

The two ex ante approaches, F2 and SL2, reveal both similarities and differences. As we have already noted, SL2 admits of ex-

---

[37] Madsen v. East Jordan Irrigation Co., 101 Utah 552, 125 P.2d 794 (1942) (blasting frightened the mother mink on plaintiff's farm and caused them to devour their young; doctrine of "proximate cause" invoked to deny liability).
[38] Ibid.

cuses bearing on the predictability of the harm and the voluntariness of the activity. F2 accommodates excuses under the analysis of the circumstances that render risks reasonable or unreasonable. Under circumstances in which the defendant's agents were excusably ignorant that a crate contained nitroglycerine, it might have been reasonable to use a hammer and chisel in opening the crate.[39]

The distinction between F2 and SL2 turns on the kind of risk that will generate liability. F2 requires an unreasonable risk, SL2 imposes liability for all abnormal or ultrahazardous risks. On the assumption that unreasonable risks are those that are socially detrimental, then a clear difference between the two standards of risk emerges. F2 exempts socially beneficial risks from liability; SL2 does not. This difference surfaces in the blasting example, for these risks might well be regarded as socially useful. SL2 imposes liability regardless of social utility.

That both fault and strict liability have two variations generates four contrasts between the two standards. The nature of the conflict differs in each of the four possible contrasts:

A. F1 and SL1: This contrast focuses solely on the relevance of excuses. As early as the seventeenth century, it became clear that the common law of trespass was based on F1 rather than SL1.[40] Epstein holds firm to SL1 as the correct standard.[41]

B. F2 and SL1: This is the conflict between the modern conception of fault and Epstein's theory of strict liability. They differ not only at the level of excuses, but as well on the principle whether socially useful activities should be exempt from liability. F2 exempts socially useful activities; SL1 does not.

C. F1 and SL2: These two converge in a single principle: unexcused and harmful intrusions entail liability. Differences arise in (1) applying the criteria of excuses, respectively, to single in-

---

[39] Parrot v. Wells, Fargo & Co., 82 U.S. (15 Wall) 524 (1872) (liability denied for causing explosion by opening crate with mallet and chisel).
[40] See Weaver v. Ward, 80 Eng. Rep. 284 (K.B. 1616).
[41] See text at notes 6–16 *supra*.

cidents as opposed to classes of similar incidents and (2) in the criteria of intrusion. F1 relies on a criterion of impact; S2, on a criterion of risk.

D. F2 and SL2: These two approaches converge on important particulars – excuses, ex ante perspective, focus on classes rather than single events – yet diverge on the important questions: should socially useful activities be exempt from liability? F2 says, "yes"; SL2, "no."

The purpose of this exercise has been to demonstrate how difficult it is to clarify the relationship between fault and strict liability. Theorists typically contrast these two "types" of liability without taking cognizance of the latent ambiguity in both theories of liability. In the course of eliciting and contrasting these four standards of liability, we have uncovered three latent tensions in the way we think about tort liability. These are worth restating, for any effort to work out a simple, consistent theory of liability would have to take a stand on these three antinomies:

1. *Ex ante vs. ex post perspective.* Where do we begin our analysis of liability, with the risk generating act or with the consummated harm?

2. *Single event or class of events.* Do we limit our focus to the single transaction causing harm or do we abstract from the single to the activity defined by taking risks of a particular sort?

3. *Exempting socially useful risks.* This exemption is incorporated in the modern conception of fault (F2). Is it right?

It is fairly clear that in order to progress beyond this welter of antinomies, the theorist has to commit himself to the lines of thought that appear most likely to generate a defensible theory of liability. In my own effort to articulate a "paradigm of reciprocity" I started from these assumptions: (1) the principle of liability must include criteria of excuses; this excludes SL1 and the simple causation formula, (2) A sound principle of corrective justice would reject utilitarian criteria for defeating liability. This excludes F2, the modern conception of negligence. These two assumptions are arguably mandated by the imperative of doing justice both to the victim and the person who causes him harm.

The additional assumption implicit in the "paradigm of reciprocity" is that the analysis of liability should proceed ex ante rather than ex post. In retrospect, this assumption seems to be mandated not by fairness, but from the synthetic power of thinking ex ante in the idiom of risk, rather than ex post in the traditional framework of trespass. In conclusion, I wish to explore some of the problems of bringing diverse tort doctrines under the umbrella of risk analysis. As we shall see, the ex ante analysis of risk does have considerable synthetic power, but nonetheless founders on some important features of the problems we seek to solve.

## 3. RISK ANALYSIS AND DEFENSES

Let us consider the implications of the following general principle for fairly redistributing losses: the defendant must pay for the consequences of subjecting another, without excuse, to an excessive risk of harm. Justice to the plaintiff is insured by recognizing compensation for the consequences of being subjected to an excessive risk; justice to the defendant is insured by recognizing the role of excuses defeating liability.

Admittedly vague, the standard of "excessive risk" has the synthetic power of accommodating not only abnormal or ultrahazardous risks, but many risks that we now call "negligent" or "unreasonable." The latter risks are always excessive relative to the conventionally acceptable level of risk in the particular arena of interaction. Modern tort analysis holds that risks become unreasonable or faultful only by reference to the Learned Hand formula – the method of balancing benefits and burdens. Yet this interpretation of "unreasonableness" is by no means compelled. Juries are not typically told of the Learned Hand formula. They are more likely to be instructed to determine, simply, what a reasonable person would have done under the circumstances.[42] If we seek an il-

[42] California Jury Instructions – Civil § 3.10 (1977) ("[N]egligence is the doing of something which a reasonably prudent person would not do....").

luminating interpretation of the "reasonable person" test, it makes just as much sense to think of unreasonable risks as excessive relative to background risks as to fit the analysis of reasonableness into a matrix of costs and benefits.

The standard of excessive risk enables us to make sense of the way in which the plaintiff's contribution or acceptance of the risk affects the analysis of liability. There are two ways in which the plaintiff's coming to the risk and subjecting himself to it might bear on the analysis of liability. The plaintiff's act might either (1) lower the standard of liability from strict liability (SL2) to fault (F2), or (2) generate a complete defense to liability. Let us take a closer look at each of these possibilities.

When *Fletcher* v. *Rylands* was litigated in the Exchequer Chamber, the intermediate appellate court, the judges had little difficulty concluding that Rylands, the owner of the reservoir, should be liable for the consequences of his reservoir's breaking through a mine shaft and flooding Fletcher's land.[43] Interpreting the case in the theory of SL2, we could identify the controlling principle simply as follows: when a landowner exposes a neighbor to an excessive risk that a large body of stored water will escape, the former is liable for the damage done to his neighbor. Against the backdrop of this interpretation, we can make sense of Blackburn, J.'s, astute reflections about why the same principle should not apply in cases in which horses on the highway bolt and injure pedestrians nearby:[44]

> Traffic on the highways, whether by land or sea, cannot be conducted without exposing those whose persons or property are near it some inevitable risk: and that being so, those who go on the highway, or have their property adjacent to it, may well be held to do so subject to their taking upon themselves the risk of injury from that inevitable danger....

Blackburn J., concludes that in these latter cases, where the

---

[43] Fletcher v. Rylands, L.R. 1 Ex. 265 (1866), aff'd Rylands v. Fletcher, L.R. 3 H.L. 330 (1868).

[44] L.R. 1 Ex. at 286.

plaintiff comes to the arena of risk, the appropriate standard of liability should be negligence, requiring "proof of want of care or skill occasioning the accident."[45] Yet where the plaintiff remains on his land and is damaged by the unusual activity of his neighbor in maintaining a reservoir, there should be no need to prove the defendant's negligence.

Blackburn, J's, analysis requires us to distinguish between two types of plaintiff: one who is on his land where he rightfully expects to be free of intrusion and another who has entered into an arena of risk. Let us suppose that a particular quantum of risk would constitute an excessive, disproportionate risk (R) against the plaintiff on his land. The same quantum R would not be sufficient against the second type of plaintiff, for the latter takes part of the risk on himself. The full quantum R is no longer chargeable to the defendant, for a part is now attributable to the plaintiff. In order to reach the standard R, the plaintiff now has to prove more: that additional quantum of risk is represented by the proof of negligence in riding the horse or driving the carriage.

The analysis developed by Blackburn, J., accounts for an important set of distinctions in analyzing the liability of airplane companies for injuries (1) to passengers in their own planes; (2) to passengers in colliding planes; and (3) to persons and property on the ground. The Restatement endorses strict liability for the latter case of ground damages,[46] but requires proof of negligence to passengers, both in the defendant's plane and in colliding planes.[47] Though all these plaintiff's might be injured in the same crash, the standard of liability differs.

The explanation for these distinctions follows readily from recognizing the plaintiff's differing posture toward the risk of a crash. The plaintiff on the ground can charge the defendant with the full quantum of risk. Those who choose to fly, however, enter in the arena of risk and therefore, like the pedestrians in Black-

---

[45] Ibid., pp. 286–87.

[46] *Restatement (Second) of Torts* § 520A.

[47] *Restatement (Second) of Torts* § 520A, comment e.

burn's example, they can hold the airplane company accountable only for a portion of the risk. To bring the quantum of risk up to the level of "excessive risk," the passengers must prove more, namely, that the defendant created additional risks of crashing by negligently flying or maintaining the plane.

The formal defense of "assumption of risk" carried Blackburn's reasoning to the logical conclusion of denying liability altogether. There are some situations, arguably, when individuals not only expose themselves to an expectable risk, but they go further: they accept the risk of injury as the price of their activity. Of course, masochists aside, no one chooses to be injured. But it is fair to say that informed patients knowingly accept the risks implicit in their operations; athletes accept the risks implicit in their contact sports. Yet accepting risks in this context merely replicates Blackburn's analysis of coming physically to the risk: ordinary risks no longer generate liability. Liability attaches only for negligent, or extraordinary risks.

Assumption of risk can, in principle, defeat liability for negligently created risks, but, typically, only in the narrowly defined cases of observable defects: wet floors, exposed wires and the like. The plaintiff chooses to confront the risk rather than forgo the activity requiring him to be at the place of the defect. The doctrine has tended, in recent years, to collapse into contributory negligence.[48] In these cases of choosing an activity at the price of a known risk, fairness requires that the importance of the activity be set off against the gravity of the risk. The plaintiff's choice to confront the known risk no longer seems an adequate basis for denying liability. The defendant's negligence forces the plaintiff, after all, to choose between the risk and forgoing the activity.

Like assumption of risk, contributory negligence would seem to fit into the matrix of risk analysis. Assuming two types of con-

---

[48] Meistrich v. Casino Arena Attractions, Inc., 31 N.J. 44, 155 A.2d 90 (1959). Cf. Carr v. Pacific Telephone, 26 Cal. App. 3d 537, 103 Cal. Prtr. 120 (1971) (reversing judgment for the defendant and restricting "assumption of risk" to cases of "knowing exposure to obvious danger").

tributory negligence, self-regarding and other-regarding, the former invites the same analysis as we applied to assumption of risk. The failure to use one's seat belt increases the risk of injury to oneself. The impact on the analysis of liability would seem to be just like coming to the risk. Exposing others to a risk by driving with bad brakes presumably qualifies as a defense for the same reason. In addition, the plaintiff's negligence towards the defendant converts the latter's excessive risk into a reciprocal, background risk common to the parties.

There is an important difference, however, between risk analysis and contributory negligence, a difference that I overlooked in my earlier paper[49] and which Jules Coleman has pointed out.[50] Assumption of risk may function as an ex ante doctrine; it is possible to know whether the plaintiff has assumed the risk before the accident occurs. But contributory negligence remains, in the traditional mold, ex post. We assess whether the plaintiff is contributorily negligent only after the accident occurs. It is not enough that driving with bad brakes exposes other drivers to a risk of accident; the bad brakes affect the plaintiff's recovery only if they contribute, causally, to the accident.

The requirement of causation bespeaks an ex post orientation. There is a rather clever way to integrate causation into an ex ante analysis of the risk, namely by specifying the ambit of the risk that renders the conduct negligent. Familiar to us in the literature on proximate cause,[51] this move could salvage my earlier effort to treat other-regarding contributory negligence as a risk that cancels out the defendant's excessive risk. The argument would be that driving with bad brakes exposes others to a risk of collision from the bad brakes. If a speeding defendant crashes into the defendant

---

[49] Fletcher, p. 549 (reporting the uncertainty in the literature about the rationale for self-regarding contributory negligence).

[50] J. Coleman, 'Justice and Reciprocity in Tort Theory,' *Western Ontario Law Review* 14 (1975): 105.

[51] See Robert E. Keeton, *Legal Cause in the Law of Torts* (Columbus: Ohio State University Press, 1963).

before he has a chance to apply the brakes, the collision falls outside the range of the reciprocal risk.

Though this reply to Coleman remains at the ready, I am afraid it misses Coleman's insight: in fact contributory negligence has functioned as an ex post rather than ex ante consideration for denying liability. This insight takes on additional strength when we turn from contributory to the ascendant doctrine of comparative negligence.[52] It is virtually impossible to make sense of this modern rationale for apportioning damages without analyzing, ex post, the relative causal contributions of plaintiff and defendant. Indeed, the ex post perspective implicit in comparative negligence accounts for the difficulty that Posner and other economic analysts have with the doctrine.[53] Economic analysis takes a jealously ex ante perspective on the value of activities as a whole and thus inevitably founders on a doctrine that focuses on particular accidents after they occur.

The conclusion that follows from these ruminations on risk analysis is that the plaintiff's contribution to the risk might account for some features of current thinking, but ex ante risk analysis runs counter to the ex post perspective implicit in the formal defenses of contributory and comparative negligence. Risk-analysis has powerful synthetic power, but it cannot serve to reduce the currently conflicted ex ante and ex post modes of tort analysis to a single framework for analyzing liability.

## 4. VINCENT REVISITED

Bringing the distinction between ex ante and ex post into focus invites further consideration of why we regard it as right to hold the shipowner liable for damaging Vincent's dock. Does the principle of liability dovetail with the Restatement's ex ante approach

---

[52] V. Schwartz, Comparative Negligence I (1974 & Supp. 1978) (in period from 1950 to 1977, number of states adopting comparative negligence increased from 5 to 32).

[53] Posner, *Economic Analysis*, p. 124.

to ultrahazardous activities? Of course, we *could* describe the risk in *Vincent* as a nonreciprocal or disproportionate risk.[54] The question is whether that is an illuminating account about why we hold the shipowner liable.

An important concept in German law suggests that a simple risk analysis does not capture the complexity of the situation in *Vincent*. Individuals forced to surrender their rights acquire what is known in Germany as an *Aufopferungsanspruch* – "a claim based on sacrifice."[55] It is an important feature of the *Vincent* situation that the dock owner had to suffer the shipowner's taking refuge from the storm. He had no right to expell him in view of the imminent damage to the ship.[56] The claim for damages derives not only from the defendant's causing harm but from the plaintiff's sacrificing his right to defend his property.

It is not so easy to extend the theory of *Aufopferung* to the cases of high risk enterprises. The potential victims of blasting and other dangerous activities must tolerate the intrusive, socially beneficial risks. Yet it is not plausible to suppose that they have sacrificed their right of self-defense. It makes no sense to say that a homeowner has a right of self-defense against overflying aircraft and, further, that he "sacrifices" this right for the sake of the common good. Self-defense presupposes an imminent danger – one that is about to materialize in harm. That danger was present in *Vincent*, but it is not typically present in the cases of ultrahazardous activities. Consequently, one has some difficulty saying that the victim of dangerous activities "sacrifices" a right in being exposed to the risk of harm.

The distinction between *Vincent* and ultrahazardous activities becomes sharper when we recall the general difference between thinking about particular cases and classes of equivalent risks. Both mooring the ship to the dock and carrying on dangerous activities might be justified on cost-benefit grounds. But the

---

54 See my earlier efforts in this direction, Fletcher, pp. 545–47.

55 See generally E. Deutsch, *Haftungsrecht* (Köln: Carl Heymanns, 1976), pp. 387–400.

justification in *Vincent* depends on the concrete circumstances of the case: the power of the storm, the danger to the dockowner, etc. The justification for blasting and airplane overflights depends on the long range social benefit of carrying on the activity. The difference in focus might make it more plausible to think of Vincent's being forced to surrender his right of self-defense, but not to treat homeowners, subject to repeated overflights, as being forced in any particular case to surrender their right to prevent intrusions.

It might be possible, however, to develop a "claim based on sacrifice" on behalf of the homeowner subject to repeated high-risk intrusions. The plaintiff does not surrender his right of self-help, but does indeed lose what might be otherwise a sound basis for enjoining the dangerous activity. Perhaps the theory of "sacrifice" could be extended to cover these cases, an extension that would bring *Vincent* and extrahazardous activities back within the same theory of liability.

## 5. CONCLUSION

In this paper I have cultivated the distinctions that hound our efforts both to interpret the existing law and to formulate sound principles of liability. Current legal thought is beset by inconsistencies between (1) ex ante and ex post perspective; (2) focusing on single incidents and classes of incidents; and (3) relying on utilitarian criteria in some contexts and not others. By bringing these tensions to the fore, I mean not to signal despair about tort theory, but to provide a basis for generating a more refined theory for justly allocating losses.

*School of Law, University of California, Los Angeles*

ERNEST J. WEINRIB

# TOWARD A MORAL THEORY OF NEGLIGENCE LAW*

ABSTRACT. This paper explores how the widely acknowledged conception of tort law as corrective justice is to be applied to the law of negligence. Corrective justice is an ordering of transactions between two parties which restores them to an antecedent equality. It is thus incompatible with the comprehensive aggregation of utilitarianism, and it stands in easy harmony with Kantian moral notions. This conception of negligence law excludes both maximizing theories, such as Holmes' and Posner's, and Fried's risk pool, which combines Kantianism with distributive rather than corrective justice.

Central to the Kantian approach is the impermissibility of self-preference. The two types of self-preference, self-preference in conception and self-preference in action can respectively account for the objective standard and the Learned Hand test, which are the two most characteristic features of negligence and which are generally (and wrongly) considered to be inescapably aggregative. This corrective justice conception of the negligence standard can then be compared to Epstein's corrective justice conception of strict liability, and arguments can be offered in favour of the superiority of the former.

A moral conception of negligence in tort law is characterized by the juncture of two features: an Aristotelian corrective justice structure and a Kantian content. Section 1 of this paper will outline what these elements are, why they are needed, and how they are related. The problematic nature of these two features is revealed in interpretations of negligence law which disregard one or both of them and in the temptation to preserve them by abandoning negligence in favour of strict liability. These interpretations will be discussed in section 2. We will then move, in section 3, to trace a

* This paper has benefited from the comments of the other participants in the Values in Tort Law symposium sponsored by the Westminster Institute. I would also like to thank Stephen Perry, Peter Benson, Jerry Bickenbach and Raymond Frey for their assistance and criticisms.

conception of negligence which will embody the two requisite features. And Section 4 will defend this conception of negligence against the rival conception of strict liability.

## 1.

Corrective justice, in Aristotle's classic account,[1] is a form of justice which bears on transactions between parties. It considers the position of the parties anterior to the transaction as equal, and it restores this antecedent equality by transferring resources from defendant to plaintiff so that the gain realized by the former is used to make up the loss suffered by the latter. In this focal and paradigmatic instance the gain is equivalent to the loss, but Aristotle recognized that corrective justice can provide a framework for compensation as well as for restitution. Corrective justice is accordingly to be contrasted with distributive justice, where a given resource is distributed among competing claimants in accordance with a ratio that states a criterion of merit. In corrective justice, a transaction creates a nexus between plaintiff and defendant resulting from a direct impingement of the one upon the other. But there is no transaction, and thus no direct impingement in distributive justice: the relationship between the claimants – who can in theory be any number – is always mediated by the scheme of distribution.

Tort law embodies corrective and not distributive justice. The requirement of factual causation establishes the indispensable nexus between the parties by relating their rights to a transaction in which one has directly impinged upon the other. Tort law does not typically pursue wrongful conduct in the abstract. It concerns itself with such conduct only when it materializes in harm to a given person so that compensation can flow from a particular tortfeasor to his particular victim.

The Aristotelian conception of corrective justice is therefore to be contrasted with a more recent version in which corrective jus-

---

1 Aristotle, *Nicomachean Ethics V* 2–4.

tice is characterized as a principle of justice requiring the annulment of wrongful gains and losses.[2] First, the non-Aristotelian version allows the gains and losses to float free from their anchorage in particular transactions. It invites us to consider each gain or each loss on its own by ignoring the nexus between a particular tortfeasor and his particular victim, and accordingly it postulates a distinction between the defendant's liability and the plaintiff's recovery. Whatever a theory founded on this version of corrective justice is, it is not a theory of tort law. Suppose, for instance, that A wrongly harmed B and that C by an identical wrong inflicted an identical harm on D.[3] In the non-Aristotelian version it would not be inappropriate in principle for B to recover from C and D from A. Tort law, however, is not concerned with recovery in the air, but with a right of recovery against a specific tortfeasor who must respond to the damage which he has caused.

Secondly, for Aristotle corrective justice is a form[4] of justice and not a principle of justice. It does not state a normative requirement which must be followed or pursued. In Aristotle's account corrective and distributive justice are parallel and different, and to regard either as a principle of justice would be to deny that status to the other and so to negate their parallelism. Rather each is a form of justice which is supported by its own structure of justification, and the significance of the distinction between them is that they indicate different justificatory structures, with distributive justice looking toward a ratio embodying a criterion of merit and corrective looking to the restoration of the antecedent equality. Thus one can say that the term "corrective" applies to the types of *reasons* for an arrangement rather than to an arrangement itself.[5]

---

[2] Jules Coleman, 'Moral Theories of Torts: Their Scope and Limits. Part II,' this issue.

[3] This example was suggested by Professor T. Benditt.

[4] Aristotle, *Nicomachean Ethics V* 1130 b31, 1131 b27: eidos.

[5] Cf. Robert Nozick, *Anarchy, State, and Utopia* (New York: Basic Books, 1974), p. 27: "the term 'redistributive' applies to the types of *reasons* for an arrangement rather than to an arrangement itself."

The status of corrective justice as a form and not a principle of justice points to its limitations as a solvent of tort controversy. A corrective justice conception of negligence will not in itself justify preferring the current system of liability based on fault to a more comprehensive no-fault compensation scheme. Inasmuch as compensation schemes implicate values of distributive justice, the decision between them and a corrective justice system must be made on the basis of considerations extrinsic to the forms of justice which they respectively embody. Moreover, since corrective justice is a matter of structure not substance, there may be no tort regime which uniquely satisfies its requirements. Restoration of equality with reference to an initial position does not specify either the relevant notion of equality or the relevant initial position. Accordingly each of the competing bases of liability in the common law – strict liability and fault liability – may be embodiments of corrective justice. The choice between them will then have to be made on further grounds of substance.

Corrective justice in itself is devoid of a specific content, which, accordingly, must be sought elsewhere. The burden of this essay is that the content which is to be infused into a corrective justice conception of tort law must be of Kantian inspiration. This is not to say that the content is a matter of exegesis from Kant's own writings or is to be justified by the precise form of universalization which characterizes the various formulations of the Categorical Imperative. But it must refer to some notion of equal membership in the kingdom of ends and the consequent impermissibility of arbitrary self-preference. It must also eschew reference to the aggregation of individual utilities which is the hallmark of utilitarian justification.

The standard objection to utilitarianism is that, by summing across individuals, it fails to take persons seriously and that individuals are regarded merely as sources of a collective and aggregate good rather than as bearers of intrinsic worth. This criticism has a reinforced piquancy in the context of a corrective justice system of adjudication. To be true to its own premises, utilitarianism must maximize the good of all the members of the collectivity who are affected by the decision. But a dispute in a corrective justice framework gives standing to only two members of that collectivity – the defendant who inflicted the injury and his victim – and thus presents an awkward vantage point for the consideration and maximization of the utility of all. The plaintiff and the defendant may not be favourably situated for the presentation of evidence of the collateral interests of all those who would be affected by the decision but are not parties to the dispute. Moreover, the utilitarian adjudicator would face the dilemma of either widening the enquiry and so blurring the significance of the particular litigants or of focusing on the particular dispute at the cost of abandoning the direct pursuit of overall utility. Corrective justice, which concerns itself with the nexus between two persons resulting from the impingement of the one upon the other, particularizes the issue and so creates a tension with the thrust to comprehensiveness which inheres in utilitarianism.

The utilitarian response might be that the theory requires the pursuit of collective welfare, but not necessarily its direct pursuit. A distinction can be drawn between the design of rules and institutions and the application of these rules to specific instances.[6] The requirements of utilitarianism would be satisfied by a utilitarian design. The application of the rules under this design according to their own internal logic would therefore instance corrective justice within a more comprehensive utilitarian framework.

This response raises notorious problems within the theory of utilitarianism in its competing versions, the exploration of which would not be to the present purpose. It will be sufficient here to indicate why it is inadequate for the foundation of tort theory. It postulates precisely what is absent from the common law of torts and turns on its head the process of legal evolution in this area.

---

6 A recent sketch of a utilitarian theory of law based on this distinction is provided by L. W. Summer, *Abortion and Moral Theory* (Princeton: Princeton University Press, 1981), p. 189. An earlier version appears in John Austin, *The Province of Jurisprudence Determined*, Lecture II (1832).

Aside from a few legislative excrescences which vary from jurisdiction to jurisdiction, the common law of torts is constituted entirely by its specific instances which assume a systematic aspect only under the pressure of the vague procedural notion that like cases ought to be decided alike. There is therefore no centralized design which can embody the general utilitarian orientation of the system. What is primary are the specific instances of dispute resolution where the concept of corrective justice – with its anti-utilitarian tendencies – is strongest.

Moreover, it is difficult, if not impossible, to design a tort system which would resolve the basic issues, such as whether liability should be absolute or fault-based, on utilitarian lines. The task was sporadically attempted in the nineteenth century with an instructive lack of success. Baron Bramwell, for instance, argued from the Benthamite premise that "the public consists of all the individuals of it, and a thing is for the public benefit only when it is productive of good to those individuals on the balance of loss and gain to all" to the conclusion that strict liability was justified as a means of ensuring that the gains from activity exceeded the losses.[7] But, as Holmes was to point out, this ignores the cost of maintaining and setting in motion the state's "cumbrous and expensive machinery"[8] of adjudication, the use of which must be justified by a benefit additional to that realized from the transaction being adjudicated. The optimal standard of tort liability might therefore not require the right to compensation for all losses, and Holmes inferred that negligence was the appropriate standard. But this conclusion was no less unsubstantiated than Bramwell's. The costs of administering the judicial machinery might show that the

---

[7] Bamford v. Turnley (1862) 122 E.R. 27, at 33 (Exch.). The case has recently been discussed by P. S. Atiyah, "Liability for Railway Nuisance in the English Common Law: A Historical Footnote" *Journal of Law and Economics* 23 (1980): 191. Bramwell's language recalls Jeremy Bentham, *An Introduction to the Principles of Morals and Legislation*, Chapter I, s. IV. Cf. also Bramwell's judgment in Powell v. Fall (1880) 5 Q.B.D. 597 (C.A.).

[8] Oliver W. Holmes, *The Common Law*, ed. M. D. Howe (Cambridge: Belknap Press, 1963), p. 77.

optimal standard was less than strict liability, but it did not demonstrate that it was so much less that the fault standard was justified. The optimal standard might be between the two or closer to the one than to the other, and the reference to administrative costs is insufficient to determine its position even approximately. Indeed the ubiquitous utilitarian pronouncements in Holmes's writings on torts illustrate the familiar temptation to adorn congenial but unsupported conclusions in language of utilitarianism without attempting the elaborate calculus which the theory requires.

The Kantian approach avoids these difficulties. It does not require conjecture or empirical demonstration concerning aggregate welfare. Moreover, since maximization across all affected persons is foreign to it, it can maintain the focus on the two litigating parties as is required by corrective justice, without concerning itself with the collateral consequences to others. And the equality of membership in the kingdom of ends which undergirds it invites speculation as to its relationship to the restoration of an initial equality which Aristotle identified as the function of corrective justice.

## 2.

Negligence is generally considered to be a utilitarian concept by contemporary theorists, and it is often rejected precisely for that reason.[9] Its foremost exponents in this century and the last – Posner and Holmes – explicitly accounted for it in maximizing terms. Indeed Holmes's justification for the objective standard – "that when men live in society, a certain average of conduct, a sacrifice of individual peculiarities going beyond a certain point, is necessary to the general welfare"[10] – conjures up a precise image which haunts utilitarianism, the sacrifice of the individual for col-

---

[9] E.g., George Fletcher, 'Fairness and Utility in Tort Theory' *Harvard Law Review* 85 (1972): 537.

[10] Holmes, *Common Law*, p. 86.

lective gain. It is hardly surprising that in the current retreat from utilitarianism the acceptability of negligence has been called into question.

The remarkable feature of Posner's defense of negligence is his claim that his theory of wealth maximization yields a corrective justice conception of negligence which rests on viable normative foundations.[11] The central legal datum in Posner's theory is the Learned Hand formulation, that negligence consists in the failure to take precautions when the burden of those precautions is less than the risk of injury times the seriousness of injury.[12] Posner concludes from this that negligence is the wasting of a social resource and that the law's role is to provide incentives for economically efficient conduct by imposing on the actor the costs which he should not have avoided. The excessive attention which this theory has received renders lengthy criticism here superfluous. Three brief comments will suffice. Firstly, the unattractiveness of utilitarianism as a moral theory is magnified by wealth maximization, which retains utilitarianism's suspect consequentialism and aggregation while discarding the comprehensiveness and the neutrality which give utilitarianism whatever plausibility it has. Secondly, the theory conceives of negligence as an offence against a maximizing scheme rather than as an injury against a particular victim, and the plaintiff's compensation is regarded not as an entitlement but as a bounty to induce his cooperation in the process of maximization. But this is incompatible with corrective justice since under corrective justice the plaintiff has a right to the restoration of the antecedent equality, and his standing is not merely an administrative adjunct to the process of imposing costs on the defendant. Thirdly, wealth maximization purports to resolve the tension between the comprehensiveness of utilitar-

---

[11] See especially Richard Posner, 'A Theory of Negligence' *Journal of Legal Studies* 1 (1972): 29; 'Utilitarianism, Economics and Legal Theory' *Journal of Legal Studies* 8 (1979): 103; 'The Concept of Corrective Justice in Recent Theories of Tort Law' *Journal of Legal Studies* 10 (1981): 187.

[12] United States v. Carroll Towing Co. (1947) 159 F2d 169, at 173 (2d Cir).

ianism and the particularity of corrective justice by postulating that the correct solution in tort litigation is what the parties would have bargained towards had bargaining been feasible. By looking upon tort litigation as a hypothetical exchange which ought to mirror an actual exchange, the theory renders a dispute amenable to adjudication since the number of parties can be restricted to two and the appearance of corrective justice preserved. But there is no plausible argument for having tort litigation mirror an actual exchange, as the theory requires, since the ethical foundations of the hypothetical exchange differ from those of the real exchange which it is supposed to mirror.[13]

As a contrast to interpretations in terms of the maximization of wealth or utility, Professor Charles Fried has attempted to ground negligence on the concept of a "risk pool."[14] The significance of Fried's view is that it represents an account of negligence on explicitly Kantian lines. As such it is unique in the current literature.

Starting from Kant's concept of justice as "the aggregate of those conditions under which the wills of all persons can be conjoined in accordance with a universal law of freedom,"[15] Fried proposes a specification of this concept which will determine when one person has imposed an excessive risk of harm on another. The moral right to impose a risk on others is explicated by reference to "the necessity for action, for the pursuit of ends and the exercise of capacities" which "requires a certain freedom to impose risk of death on others," so that "we are justified in imposing that degree of risk on others which we would all agree to so that we would have the maximum degree of freedom to pursue our ends and exercise our capacities." Combined with this

---

13 The first and third of these criticisms are developed more fully in Ernest Weinrib, 'Utilitarianism, Economics, and Legal Theory,' *University of Toronto Law Journal* **30** (1980): 307; the second in Ernest Weinrib, 'Corrective Justice and Tort Theory' (forthcoming).

14 Charles Fried, *An Anatomy of Values* (Cambridge: Harvard University Press, 1970), pp. 183ff.

15 Immanuel Kant, *The Metaphysical Elements of Justice*, tr. John Ladd (Indianapolis: Bobbs-Merrill, 1965), pp. 33–37.

specification of a Kantian principle of equal right is a view that the justifications for imposing the risk on others are analogous to those governing the rationality of imposing it on oneself. Just as each individual has a risk budget which orders the risks he is willing to undergo against the ends which are important to him, so there is a correlative interpersonal risk pool to which all persons contribute and on which they may draw in the pursuit of ends of the appropriate degree of seriousness. The risk pool is reflected in the balancing of the significance of the end against the degree of risk which, in Fried's view, characterizes the law of negligence.

This interesting approach cannot, however, provide a moral theory for negligence law. Even if it had an appropriate Kantian content, it would lack the required structure of corrective justice. Indeed the risk pool is a scheme of distributive rather than corrective justice, and it cannot be incorporated into a theory of tort law without intolerable tension. Because distributive justice presents an aggregation of claimants against a common pool, it provides no direct linkage of plaintiff to defendant. Morever, distributive justice has a conceptual dynamic of its own which in its focal and ideal form arrays the subject matter of the distribution, the criterion of distribution, and the beneficiaries of the distribution in an interrelated and purposive ordering. But in the tort system the litigants are linked by the random occurrence of the accident rather than by membership in a purposively constituted group.

The difficulty of establishing a nexus between plaintiff and defendant surfaces in a number of ways. Fried recognizes that conformity with the law of negligence requires that a stupid, incapacitated, or accident-prone person not be allowed to withdraw from the pool the large amount which would accord with his subjective needs. But there is no argument of right which can prevent a person from making an extraordinarily large single withdrawal provided that the total amount of risk withdrawn over his lifetime is within his allotment. The cautious and prudent recluse whose withdrawals from the pool have been minimal would be entitled to go on a single wild spending spree which could impose risks beyond what would be countenanced by the law of negligence. The idea of the risk pool is not sufficiently powerful to calibrate the withdrawals into amounts which would be acceptable for individualized transactions.

Moreover, the very notion of excessive withdrawal is problematic. Here the difficulty is the lack of correlation between what each person contributes to the pool – life, health, and property – and the risk which he withdraws. Since risk is as varied and as inexhaustible as the human actions which generate it, an extraordinary withdrawal does not mean that other members of the risk pool suffer from a consequent deficiency. The spending of risk does not diminish the risk available to others: it diminishes rather the contributions which others have made, and it is these contributions which are exhaustible. But it is implausible to suppose that the wrong which inheres in excessively risky behaviour is the failure to leave over a fair share of lives to be consumed by the risky activities of others. A Kantian notion of freedom may perhaps lead to the right to impose risk in its exercise, but it cannot lead to a right to have lives available for extinction.

The disparity between what is put into the pool and what is taken out of it suggests another difficulty: does the distributive scheme distribute life or risk? Here we have a choice between looking to the losses of potential victims or the activity of potential actors, and either alternative washes us away from negligence law. Concentration on the distribution of the risk-imposition would require the excogitation of a scheme in which the central fact of tort litigation – the materialization of risk into injury – is irrelevant.[16] On the other hand, attention to life suggests a no-fault or social insurance programme which need have no connection with unreasonably risky behaviour, which constitutes only one of the many ways in which life and health can be consumed. Corrective justice, with its focus on the transactional nexus between actor and victim, constrains the inquiry through its very structure, and the removal of this structure by viewing the matter as one of

---

[16] Cf. Joel Feinberg, *Doing and Deserving* (Princeton: Princeton University Press, 1970), p. 215.

distributive justice opens up possibilities which transcend and overwhelm the specific concerns of negligence law.

Aside from these difficulties, there are problems with the relationship between the risk pool and the Kantian conception of equal right. Fried seeks to operationalize the Kantian principle by attending to what we, as rational persons, would agree to as the price for allowing our own freedom of action. Since a prospective victim would not agree to subjection to any life-threatening risk at the moment of action, we must imagine the hypothetical agreement taking place in some sort of Rawlsian original position. But if the persons in the original position choose to set up a risk pool for the grounds given by Fried – that there is a symmetry between an individual's choosing to expose himself to risk in the realization of his own ends and a social decision to allow risk in order to promote more important societal ends – they will in fact have chosen a utilitarian principle on utilitarian grounds. The parallel between the intrapersonal risk budget and the interpersonal risk pool seems to present the very failure to take persons seriously which a contractarian framework is designed to avoid.[17]

Fried is aware of this difficulty and indicates a different relevance for the risk budget. He is concerned that a person in the original position might be unwilling to purchase his freedom of action at the cost of having his own life subject to the random interruptions occasioned by the behaviour of others and might accordingly opt for strict liability. In Fried's view this risk-aversiveness would be irrational because it would make all action impossible and because it is belied by the choice of risk which each person incorporates into his own risk budget. But these factors cannot bear the weight which the argument requires. Strict liability does not necessarily make action impossible; it merely imposes costs – high costs to be sure – on action. There is no reason to believe that a person in the original position would not consider the high cost to be worth the security gained in exchange.

[17] John Rawls, *A Theory of Justice* (Cambridge: Harvard University Press, 1971), pp. 22–27.

And the fact that persons are not risk averse in their own choices in no way shows that they would not be averse to the risk imposed upon them by the choices of others. The idea of the risk pool cannot lead to a determinate conclusion yielding a moral justification of negligence.

The inadequacy of these maximizing and Kantian approaches to negligence seems to open the way for elaborating a tort theory on a different basis of liability, and Professor Epstein's elucidation of strict liability constitutes the most ambitious contemporary project in this vein.[18] Indeed the credentials of this version of strict liability are impressive, for it manifestly satisfies the two criteria for a moral theory. Strict liability in this version is single-mindedly concerned with causation as a necessary and sufficient condition of liability. In thus focusing on the impingement by defendant on plaintiff in a particular transaction and regarding the *status quo ante* as the point of equality towards which the law restores, it readily conforms to the structure of corrective justice. Furthermore, in isolating these two parties and analysing their relationship in terms of the harm which one transitively imposes on the other, recourse to an aggregation involving the interests of everyone affected is excluded. But it will be recalled that, in the Aristotelian conception, corrective justice is a form and not a principle of justice, and that therefore an embodiment of this form need not be exclusive. We are thus justified in continuing to seek a Kantian and corrective justice account of negligence.

3.

At the heart of a Kantian approach lies the recognition of equal membership in the kindom of ends and the consequent impermis-

---

[18] Richard Epstein, 'A Theory of Strict Liability,' *Journal of Legal Studies* 2 (1973): 151; and 'Defences and Subsequent Pleas in a System of Strict Liability,' *Journal of Legal Studies* 3 (1974): 165. The two papers have been reprinted by the Cato Institute as *A Theory of Strict Liability: Toward a Reformulation of Tort Law* (San Francisco: Cato Institute, 1980).

sibility of self-preference. In willing that the maxim of one's action become a universal law of nature, the individual imposes no law upon others which he would not impose upon himself and arrogates to himself no privilege which he would not allow to others. One can distinguish, as Kant did,[19] two forms of the impermissibility of self-preference which we might term self-preference in action and self-preference in conception. The first form is linked to the fact that man acts in the world in a purposive way, and in willing his particular ends he must also will the means necessary for them. But he cannot will those means for himself without conceding them to others, and inasmuch as the realization of his purposes requires the forebearance or consideration of others, he must extend to others an equal forebearance or consideration. As he acts in the world, a person must not grant to himself an advantage that he would deny to others. The rationality of his own purposive actions must mesh with the equality of persons generally. The other form of self-preference involves the use of a concept in a manner whose idiosyncracy would destroy the very concept being used if such use were to be universal. Invocation of a concept in itself imposes constraints, and the actor must attorn to the concept which, expressly or by implication, is an element in the maxim being universalized.

Now there are two features of negligence which a Kantian theory must explain: the rejection of the subjective standard and the existence and ingredients of the objective standard. The first derives from *Vaughan* v. *Menlove,*[20] where the defendant argued that the appropriate standard was "whether he had acted bona fide to the best of his ability" since if he had, "he ought not to be responsible for the misfortune of not possessing the highest order of intelligence." The argument was not accepted, and a jury direction couched in terms of "such reasonable conduct as a

---

[19] Immanuel Kant, *Fundamental Principles of the Metaphysic of Morals,* tr. Abbott (Indianapolis: Bobbs-Merrill, 1949), p. 41 (distinguishing contradictions in the will from contradictions in the conception).
[20] (1837), 132 E.R. 490 (C.P.).

prudent man would have exercised" was upheld. The second was formulated in Learned Hand's famous test that there is negligence when the burden of taking precautions is less than the probability of injury multiplied by the gravity of injury. As we have seen, maximization is generally supposed to justify both features: the Learned Hand formula is regarded as an economic or utilitarian comparison of costs and benefits which encourages individual activity tending to efficiency or the public good, and the rejection of the subjective standard is thought to embody a sacrifice of individual peculiarities for the sake of the common welfare. In a corrective justice analysis on Kantian lines, a new justification for each of these features must be offered.

The defendant's argument in *Vaughan* v. *Menlove,* that he ought not to be responsible for the misfortune of his own stupidity, unsuccessfully attempted to make tort liability coterminous with subjective capacity. The holding in this case has been criticized as being inherently unfair to the particular defendant who may be unable to act in accordance with the objective standard which it mandates.[21] This criticism is misguided. It assumes that the issue is the morality or immorality of the defendant's action when considered in itself and without reference to the person injured by the action. But the real issue for corrective justice is the setting of fair terms of interpersonal impingement, and this requires attention both to the actor and to the person affected by his acts.

In this connection the Kantian prohibition against self-preference in conception can be helpful. The defendant's argument in *Vaughan* v. *Menlove* that the standard should not be set beyond the limits of his ability constituted a claim that the boundary between the defendant's right to act and the plaintiff's right to freedom from the effects of that action is marked by the defendant's subjective powers of evaluation. By this claim the ambit of the plaintiff's right is confined to, and thus defined by, the space remaining after the defendant's occupation. The defendant is thus the sole determinant of the plaintiff's rights, and the plaintiff's right is dependent

---

21 Epstein, 'A Theory of Strict Liability,' p. 153.

on the defendant's subjectivity. But this version of the parties' rights cannot be willed to be a universal law since it contradicts the very conception of a right. On a Kantian view, a right is something which a person has "in his own right," by virtue of his being an end in himself. Since a person has an independent claim to it, it cannot be dependent on someone else's subjectivity. By claiming the right to be the subjective arbiter of another's rights, the defendant was giving himself a preference which, if universalized, would destroy the very concept of right and, with it, his own claim.[22]

The rejection of subjectivity as a standard is thus based on the immorality of self-preference in conception. But the ingredients of the objective standard, as formulated in the Learned Hand test, are to be explicated by reference to self-preference in action. Here we must imagine a hypothetical inquiry of two stages, the first centering on rationality and the second on equality. First, we ask how the defendant ought to have acted if he were affected by his own action. If, for instance, the issue is whether the defendant is negligent in making a combustible hayrick close to the plaintiff's cottage,[23] we ask how the defendant would have acted if he were also the owner of the cottage. Since a subjective standard is excluded, the question becomes what would he, as a reasonable person, have done if he had owned the cottage near the hayrick which he was contemplating making. And the answer is that he would have compared the probability of the hayrick's ignition and the damage his cottage would suffer if it did ignite with the cost of taking precautions against this damage by making the rick elsewhere. In other words, the rational thing for the defendant in the hypothetical situation to have done is to have applied the Learned Hand test to himself. The second stage then moves from this hypothetical situation to the actual one and operates to deny the validity of the defendant's plea that he did not in fact own the plaintiff's cottage and that there is thus no need for him to include

22 The argument is modelled on Kant's discussion of promises, *Fundamental Principles*, pp. 39, 46.

23 The facts of Vaughan v. Menlove, supra n. 20.

the risk to the cottage in his calculations. It would be a violation of equality for the defendant to refuse to extend to the plaintiff the consideration which he would have extended to himself. For the defendant to claim that he would have moved his rick to protect his own cottage but not to protect the plaintiff's is to violate the Kantian injunction against self-preference in action.[24]

It is thus possible to explicate the Learned Hand formula in a way that makes no reference to utilitarian or aggregative considerations. The balancing of the risk against the measures needed to eliminate or avoid the risk stands at the junction of the paradigmatically deontological elements of rationality in a hypothetical situation[25] and equality as between actor and victim. There is here no end-state which is being promoted, no good which is being maximized, and no aggregation of individual interests.

Moreover, the Kantian interpretation fits readily into, and provides content for, corrective justice. It will be recalled that corrective justice requires the cancellation of gains and losses which have occurred through the violation of equality in transactions. The relevant loss is the damage suffered by the plaintiff as a result of the defendant's failure to give him equal consideration, and cause-in-fact is the concept by which tort law traces the causal nexus between the defendant's violation of equality and the plaintiff's loss. The defendant's gain is that he did not carry the burden

---

[24] This notion of impartiality is explicit in the concept of *culpa levis* in Roman Law. The avoidance of *culpa levis in concreto* required the defendant to have treated the property of others with the same care with which he treated his own *(diligentia quam suis rebus)*, and *culpa levis in abstracto* was the absence of *talis diligentia qualem quisque diligentissimus pater familias suis rebus adhibet* (*Digest* 13.6.18pr). See J. A. C. Thomas, *Textbook of Roman Law* (New York: North-Holland, 1976) 250. An application in tort law is given in *Digest* 9.2.39.1 (Pomponius): *quamvis alienum pecus in agro suo quis deprehendit, sic illud expellere debet quomodo si suum deprehendisset.*

[25] Reference to a hypothetical situation can be derived from the first version of Kant's categorial imperative ("Act as if...") and in his distinction between moral freedom and physical causation in his *Critique of Practical Reason*, tr. L. W. Beck (Indianapolis: Bobbs-Merrill, 1956), p. 101.

of appropriate precautions as he implicated the plaintiff into the web of his own projects. And the notion of equality against which these gains and losses are measured is the Kantian prohibition against self-preference in action which the defendant has violated by treating the plaintiff less advantageously than he would have treated himself. The gain and loss are not equal because the former is *ex ante* and the latter *ex post*, but the litigation itself takes place *ex post*, as it must if it is to deal with an actual rather than a possible loss, and so the plaintiff's loss is the measure of recovery. In this way, the Kantian conception of equality dovetails with the Aristotelian version of corrective justice.

Since this account of negligence bears a suspicious resemblance to Posner's economic one, it is appropriate to remark on the difference. Both interpretations locate the defendant's wrongful gain in the foregone burden of precautions. But the economic interpretation exhibits no essential connection between negligence and equality, and as a consequence it must portray negligence not as a wrong against a particular plaintiff but as wastefulness under a maximizing scheme. In contrast, on the Kantian interpretation the defendant's failure to exercise due care is a failure to give equal consideration to the plaintiff and is thus a wrong directed against him.[26] When this wrong materializes into injury the plaintiff's standing to sue derives from his being wronged and not from his being strategically situated for the imposition of incentives for wealth maximization.[27]

---

[26] Cf. Ronald Dworkin, *Taking Rights Seriously* (Cambridge: Harvard University Press, 1978), p. 98; Gary Schwartz, 'Contributory Negligence and Comparative Negligence: A Reappraisal,' *Yale Law Journal* 87 (1978): 703.

[27] The difference can lead to a different handling of specific problems. On the economic approach, rules of contributory and comparative damages must provide the greatest incentive for accident prevention at the lowest joint cost to the plaintiff and defendant, and it seems difficult to formulate the appropriate rule; see Richard Posner, *Economic Analysis of Law*, 2nd ed., (Boston: Little Brown, 1977); Schwartz, 'Contributory Negligence', pp. 703–10. On a Kantian approach, comparative negligence on the Anglo-Canadian model is satisfactory because it holds the plaintiff to the same standard of rationality which his suit is imposing on the defendant.

Similarly, the Kantian account of negligence can be distinguished from utilitarianism. The one requires the aggregation of any number of individual interests, whereas the other involves merely a comparison of the interests of two initially equal parties. The distinction between aggregation and comparison is an important one. That comparison is the more fundamental of the two procedures is evidenced by the mistake committed by utilitarian thinkers who have assumed that agreement with the latter entails acceptance of the former. Sidgwick's proof of utilitarianism against the egoist is illustrative:

> If the egoist strictly confines himself to stating his conviction that he ought to take his own happiness or pleasure as his ultimate end, there seems to be no opening for any line of reasoning to lead him to universalistic Hedonism as a first principle... When, however, the Egoist puts forward, implicitly or explicitly, the proposition that his happiness or pleasure is good not only *for him* but from the point of view of the Universe... it then becomes relevant to point out to him that *his* happiness cannot be a more important part of the Good, taken universally, than the equal happiness of any other person.[28]

From this "proof" one can conclude only that the actor must be impartial between his own happiness and that of any other person, not that he must promote the aggregate happiness of all persons. Comparison, which presupposes the equality of persons, constitutes the deeper Kantian[29] foundations upon which utilitarianism attempts to build – at the cost of inescapable incoherence[30] – an aggregative structure. The Kantian theory of negligence, which invokes comparison but not aggregation, should not be confused with utilitarianism.

---

[28] Henry Sidgwick, *The Methods of Ethics*, (London: Macmillan & Co., 7th ed., 1907), p. 420.

[29] For Sidgwick's acknowledgement of Kant's influence on him, see ibid., xvii.

[30] The incoherence consists in regarding a person's subjective state – pleasure, desire, experience, or happiness – as expressive of ultimate value and then requiring an aggregation of subjective states which does not represent the subjective state of anyone. Cf. John Taurek, 'Should the Numbers Count?' *Philosophy and Public Affairs* 6 (1977): 293.

It is a commonplace of textbooks that the negligence concept is "clearly utilitarian."[31] The language of utilitarian justification in judicial opinions is, however, usually restricted to the exoneration of public authorities or public champions who have caused injury while attending to an emergency. This language should not be regarded as the germ of a comprehensive theory of negligence for two reasons. First, the involvement of public authorities moves the litigation away from private law adjudication and closer to the model of judicial review of administrative action. Here a court might properly feel deferential about substituting its assessment for that of the officers of a coordinate branch of government with specialized expertise acting for the good of others and not self-preferentially.[32] Secondly, even here the facts often feature a pair-wise comparison between the person whose imminent danger motivates the official action and the plaintiff whom the official action puts at risk.[33] In these situations the court is still concerned with the propriety of preference, although not of self-preference, and it is not engaged in the aggregation which characterizes utilitarianism.

The point is also relevant to Fried's risk pool. Fried regards negligence law as involving a balancing of the significance of the end against the degree of risk and so takes the superficial textbook utilitarianism as paradigmatic. This has the advantage of allowing for the symmetry between the interpersonal risk pool and the intrapersonal risk budget, and the disadvantage of requiring a further move to rescue the risk pool from the utilitarianism which is embedded in its foundations. A contractarian original position is then set up, but there is no secure ground for discounting the risk aversiveness which rational persons in this position might display. By contrast the Kantian theory proposed here retains the deontological elements of rationality and equality but without an original

---

[31] E.g., John Fleming, *The Law of Torts*, 5th ed., (Sydney: Law Book Co., 1977), p. 117.

[32] The leading Canadian case is Priestman v. Colangelo [1959] S.C.R. 615.

[33] E.g., Watt v. Hertfordshire Country Council (1954) 2 All E.R. 368 (C.A.).

position and thus without the need to deal with the possibility of aversion to risk as a ground for choice under conditions of uncertainty. Here negligence law can be seen as imposing a hypothetical calculation in an actual, not in a hypothetical, situation. In this actual situation the problem is not risk aversion but extraordinary susceptibility to injury, and this can be accounted for in accordance with the particular fact contour. Where the actor knows or ought to know of the susceptibility, it is worked into the interpersonal comparison.[34] Otherwise, it does not play a role until the actor crosses the threshold of negligence.[35]

4.

The Kantian account of negligence requires that the defendant, at the time of his acting, hypothetically place himself in the position of the person affected by the prospective action. The hypothetical consideration intervenes at the point of conduct and provides a means for assessing the propriety of the defendant's harm-causing action. In this it is to be compared with strict liability, which takes the pre-existing holdings as the starting point of equality towards which corrective justice must restore.

Now a theory of strict liability, on Professor Epstein's elucidation, also involves a hypothetical. The defendant is required to treat the harm he has inflicted upon others as though it were inflicted on himself.[36] He would have borne the consequences of

---

34 Paris v. Stepney Borough Council (1951) A.C. 367 (H.L.) (for one-eyed man the consequence relevant to assessment of the risk is loss of sight not the loss of an eye).

35 Smith v. Leech Brain (1962) 2 Q.B. 405.

36 Epstein, 'Defences and Subsequent Pleas in a System of Strict Liability,' p. 170; cf. Epstein, 'A Theory of Strict Liability,' p. 158. The strict liability hypothetical was invoked by Baron Bramwell in Bamford v. Turnley, (1862) 122 E.R. 27, at 33: "If, though the wood were their own, they still would find it compensated them to run trains at the cost of burning the wood, then they obviously ought to compensate the owner of such wood, not being themselves, if they burn it down in making their gains."

his action regardless of whether he was justified in doing it on the negligence calculus, and since he cannot transfer his problems to someone else, tort law forces the defendant to bear in the real world the losses which he would have borne in the hypothetical one. The difference between negligence and strict liability thus becomes a difference in the operation of two hypothetical situations. In negligence law the hypothetical focuses on conduct at the point of action, whereas the strict liability hypothetical focuses on the results of the defendant's behaviour.

Both negligence liability and strict liability aspire to satisfy the two criteria of a Kantian content and a corrective justice framework. Both attempt to do this by means of a hypothetical, and the contest between them can be looked upon as requiring determination of which of the hypotheticals is more compelling. Are there any advantages which a hypothetical oriented towards the actor's conduct has over a hypothetical oriented towards the results of conduct? The more obvious implication of notions of responsibility in the former suggests two considerations.

First negligence, with its focus on conduct and choice, can accommodate the absence of liability where there is no act in the technical tort sense of a manifestation of the will.[37] Under the Kantian approach lies the view that moral personality is marked by the capacity to form and advance a conception of the good.[38] Liability should not be visited on actions that cannot plausibly be regarded as instances of the exercise of this capacity. This does not excuse the fool who makes a hayrick beside another's cottage, or the person who drives a car after unknowingly suffering a stroke which impairs his capacity.[39] He is pursuing his own purposes albeit in a foolish or impaired manner. But it does exclude cases where the actor is unconscious[40] or where his limbs are

---

37 *Restatement (Second) of Torts* 2 (1965).

38 John Rawls, 'Kantian Constructivism in Moral Theory,' *Journal of Philosophy* 77 (1980): 525.

39 Roberts v. Ramsbottom (1980), 1 All E.R. 7 (Q.B.D.).

40 Slattery v. Haley (1923) 3 D.L.R. 156 (Ont. App. Div.); Stokes v. Carlson (1951) 240 S.W. 2d 132 (Mo.S.C.).

being forcibly moved by someone else,[41] since the conduct is not a step in the realization or promotion of his own end whatever it may be. He cannot appropriately be regarded as having gained anything through the infliction of injury and there is accordingly no room for the operation of corrective justice. Nor can he be looked upon as having committed a self-preference in conception: his behaviour can no more plausibly be construed as implying contradictory claims than can the epileptic who in the course of his convulsions emits the sounds "X" and "not X" be regarded as having contradicted himself.

In contrast, it is hard to see how a result-oriented theory can exclude from liability those results which are a consequence of nonvoluntary behaviour. Professor Epstein himself acknowledges the need for this exclusion,[42] but does not indicate how it can be integrated into the theory. The epileptic who in the course of an unanticipated convulsion injures another would have had to bear the consequences if he had injured himself, and accordingly is caught by the strict liability hypothetical. The attention to results in strict liability renders irrelevant not only the process of choice envisaged in the negligence calculus but also the volitional basis of choice which is embodied in the tort concept of an act.[43]

The other difficulty is more fundamental. Since thc Kantian account of negligence takes hold at the level of conduct and ties

---

[41] Smith v. Stone (1647) 82 E.R. 533 (K.B.).

[42] Epstein, 'A Theory of Strict Liability,' p. 166.

[43] Cf. Holmes, *Common Law*, p. 96: "Unless my act is of a nature to harm others, unless under the circumstances a prudent man would have foreseen the possibility of harm, it is no more justifiable to make me idemnify my neighbour against the consequences, than to make me do the same thing if I had fallen upon him in a fit, or to compell me to insure him against lightning."

Epstein might explain absence of liability in terms of causation, but causation is itself treated as something reflected in language usage. It is not impossible to say that the epileptic struck another. At most, an argument from causation as based on language usage would apply to situations where the immediate physical origin the person's behaviour is in another person (A moves B's hand so that it strikes C) and not where the origin is internal (epilepsy etc.). But the legal category of "no act" applies to both.

its notion of propriety in action to a moral theory, it provides a positive reason for shifting losses in accordance with it. The wrongfulness of the action, consisting here of the defendant's self-preferential violation of the equality he ought to have accorded to the plaintiff, supplies a ground for the restoration of the antecedent equality which was wrongly disturbed. Negligence constitutes the measure of wrongfulness which justifies judicial intervention. But strict liability looks to results, and, unless one is upholding strict liability on consequentialist grounds, there may be nothing either moral or immoral about differences in results. They may merely be different states of the world, and on a nonconsequentialist view they may in themselves not provide a positive reason, or even a prima facie one, for using the machinery of state to effect a change. If corrective justice is regarded as operating against a baseline of equality of result, there must be some positive reason for restoring the *status quo ante* beside the fact that it *is* the *status quo ante.*

The intuitively appealing solution to this difficulty fastens on the impermissibility of a transfer without the transferor's consent. The argument would be that consent has a special and indispensible status and that unless there is a strict liability tort regime, the defendant's property will be appropriated by another without the defendant's consent. Thus lack of consent is supposed to constitute the independent ground of wrongfulness, parallel to negligence's wrongful self-preference in action, which provides a positive reason for shifting losses. But there are two related difficulties with this argument. First, it is circular. The defendant can have a right to protection against nonfaulty diminutions of his holdings only if the property is protected by a tort regime of strict liability. If, however, the boundaries of one's holdings are demarcated by the principle of fault, there would be no need to secure the defendant's consent to the diminution since he would have no entitlement to protection against it. Any tort regime establishes the conceptual nature of the boundaries of one's holdings, and thus a normative argument about the appropriate tort regime cannot proceed from the fact that one has holdings. Secondly, the argument meshes the existence of property with the centrality of consent, but the centrality of consent calls into question the legitimacy of property which by its nature creates the right to exclude others without *their* consent.[44] The proposed positive argument in favour of strict liability, that it protects property from unconsented to depredations, is caught on the horns of a dilemma: if property is prior to consent, there is no objection to a tort standard of negligence which defines property so as to reduce the occasions for the securing of the owner's consent, whereas if consent is prior to property the justification of property in itself becomes problematic.

The reconciliation of property and consent has been a major theme in political theory for several centuries, and it will be sufficient for present purposes to indicate that the terms in which the problem is discussed are not auspicious for the resolution of the objections to the proposed positive argument for strict liability. The usual approach for justifying the institution of property against the unconsented exclusion of others is to argue that there is a way of effecting the transition from a property-less state of nature to a system of property holding such that everyone would agree to it. Thus it is claimed that everyone, including those whom property rules exclude, is better off under a system of property holding than in the property-less state of nature, so that the former is Pareto-superior to the latter.[45] The comparison is systemic in that what is compared to a state of nature is property, not any specific property regime. Both strict liability and negligence might be preferable to a state of nature without there being any implication as to which was preferable to the other.[46] Thus, even if as a matter of political theory, property can be reconciled

---

44 Hillel Steiner, 'A Libertarian Quandary", *Ethics* 90 (1980): 257.

45 Nozick, *Anarchy, State, and Utopia*, pp. 175–82 provides a contemporary version.

46 In Losee v. Buchanan (1873) 51 N.Y. 476 (C.A.) the court assumed that the Pareto superiority of civilized society to a state of nature would favour negligence over strict liability.

with consent, there seems to be no way to extract from political theory a positive argument for strict liability. The existence of property does not imply that nonnegligent injuries constitute morally impermissible transfers. The positive argument for strict liability remains to be made.

*Faculty of Law, University of Toronto*

J. ROBERT S. PRICHARD AND ALAN BRUDNER

# TORT LIABILITY FOR BREACH OF STATUTE: A NATURAL RIGHTS PERSPECTIVE

ABSTRACT. This essay applies Hegel's theory of remedies to the question of whether and when breach of a penal statute should attract civil liability in tort. For Hegel, the purpose of a remedy is to vindicate the human right to self-determination by refuting the claim to validity implied in intentional or negligent acts that infringe this right. Accordingly, in determining the civil effect of legislation, a distinction must be made between statutes that effectuate pre-existing rights and those which create new rights in the attempt to maximize aggregate welfare. The former should confer a civil right of action, the latter should not. Statutes that impose a duty of affirmative action should be enforced civilly if their purpose is to protect individual autonomy in circumstances where one person has gained control over the welfare of another. And statutes that protect persons from exposure to unreasonable risk should confer a civil right of action provided that the conditions of ordinary negligence liability are met. These conditions ought to supplant those connected with the legislative intent theory of statutory torts.

## 1.

This essay considers from a natural rights perspective whether, and under what circumstances, breach of a penal statute should give rise to a civil cause of action in tort. Two separate questions are involved here. Where the injured party has no cause of action at common law, the question is whether the courts should use the statute to create one. Where, on the other hand, the plaintiff has a cause of action in negligence, the question concerns the appropriate procedural effect of a breach of the statutory standard of care. Should it be conclusive, presumptive, or merely some evidence of negligence?

It cannot be said that these issues have been ignored by the common law or even by academic commentators. On the contrary, they have given rise to a complex body of legal doctrine as well as to a rich and extensive literature.[1] Nevertheless, two considerations justify a reexamination of the problem.

First, there is widespread agreement among both judges and academic lawyers that the common law response to these issues is inadequate. Two broad lines of cases are discernible. According to one, breach of a statute causing injury to a person is prima facie actionable unless a contrary legislative intent has been manifest;[2] according to the other, the stipulation of a penal sanction prima facie excludes any further remedy unless the legislature intended otherwise.[3] We can see that, whichever of these approaches is taken, the decisive factor in determining the civil effect of statutes is the intent of the legislature. Since, however, the statute is usually silent with respect to civil liability, the courts have developed a number of indicia by which to divine an unexpressed and (one may assume) nonexistent legislative intention. Thus, if the statute

---

[1] See E. R. Thayer, 'Public Wrong and Private Action,' *Harvard Law Review* 27 (1914): 317, L. B. Lowndes, 'Civil Liability Created by Criminal Legislation,' *Minnesota Law Review* 16 (1932): 361; C. Morris, 'The Relation of Criminal Statutes to Tort Liability,' *Harvard Law Review* 46 (1933): 453; C. Morris, 'The Role of Criminal Statutes in Negligence Actions,' *Columbia Law Review* 40 (1949): 21; G. Williams, 'The Effect of Penal Legislation in the Law of Tort', *Modern Law Review* 23 (1960): 233; G. L. Fricke, 'The Juridical Nature of the Action Upon the Statute,' *Law Quarterly Review* 76 (1960): 240; E. R. Alexander, 'Legislation and the Standard of Care in Negligence,' *Canadian Bar Review* 42 (1964): 243; A. M. Linden, 'Tort Liability for Criminal Negligence,' *Canadian Bar Review* 44 (1966): 25.

[2] Couch v. Steel, 3 E & B 402, 118 E.R. 1193 (1854); Groves v. Wimborne, [1895–9] All E.R. 147; Britannia Merthyr Coal Co. v. David, [1909] 2 K.B. 164; Butler (or Black) v. Fife Coal Co. Ltd., [1912] A.C. 149; Lochgelly Iron and Coal Co. v. McMullan, [1934] A.C. 1; Galashiels Gas Co. Ltd. v. O'Donnell or Millar, [1949] A.C. 275.

[3] Atkinson v. Newcastle and Gateshead Waterworks, 2 Ex. D. 441 (C.A. 1877); Brain v. Thomas, 50 L.J.Q.B. 662 (C.A. 1881); Pasmore v. Oswald Twistle Urban, [1898] A.C. 387; Phillips v. Britannia Hygienic Laundry, [1923] 2 K.B. 832; Cutler v. Wandsworth Stadium, [1949] 1 All E.R. 544, [1949] A.C. 398, [1949] L.J.R. 824; Wolfe v. Dayton, [1975] 1 W.W.R. 665 (B.C.S.C.).

was enacted for the benefit of a class as distinct from the public as a whole, an intention to confer a civil right of action is inferred.[4] Obversely, a plaintiff will have an action only if he is a member of the class protected by the statute, and only if his injury was both proximately caused by the statutory violation and of a type that the statute was designed to prevent.[5] The nature and severity of the statutory penalty are also deemed to be clues to what the legislature intended. A statutory provision for a civil remedy, or a penal sanction thought to be sufficient for deterrence are often said by the courts to indicate a legislative intent to exclude any further remedy.[6]

The principal indictment against this approach is that it has failed to produce a coherent body of decided cases or a set of principles by which to structure judicial discretion. Consider, for example, the rule that makes the availability of a civil remedy depend on whether the statute was enacted for the benefit of a class or for the public as a whole. The only certain result of the application of this rule is that a breach of safety regulations for factories and mines will give a cause of action to factory workers and miners injured by the breach.[7] In other areas the application of the rule has yielded decisions that challenge one's powers of synthesis. Occupiers of buildings, we have been told, constitute a

---

4 Atkinson v. Newcastle and Gateshead Waterworks (1877), 2 Ex. D. 441 (C.A.); Groves v. Wimborne [1895–9] All E.R. 147; Phillips v. Britannia Hygienic Laundry, [1923] 2 K.B. 832.

5 Kelly v. Henry Muhs Co., 71 N.J.L. 358 (1904); Leask Timber and Hardware Pty. Ltd. v. Thorne, 106 C.L.R. 33 (1961); Gorris v. Scott, L.R. Exch. 125 (1874).

6 Board of Governors of the Seneca College of Applied Arts and Technology v. Bhadauria (1981), 124 D.L.R. (3d) 193 (S.C.C.); Cutler v. Wandsworth Stadium, [1949] 1 All E.R. 544; Cofield v. Waterloo Case Co. Ltd., 34 C.L.R. 363 (1924).

7 Groves v. Wimborne, [1895–9] All E.R. 147; Britannia Merthyr Coal Co. v. David, [1909] 2 K.B. 164; Butler v. Fife Coal Co. Ltd., [1912] A.C. 149; Lochgelly Iron and Coal Co. v. McMullan, [1934] A.C. 1; Galashiels Gas Co. Ltd. v. O'Donnell, [1949] A.C. 275; Potts v. Reid, [1943] A.C. 1; Brown v. National Coal Board, [1962] A.C. 574.

special class of the public,[8] but used-car purchasers do not.[9] A statute requiring, inter alia, that racetracks provide adequate facilities for bookmakers was said to have been intended for the public as a whole,[10] but a law forbidding the excessive extraction of underground water was held to have been intended for the specific class of landowners who could be harmed by such conduct.[11]

The lack of consistency in the decided cases is ultimately attributable to the court's pretense that it is the legislature that controls the civil effect of statutes. By invoking the fiction of legislative intent, the courts dissemble their own creative role in determining the civil consequences of criminal offences and thereby suppress or fail to bring to full consciousness the considerations they are really applying. Some judges, it is true, have frankly acknowledged that it is the court and not the legislature that decides whether a civil remedy will supplement a penal one.[12] However, the ascendancy of the intention theory has meant that, even where the judicial basis for the action upon the statute is recognized, no attempt is made to reformulate the appropriate principles. The result is that judges continue to justify their decisions in terms of a theory that bears no connection to the real process by which the decisions are reached. It is not surprising, therefore, that adjudication in this area has produced cases so apparently bereft of logical coherence as to cause judges themselves to despair of ascertaining the law.[13]

The other consideration justifying a reexamination of this

---

8 Solomons v. Gertzenstein Ltd., [1954] 2 All E.R. 625.

9 Henzel v. Brussels Motors Ltd., [1973] 1 O.R. 339.

10 Cutler v. Wandsworth Stadium, [1949] 1 All E.R. 544, [1949] A.C. 398, [1949] L.J.R. 824.

11 Pugliese v. National Capital Commission, [1979] 2 S.C.R. 104.

12 For example, Lord Wright in London Passenger Transport Board v. Upson, [1949] A.C. 155 at p. 168, and Mr. Justice Traynor in Clinkscales v. Carver, 22 Cal. App. 2d 72 (1943).

13 See the judgment of Lord Denning, M. R. in *Ex parte Island Records Ltd.* [1978] 3 All E.R. 824 (C.A.).

problem is the lack in the existing literature of any attempt to deal with it from the perspective of the philosophical foundations of tort and criminal law. That the problem requires such an approach is suggested by the shortcomings of alternative perspectives. Once we discard the intention theory, we are left with the fact that judges must decide on their own whether and when tort liability will supplement criminal liability. What criteria are to guide them? Deference to the legislature is of little use as a principle, because it can lead indifferently to a judicial activism that strives to advance the policy behind the statute or to a passivity that refuses to do anything not expressly authorized by statute.[14] Equally indeterminate is the democratic principle of the supremacy of legislation vis-à-vis the common law.[15] For while this principle univocally sanctions the courts' implementation of legislative policies even at the expense of judge-made law, it provides no guidelines for determining when and how to do this, so that in the end it leaves the courts with freedom but no direction. It cannot be every provision of the common law that must bow to the latest expression of the general will. It would, for example, be to take an unduly sanguine view of democratic majorities to believe that we can now dispense with the protection afforded individual rights by such common-law limitations on liability as fault and causation. Considered by itself, the theory of statutory supremacy is a justification of legislative despotism because it implies no requirement that the judicial implementation of legislative policies be circumscribed by such limitations.

Ultimately the question as to when someone who violates a penal statute should incur civil as well as criminal liability forces us to consider the fundamental purposes of legal sanctions as well as the relationship between civil and criminal remedies. One theory

---

[14] See Thayer, 'Public Wrong and Private Action,' and Lowndes, 'Civil Liability Created by Criminal Legislation.'

[15] R. Pound, 'Common Law and Legislation,' *Harvard Law Review* 21 (1908): 383; S. M. Landis, 'Statutes and the Sources of Law,' *Harvard Journal on Legislation* 2 (1965): 7.

of law enforcement that has traditionally oriented thinking about the appropriate scope of legal liability is the retributivist theory, which derives from the natural rights stream of legal philosophy and which received its classical formulation in G. W. F. Hegel's *Philosophy of Right.* We shall not attempt here to defend this perspective against the rival deterrence theory of legal sanctions;[16] rather our purpose is simply to fashion a coherent approach to the problem of statutory breach by tracing the implications of a natural rights theory of law enforcement for the civil consequences of a criminal violation.

## 2.

For Hegel, the purpose of law enforcement, both civil and criminal, is the vindication of the human being's natural right to objective

---

[16] For a deterrence approach to the problem of tort liability for breach of statute see Morris, 'The Relation of Criminal Statutes to Tort Liability,' and Morris, 'The Role of Criminal Statutes in Negligence actions.' Consistently applied, the deterrence perspective would emancipate private actions for breach of statute from certain limitations that seem demanded by a common sense intuition of fairness. There is, for example, no basis in social utility for an absolute rule requiring a causal link between the injury suffered and the criminal violation. The aim of deterrence would be admirably served by holding the defendant strictly liable for the damages incurred by the plaintiff once a breach of statute has been proved and whether or not the damage was caused by the unlawful conduct. All that would be required to legitimate such liability would be a social interest sufficiently important to justify the heavy cost to the defendant. Furthermore, it is not clear, as Morris seems to think, that the fault requirement of tort liability is supported in most cases by a deterrence theory of remedies. The same utilitarian rationale underlying strict liability in criminal cases can also support absolute duties in correlative civil actions. The imposition of liability on an innocent lawbreaker might constitute superfluous admonition for him, but it will arguably serve to warn less conscientious persons of the consequences of similar conduct.

In further work we plan to undertake a thorough analysis from a utilitarian perspective.

freedom.[17] Objective freedom is distinguished from the merely formal freedom to do as one pleases in that it includes within its definition the security against external coercion that makes freedom of choice meaningful. Objective freedom is freedom so circumscribed as to be compatible with the equal freedom of all. For Hegel as for Kant, human beings have a natural right to such freedom, because the autonomy of the will defines man's essential nature; it is that potentiality which distinguishes him from other animals and which thus endows him with dignity.

The freedom of the individual from subjection to the egoistic will of others is thus the basic value of the legal order. The essence of wrong is the violation of rules by which each person's independence is reciprocally guaranteed by an act to which the agent, by virtue either of intending or disregarding its probable consequences, claims a right. The show of right made by a particular (i.e., selfish) will constitutes the mental element of wrongdoing and alone justifies a legal response. For without the wrongful claim of right there is no challenge to the validity of the right that has been infringed, hence no need for its vindication. Where this claim is made, however, law enforcement is needed to refute it. The penalty annuls the wrong in the sense of revealing its claim to validity to be false. The annulment of the wrong is simultaneously the confirmation or objective realization of the individual right.[18]

If civil and criminal law enforcement have a common aim, what distinguishes them? In the case of wrongs involving the violent interference with another's freedom, civil enforcement is an adjunct of criminal; that is to say, the wrong is essentially a crime, but a civil remedy that compensates the victim at the expense of the wrongdoer is needed to supplement the effect of punishment.

---

[17] Hegel, *Philosophy of History*, trans. J. Sibree (New York: Dover Publications, Inc., 1956), pp. 442–43; *Philosophy of Right*, trans. T. M. Knox (Oxford: Oxford University Press, 1952), pars. 82–103; cf. Kant, *The Metaphysical Elements of Justice*, trans. John Ladd (Indianapolis: Bobbs-Merill, 1965), pp. 99–107.

[18] Hegel, *Philosophy of Right*, pars. 82–3, 92–101.

Why a civil supplement to punishment is necessary will be explained in a moment. For now we need only observe that in the case of such wrongs, compensation and punishment are complementary, though independently necessary, means of annulling a crime. There are, however, wrongs that are distinctively civil and for which the remedy is not compensation plus punishment but compensation only. What is the difference between a civil wrong simpliciter and a crime, and why the difference in their remedies?

In both a civil wrong and a crime the wrongdoer claims validity for his act. In crime, however, he does so to the extent of denying the authoritative validity of the general will and hence of the entire framework and basis of rights.[19] The essence of crime is the assertion of a right to the untrammelled freedom of the will. The effect of this assertion is to deny any objective basis for the distinction between mine and thine, right and wrong, good and evil. Accordingly, state rather than merely private action is demanded, because the crime challenges not only the victim's right but the authoritative validity of human rights in general. The sole adequate response to this challenge is one that reveals its inner nullity. By denying the validity of human rights, the criminal simultaneously denies the validity of the right to liberty which he himself has asserted. The implicit forfeiture of his own rights is the inner consequence of the criminal's claim and shows that claim to be null. The means by which what is implicit is made explicit is punishment. By taking away his freedom, punishment reveals the latent contradiction in the criminal's claim, and, in doing so, confirms the validity of that which the claim denied.[20]

A civil wrong is different. Here the wrongdoer infringes a particular right but without denying the sovereignty of the legal order constitutive of rights in general. Rather, that sovereignty is acknowledged and the question is simply which of two conflicting claims to right has the sanction of the general will.[21] The degree

---

[19] Ibid., par. 95.

[20] Ibid., pars. 99–100.

[21] Ibid., pars. 85–6.

of a tortfeasor's moral guilt is thus less than that of a criminal, because he has not set his particular will above the general. Nevertheless, an element of moral guilt is present. The guilt of the tortfeasor consists in a kind of mistake or ignorance. While recognizing the authority of the general will, he nonetheless mistakes a selfish assertion of liberty for one consistent with the common good.[22] Such a mistake is morally blameworthy because it is not a mistake as to external facts or circumstances but one as to the content and dictates of justice. More formally stated, if moral rectitude consists in the identification of the particular with the general will, then the reverse identification is wrongful whether or not it is consciously intended. The liability of the tortfeasor is thus based on what might be termed objective fault. It is not strict because, for vindication to be necessary, there must have been such a disregard for the probable consequences of one's act as to evince a belief in the rightness of conduct inconsistent with the freedom of others. But neither is it dependent on subjective *mens rea.* Ignorance of right and wrong is no excuse for a tortfeasor because it is this which precisely constitutes the essence of tort.

If liability in tort is based on moral ignorance rather than on moral rebellion, then clearly it is not sufficient to call forth punishment. Not having subjectively denied the sovereignty of law, the tortfeasor has done nothing that logically entails the forfeiture of his rights. Here the wrong is annulled (and the right vindicated) simply by shifting the loss due to the tortfeasor's action onto the tortfeasor himself. This transfer is more accurately characterized as serving corrective rather than retributive justice, for although both compensation and punishment aim at vindicating rights, only the latter is properly retributive. It is retributive in the sense that it is the inward and inexorable consequence of the criminal's own will and in the sense that, being the recoiling of the deed upon itself, its measure is inwardly derived from the moral seriousness of the wrong. Because, on the other hand, a purely civil wrong does not notionally imply its own remedy, the latter is left depen-

---

22 Ibid., par. 86 and Addition.

dent on the victim's decision to defend his right, while its measure is likewise contingently determined by the plaintiff's losses.

What consequences does the foregoing account of law enforcement have for the question of civil liability for breach of statute? The first thing to observe is that the crystallization by statute of a preexistent civil duty effects a change not simply in civil procedure but in the very meaning of a breach of duty. Whereas formerly a breach was a civil wrong simply, it is now a crime with civil consequences. This means that the availability of a civil remedy can no longer be justified in terms of corrective justice taken by itself, or in terms of the pure tort analysis given above. Rather, if justified at all, it must be justified in terms of retributive justice – that is, in terms of the requirements for the annulment of a criminal wrong.

But why should a civil remedy be needed to enforce the criminal law? It would appear that, on the retributive theory, if the criminal statute prescribes a penalty, then this should be the only one, for any further civil remedy would be redundant. Since the purpose of remedies is the vindication of right, the achievement of this end by the criminal law leaves nothing further to do. However, this result is counterintuitive and ignores the twofold character of the criminal's challenge. According to Hegel, human beings are coercible only because their independence as persons requires an objective embodiment in property.[23] That is, the will can be coerced only because it needs things (including a body) that can be destroyed, damaged, or taken away. Because freedom requires an external embodiment, the criminal act not only involves a challenge at the conceptual level, that is, as an implicit denial of human rights; it also has existential significance as an apparent injury to one individual's human dignity and hence as an ostensibly meaningful alteration of things in the world. Inherently the crime is insignificant, because the individual's dignity does not depend on external things, but is inwardly secured by the ontological supremacy of law, which guarantees his human right to the things necessary for

[23] Ibid., pars. 90–1, 96.

his independence. But the appearance of injury is once again a show of validity made by the criminal act, a show that must be revealed as such. Stated otherwise, the pretended validity of the crime, its claim to positive reality, is voiced partly by the subjective will of the criminal (his denial of rights in general) and partly by the altered state of things that the criminal act has brought about in the world. The refutation of the claim must correspondingly be double. Punishment annuls the wrong by revealing the self-contradictoriness of the criminal's will; compensation does likewise by restoring (as far as possible) the victim to his condition before the crime.[24]

## 3.

The retributive account of law enforcement thus confirms the practice of redressing crimes both by punishing the lawbreaker and by compensating the victim. It is also consistent with certain common-sense notions concerning the appropriate restrictions on civil liability for criminal violations. The plaintiff must, first of all, have suffered special or particular damage, for otherwise there is no existential challenge to the dignity of the person in addition to the conceptual one. Secondly, the damage must be to an interest essential to the independence of the person, for otherwise it constitutes no injury to his dignity, not even an apparent one. And thirdly, the injury must have been proximately caused by the defendant, for without such a link the injury has no symbolic significance as a concrete manifestation of the criminal's will and hence as a witness to the latter's claim to validity.

However, the analysis of criminal wrongdoing thus far given seems peculiarly applicable to offences normally found in a Criminal Code, in particular to the so-called offences against the person and against property. What, however, if a statute criminalizes conduct irrespective of whether it actually infringes upon another person's right? There are at least two types of such statutes: those which enshrine a natural duty to take care (or a natural

---

24 Ibid., par. 98–99.

right to be free from exposure to unreasonable risks arbitrarily imposed by others) and those which, rather than protecting a universal human right, merely articulate a social policy aimed at maximizing aggregate welfare.[25] Highway safety regulations are examples of the former, while statutes that confer economic privileges on certain classes of the public illustrate the latter. What distinguishes both types of statute from laws proscribing violence to the person and property is the emancipation of public from private wrong. Whereas ordinarily a criminal violation will entail a civil wrong to a person, here no such connection need exist. Breach of the statute may cause no injury at all; or it may cause injury that, either because of its remoteness, its unavoidability, or the triviality of the interest interfered with, is not a wrong; or it may cause harm that is tortious. The possibility and equal likelihood of these eventualities would preclude the formulation of a general rule as to whether a civil remedy is available for breach of a statute. At most one would want to say that prima facie there is such a remedy unless circumstances dictate otherwise, or that prima facie there is not. But whichever way one wished to state the principle, one would insist on the satisfaction of a number of conditions before imposing a civil penalty.

If a breach of a regulatory statute is itself to give rise to a civil cause of action, the common law must, on retributive principles, build in limitations on tort liability lacking in the statute – limitations that restrict such liability to cases of civil wrongdoing. Thus, for the statute to be applicable in a civil suit, the interest protected by it must be one that is vital to the independence of all human beings, and to whose protection the individual is thus entitled as a matter of right. This means that a civil remedy would ordinarily not be available for breach of a statute the purpose of which is to maximize aggregate welfare rather than to protect a universal right.

---

[25] The distinction we draw between statutes that embody rights and those which seek to maximize welfare in the aggregate corresponds to Dworkin's distinction between principle and policy as grounds for the justification of political decisions. See *Taking Rights Seriously* (Cambridge: Harvard University Press, 1977), pp. 82–84.

For though the violation of such a statute might result in injury to a private interest, no civil wrong is committed as long as the right infringed is a contingent one of purely statutory origin and not a natural one essential to the autonomy of the person. Thus, for example, the violation of a municipal by-law restricting one's freedom to construct additions to one's home might (if the law is well-conceived) injure the public welfare; unless, however, it amounts to nuisance, this type of offence does not injure the person as such, even though it might decrease the market value of his property.[26]

The distinction between statutes that enforce rights and those which maximize welfare seems to underlie the judicial distinction between statutes intended to benefit specific persons and those intended to benefit the community as a whole. At a minimum, it helps to explain decisions that cannot be accounted for using the latter criteria. In *Cutler* v. *Wandsworth Stadium,*[27] for example, a bookmaker was denied a remedy for the defendant's breach of its statutory duty to provide facilities for bookmakers at its racetrack if a totalisator (a mechanical betting device) were in operation. The House of Lords reasoned that although the statute incidentally conferred a benefit on bookmakers, its main purpose was the regulation of betting in the public interest. The real ground of the decision, it is submitted, is that the purpose of the statute was not the protection of a right naturally inhering in persons but the balancing of competing interests in order to maximize public welfare. Parliament was apparently concerned that the authorization for the benefit of racetrack owners of hitherto illegal totalisators would damage the economic interests of bookmakers as well as create a monopoly of betting facilities hurtful to the betting public.

The notorious case of *Monk* v. *Warbey*[28] is also explicable within this framework. There the plaintiff was injured by the negligent

---

[26] Orpen v. Roberts, [1925] S.C.R. 364.

[27] [1949] 1 All E.R. 544, [1949] A.C. 398, [1949] L.J.R. 824.

[28] [1934] All E.R. 373.

driving of someone whom the owner of the automobile had failed, contrary to statute, to insure against public liability. Alleging breach of statutory duty, he sued the owner for his damages and succeeded. Viewed in light of the traditional criterion of statutory tort, the decision is mysterious, since no class can be identified as uniquely benefited by the legislation. Nevertheless, the case is rightly decided on the ground that a person whose freedom is infringed by tortious conduct has a natural right to a remedy, and the purpose of the statute was simply to make good this right.

The first condition, then, for the civil enforceability of a statute is that the latter confer a benefit to which persons are *qua* persons naturally entitled. This way of stating the principle preserves what is true in the insights of Dixon, C. J.[29] and G. L. Fricke,[30] both of whom argue that it is the existence of a duty independent of the legislation that explains the action upon the statute, but who understand by independent duties those recognized by the common law. It is not, however, the existence or nonexistence of a common-law duty that determines when statutes will (or should) be civilly enforced, for in many cases a civil remedy is awarded for breach of a statutory duty of affirmative action for which no common-law parallel exists. *Monk* v. *Warbey* is a case in point, as are the cases involving a landlord's statutory obligation to maintain rented premises in a good state of repair,[31] and that of a motor-vehicle driver to stop and render assistance when involved in an accident.[32] On the other hand, the cases concerning the statutory duty to remove snow and ice from public sidewalks abutting one's property are ones in which the absence of a common law duty has frequently been cited in support of a refusal to impose civil liabili-

[29] O'Connor v. Bray, 56 C.L.R. 464 (1937).

[30] Fricke, 'The Juridical Nature of the Action Upon the Statute.'

[31] See Cunningham v. Moore, 28 D.L.R. (3d) 277 (1972); Lindstrom v. Bassett Realty Ltd., 90 D.L.R. (3d) 238 (1978); Fleischmann v. Grossman Holdings Ltd., 16 O.R. (2d) 746 (1976).

[32] Langenstein v. Reynand, 13 La. 272, 127 So. 764 (C.A. 1930); Battle v. Kilerease, 189 S.E. 573 (1936); Summers v. Dominique, 29 Cal. App. 2d 308, 84 P.2d 237 (1938).

ty.[33] Can the natural rights perspective reconcile these apparently conflicting cases?

It is beyond the scope of this paper to determine whether or not a natural rights theory of law enforcement supports the common-law distinction between misfeasance and nonfeasance together with the general immunity from liability for the latter.[34] For the purposes of argument we shall accept the common-law premises regarding these matters. Even granted these premises, however, the principle of autonomy that underlies the legal distinction between permissible and wrongful conduct provides grounds for a more expansive definition of misfeasance than has traditionally been adopted by the common law. For example, it used to be the case that someone who without fault exposed another to danger owed no duty to make reasonable efforts to prevent the danger from materializing.[35] Thus, prior to statutory intervention, a motor-vehicle driver owed no duty to stop and render aid to someone whom he had innocently incapacitated. A theory of justice that makes the autonomy of the human person the fundamental value of the legal order cannot, however, support such a principle. For if A places (or contributes to placing) B in a position of peril, then, notwithstanding that the act whereby he did so was innocent, he has deprived B of his power of self-help and placed him in a position of dependence on others. This dependence is compatible with B's autonomy only if he can rely on assistance as a matter of enforceable right rather than of chance benevolence. The right to assistance entails a corresponding duty resting, if not on every passer-by, then at least on two pairs of shoulders. It rests on public authorities, for the latter's power is legitimate only to the extent that it is used to realize the common good, which is autonomy. And it rests on A as the person who caused B's dependence. Al-

---

33 Commerford v. Board of School Commissioners of Halifax, [1950] 2 D.L.R. 207 (N.S.).

34 See E. J. Weinrib, 'The Case for a Duty to Rescue,' *Yale Law Journal* 90 (1980): 247.

35 Vanvalkenburg v. Northern Navigation Co., 19 D.L.R. 649 (1913).

though the incapacitating act was originally innocent, the fact that A subsequently fails to render assistance transforms it into a case of misfeasance. This is because A's having placed B in a position of dependence on his will is innocent only if A renounces his liberty to choose whether or not to assist B in his need and acknowledges a categorical duty to do so. If A reserves his liberty as a matter of principle, then he has as surely subjected another to his pleasure as if he had intentionally or negligently harmed him.

The principle of self-determination thus explains the judicial imposition of civil liability for a breach of a hit and run statute. Here the legislation permits the courts to enforce a moral duty by freeing them from a common-law tradition too entrenched to be overthrown by judges acting completely on their own. However, the principle of autonomy also accounts for the various relationships recognized by the common law itself as creating exceptions to the general immunity from liability for nonfeasance. It has been held that the failure of an employer,[36] an occupier,[37] and a boat operator[38] to go to the rescue respectively of an employee, a guest, and a passenger is a tort regardless of whether the peril was the fault of the defendant. What is common to all these relationships is a tacit invitation to reliance whereby one party is induced to surrender to another control over the instruments affecting his well-being. Again, such an inducement to dependence is innocent only if one submits to a duty to assist the other in the relevant contingencies, at least to the extent that such assistance can be effected without subjecting one's own life to the pleasure of the person in peril.

Both the landlord-tenant and the abutter cases can be explained from this perspective. The former is a relationship wherein one party, in circumstances of necessity, alienates to another control over the factors affecting his welfare, including control over the safety of his living environment. In these circumstances, the land-

---

[36] Harris v. Pennsylvania Railroad Co., 50 F.2d 866 (1931).
[37] Ayres and Co. v. Hicks, 40 N.E.2d 334 (1942).
[38] Horsley v. MacLaren, 22 D.L.R. (3d) 545 (1971).

lord's reservation of liberty is destructive of the independence of the tenant, which is to say that he is under a natural duty to keep rented premises safe and fit for habitation. At common law the only basis for a landlord's obligation in this respect is a contractual one. Contract, however, enshrines the very arbitrary liberty that constitutes the self-alienation of the tenant, which is why the statute had to intervene to take away that liberty and replace it with a categorical duty corresponding to the natural one. Here again, therefore, the statute enabled the courts to enforce civilly a moral duty whose recognition by the common law had been blocked by the weight of tradition.

The abutter cases are different. Between the owner of a dwelling and a user of public sidewalks there is no relationship of dependence to ground a duty of affirmative action. The pedestrian does not alienate his power of self-reliance to secure a benefit for himself. Rather the pedestrian relies for the safety of public sidewalks on municipal authorities, which, for the sake of economy and administrative convenience delegate the responsibility to private citizens. The courts have thus rightly decided that the statutory duty to clear public sidewalks fronting one's premises is not enforceable by a civil remedy.

4.

If it is accepted that those statutes are alone civilly enforceable that enshrine a natural right to be free from subjection to the arbitrary will of others, then statutes that protect persons from exposure to unreasonable risk should in principle be available to support a civil cause of action. They should not, however, confer a right of action unconditionally. For if the purpose of enforcement is to vindicate right against wrong, then the civil enforceability of safety statutes must be subject to the fault limitations of ordinary negligence liability. Thus, for a safety statute to be applicable in a civil suit, the plaintiff must have been foreseeable as one likely to be harmed by a breach of the statute, and the plaintiff's injury must be one the risk of which was sufficiently likely to warrant the standard of care fixed by the legislature. Transmuted by the intention theory, these familiar limitations become the rules that the plaintiff must be a member of the class protected by the statute and that his injury must be of a kind that the statute was designed to prevent. Accordingly, the common-law rules governing the applicability of statutes to civil actions are defensible not as indicia of legislative intent but as means by which the fault criteria of tort liability are introduced into a criminal statute, breach of which may or may not constitute a civil wrong. These rules are the links by which criminal and civil wrongdoing, separated in regulatory statutes, are reunited.

On the other hand, when translated into the language of legislative intent, these rules become separated from their animating spirit. What in ordinary negligence law are flexible criteria permitting latitude for judicial discretion become in the law of statutory negligence reified principles whose working of justice in particular cases seems quite accidental. Sometimes, as in the case of factory safety legislation, the rules work well, producing results that would be obtained through the application of common-law negligence principles. In most instances, however, they work badly. The unpredictability of the cases can in large measure be explained by the frequent clash between the results required by the rules of statutory negligence and those demanded by the natural tort principles they represent. Sometimes the court will adhere rigidly to the formal rule; sometimes it will burst through the formula to the living principle it embodies, while still paying lip-service to the rule. A few examples will make this point clearer.

In *Henzel* v. *Brussels Motors Ltd.*[39] the plaintiff had purchased a used truck from a dealer who had neglected, contrary to statute, to inspect the brakes. The latter were defective, and the plaintiff was injured in an accident shortly after the purchase. While finding for the plaintiff on the basis of breach of warranty, the court denied a cause of action for breach of statutory duty. Fogerty Co. Ct. J. reasoned that used car purchasers do not constitute an

---

[39] [1973] 1 O.R. 339.

identifiable group for whose benefit the statute in question was enacted. Not only was such a category "too vague" to be considered a class, but the statute was designed for users of the road generally and not solely for purchasers.

The point, it is submitted, was wrongly decided. The plaintiff was certainly foreseeable as one likely to be harmed by a failure of the truck's brakes; hence the defendant was under a natural duty to inspect them for any hidden defect, a duty that is crystallized in the statute. There can be no doubt, moreover, that the plaintiff's accident was of a type that the statute was designed to prevent, nor that the defendant's breach of duty was a proximate cause of the plaintiff's injuries. In this case, therefore, the criminal violation was accompanied by a civil wrong. But by the rule which requires that the statute be enacted for the benefit of a specific and ascertainable class, the plaintiff was denied a cause of action for breach of the statute. The rule was thus adhered to in the face of the demands of natural tort principles even though its only function is to import these principles into civil actions for breach of statute.

The decision in *Solomons* v. *Gertzenstein*[40] provides a useful contrast. There the plaintiff suffered injuries when a fire broke out in rented premises. Under an order made pursuant to the *London Building Act,* a trap door had been installed some years earlier together with a ladder allowing access to the roof. The ladder, however, was seldom in place, and at the time of the fire was unavailable to anyone needing it for an emergency escape. The trial judge held both the landlord and his receiver civilly liable for breach of their statutory duty to maintain the means of escape in efficient working order. Although the receiver's appeal was allowed on the ground that the statutory duty that was violated did not apply to him, the English Court of Appeal addressed the question of whether an offence under the *London Building Act* conferred a right of action upon someone injured as a result of its breach. A majority of the Court held that it did. In the course of his judgment, Birkett

---

40 [1954] 2 All E.R. 625.

L. J. stated "that the duty imposed in the present case was imposed for the benefit of a particular ascertainable class, namely, the persons in the building, and those persons have a right of action for a breach of statutory duty... ."[41]

Now nothing can be more certain than that the London Building Act was not enacted for the specific benefit of the occupants of No. 36, Gerrard Street, Soho. On the other hand, those residents were certainly foreseeable victims of a failure by the landlord to take adequate precautions against the risk of fire. The Court appears to have decided the question on natural tort principles, although it obscured this fact by pretending to apply the criteria associated with the intention theory.

A similar contrast can be drawn with respect to the application of the rule in *Gorris* v. *Scott.*[42] The rule is that a defendant is civilly liable for breach of a statute only if his offence caused damage of the type that the statute was designed to prevent. Early in the century two Canadian cases dealt with the question of a railway's civil liability for breach of its statutory duty to fence its right of way. In *Hunt* v. *Grand Trunk Pacific Railway,*[43] the plaintiff's crops were damaged by cattle that had strayed onto his field via the railway lands. Although the defendant was found to be in breach of its statutory duty to erect fences "suitable and sufficient to prevent cattle and other animals from getting on the railway," no civil liability was imposed. The Manitoba Court of Appeal held that the purpose of the statute was only to prevent animals from straying *onto* the railway tracks and from suffering injury in collisions with trains. By contrast, in *Winterburn* v. *Edmonton, Yukon and Pacific Railway Co.,*[44] the Alberta Court of Appeal held for the plaintiff on virtually identical facts. "The danger caused," said Harvey J., "being the natural and probable consequence of the

---

41 Ibid., at pp. 634–35.

42 L.R. Exch. 125 (1874).

43 18 Man. R. 603 (1909).

44 [1980] 1 A.L.R. 92.

defendant's neglect, there can be no doubt of (its) liability."[45] In *Hunt*, therefore, the express intention of the legislature as to the mischief to be avoided was held to define the limits of liability, even though this limitation seems justified only as a means of preserving the right relationship between the required standard of care and the degree of probability and seriousness of the injury. In *Winterburn*, on the other hand, the intention formula was rejected when it entailed a conclusion contrary to the one required by the "natural and probable consequence" test. The Alberta Court apparently believed that the damage caused by the defendant's neglect was analogous in foreseeability and seriousness to the type contemplated by the legislature, so that the statutory standard of care was as relevant to the one situation as to the other. Even so, the Court felt the need to rationalize its decisions in terms of legislative intent, which it determined by a rather tortuous piece of statutory interpretation.

If the rules governing the relation of statutes to civil actions are less workable counterparts of natural tort principles, the solution indicated is to abandon those rules together with the intention theory with which they are connected and to apply the liability criteria of ordinary tort law. Thus the first question to ask in determining whether civil liability should be added to criminal is not whether the statute protects the public or only a class thereof, but whether it protects a basic human right to freedom from subjection to the arbitrary will of others or merely seeks to maximize social welfare in the aggregate. Secondly, if the statute protects a natural right, then civil liability should depend not on whether the plaintiff is a member of the class expressly protected by the statute but on whether or not he was foreseeable as one likely to be harmed by a violation of the law. Thirdly, breach of a statute should give rise to civil liability only if it caused the injury complained of, and fourthly, only if the injury was either foreseen by the legislature in formulating the standard of care or is comparable in probability and seriousness to the type that was foreseen.

---

[45] Ibid., at p. 96.

5.

It remains to consider the appropriate effect in a negligence action of a violation of a safety statute. The question here, it will be recalled, is whether a criminal violation should be treated as conclusive of, presumptive proof of, or merely some evidence of, negligence. We have already seen that the retributive theory of law enforcement both accounts for and supports the fault limitations on both tort and criminal liability. On this theory, the purpose of both reparation and punishment is to nullify the claim to validity of an assertion of freedom inconsistent with the equal freedom of others. The claim of validity is expressed either by intending or showing indifference to the probable consequences of an invasive act. Without such a claim there is no challenge to the validity of the rights that have been *de facto* violated and hence no commission of a wrong.

However, this confirmation of the fault principle is only an incidental result of an explanatory theory of wrong and the rectification of it. It is not yet a direct moral justification in terms of a supreme normative principle. For Hegel, as we have seen, the fundamental value of the legal order, that in terms of which all laws and processes are to be evaluated as just or unjust, is the autonomy of the human person. Autonomy is the basic right of the individual and provides a criterion for distinguishing between interests that are properly the subject of rights and those whose protection is merely a contingent benefit or privilege. The question we must now ask is whether this principle demands liability only for fault as a right of the individual, and if so, whether it confirms common-law notions concerning the appropriate ambit of individual responsibility.

In the *Philosophy of Right* Hegel writes:

> The freely acting will, in directing its aim on the state of affairs confronting it, has an idea of the attendant circumstances. But because the will is finite ... the objective [state of affairs]...may contain something other than what the will's idea of it contains. The will's right, however, is to recognize as its action, and to accept responsibility for, only those presuppositions of the

deed of which it was conscious in its aim and those aspects of the deed which were contained in its purpose. The deed can be imputed to me only if my will is responsible for it . . . .[46]

The principle of autonomy raises action to philosophical significance as an integral element of human nature. This is because the very concept of self-determination implies action in accordance with an idea formed in the imagination. It implies, in other words, a bond between thought and deed, where the latter is the outward realization of an idea and the idea is the soul or guiding principle of the external, physical movements. Action, however, is intrinsically paradoxical. While essential to the individual's freedom, it is also that in virtue of which he steps out into a world of external causal connections, a world over which he has only limited control and where his deed begets consequences impossible to foresee.[47] This means that the alteration in the external world brought about by his act will be partly due to his will, but also partly due to forces and circumstances of which he was not aware. Now it is clear that the autonomy of the individual requires not only that he be free from external coercion by the will of others, but also that he be free from subjection to the blind and incalculable caprices of fortune or (more technically) to the sphere of external causal necessity. Accordingly, the right of the individual is to be held accountable only for those consequences of his act that were originally present in his will.

Does not, however, this justification of the fault principle prove too much? Does it not lead to the conclusion, for example, that if A stores hay in a combustible condition next to B's field, he can escape liability for fire damage caused to B's property if such damage were not foreseen and hence not willed?[48] Hegel avoids this result by drawing a distinction between purpose (*Vorsatz*) and intention (*Absicht*).[49] An act is a complex whole composed of

---

[46] Hegel, *Philosophy of Right*, par. 117.
[47] Ibid., par. 118.
[48] Vaughan v. Menlove, 3 Bing. N.C. 467 (1837).
[49] Hegel, *Philosophy of Right*, pars. 114, 119.

discrete units connected by causal necessity. Any one of these units might form the content of my purpose, but intention encompasses the act in the entirety of its probable consequences.[50] Thus, my purpose might be to store my hay, but if it is highly probable that the manner of my doing so will cause damage to my neighbour, then this damage too must be imputed to my intention. To do so is not to compromise the principle of autonomy, but, on the contrary, to honour it in a way more adequate to its concept. This is so for two reasons. First, an individual is more or less master of his fate according to the degree to which he can limit the influence upon his life of accidents. This he can do by pulling back (*Ab-sicht*) from narrow attention to his immediate purpose and by surveying the whole of his projected act in its probable consequences. Because self-determination requires such foresight and circumspection, and because autonomy is definitive of human nature, respect for the humanity of the individual demands the imputation to him of the foreseeable consequences of his act.

Second, such an imputation is justified because of the paradox lying at the heart of action. It is in the nature of action to be both a requirement of autonomy and a contradiction thereto. When we act to fulfill our goals we simultaneously surrender ourselves to a chain of causal connections independent of our rational control. While a particular effect may be contingent, therefore, the exposure to such effects is inwardly necessary and, because necessary, imputable to the will. Hence the individual cannot disavow responsibility for a consequence simply because it was not present in his immediate purpose. "To act," says Hegel, "is to expose oneself to bad luck. Thus bad luck has a right over me and is an embodiment of my own willing."[51] In sum, the individual has a right to be held responsible only for those consequences which he intended, but he also has a right to have imputed to his intention the foreseeable consequences of his act. To do less is to treat the agent

---

[50] Ibid., par. 119.

[51] Ibid., Addition to par. 118.

"as devoid of the dignity of being a thinker and a will."[52]

If an individual may legitimately be held liable only for damage reasonably imputable to his intention, then the mere fact of non-conformity with a statutory standard of care can never be conclusive of negligence. For it is certainly possible to break a safety statute even though one has inteded to comply with it and made strenuous efforts to do so. A classic illustration is the case of *Phillips* v. *Britannia Hygienic Laundry*.[53] An axle of the defendant's truck broke while the vehicle was in motion, causing the wheel to come off and to strike the plaintiff's van. The defendant was found to be in breach of a statutory prohibition against operating a defective motor vehicle. Only two days prior to the accident, however, the truck had been returned from the manufacturer's, where one axle had been replaced and the other repaired. The Court of Appeal denied the plaintiff a civil remedy – ostensibly because highway users did not constitute a specific class but in reality because of an unwillingness to impose strict liability. "It is not likely," said Lord Atkin, "that the legislature intended by these means to impose on the owners of vehicles an absolute obligation to have them roadworthy in all events even in the absence of negligence."[54]

However, if breaches of safety statutes cannot, on the principles just elaborated, be conclusive of negligence, neither can they be merely some evidence of negligence. For to treat them in this way is, as E. R. Thayer saw, to subordinate the reason of the legislature to that of the individual.[55] It is to suggest that, even where the legislature has spoken on the matter, the private conscience remains the arbiter of what constitutes reasonable care in the circumstances, so that breaking the law is in principle justified. This is to push the principle of individual autonomy to the point where it contradicts itself, resembling nothing so much as the principle of

---

52 Ibid., par. 120.
53 [1923] 2 K.B. 832.
54 Ibid. at p. 842.
55 Thayer, 'Public Wrong and Private Action.'

crime. The latter, we have said, is the claim to a right to the untrammelled freedom of the will. Similarly, the claim to a right to decide for oneself the content of one's duties leads, when generalized, to the total subjection of all to the caprices of each. No doubt the individual is still answerable before the court to the objective standard of the reasonable man. But if the reasonable man is justified in breaking the law whenever its commands do not conform to his private judgment, then everyone is so justified who can persuade a jury that he acted conscientiously. The evidence-of-negligence rule is thus not only a judicial affront to the legislature; it is antithetical to the rule of law.

The approach which respects the fault principle on the one hand and the sovereignty of law on the other is the one which treats a breach of a safety statute as prima facie proof of negligence. Opponents of this doctrine have argued that it is only the evidence-of-negligence rule in disguise, since to allow a defence of reasonable care is once again to substitute the reasonable man standard for the statutory one. This, however, need not be the case. Whether or not the statutory standard remains authoritative depends on what counts in law as a defence to the action. If the defendant may exonerate himself by a showing that, notwithstanding his violation of the statute, he took alternative steps that were reasonable in the circumstances, then private opinion has indeed displaced the legislature as the authoritative source of right. If, on the other hand, nothing will exculpate the defendant save a showing that he took all reasonable steps to comply with the law, then the statutory standard remains sovereign. An example of the latter approach is *Schofield* v. *Town of Oakville.*[56] There the defendant municipality was held liable to a truck driver for breach of a statutory duty to post loadlimit signs at each end of a defective bridge. The Ontario Court of Appeal rejected the defendant's argument that it had placed signs on a hill leading down to the bridge, that this measure satisfied the demands of ordinary prudence, and that it was the theft of these signs by an unknown

[56] 69 D.L.R. (2d) 441 (1968).

person that caused the accident. Where the range of acceptable excuses for statutory negligence is limited in this fashion, there is nothing to distinguish the presumption-of-negligence rule from the doctrine of the *Restatement of Torts* that the "unexcused violation of a legislative or an administrative regulation, which is adopted by the court as defining the standard of conduct of a reasonable man, is negligence in itself."[57]

6.

In his classic essay on 'Statutes and the Sources of Law', Dean Landis argued that the imposition of tort liability for breach of statute indicated a "recognition by judges that behind the formal fiat of the statute [lies] an aim that challenge[s] their sympathetic attention, and the appropriate exercise of judicial power permit[s] courts to advance ends so emphatically asserted."[58] Earlier we remarked that this encouragement of the courts' implementation of legislative policies is too permissive in that it fails to specify any constraints on the judicial advancement of social objectives. On the other hand, an approach that would determine the incidence of tort liability by sole reference to the common law would be too restrictive, for it would fail to distinguish between those elements of the common law that embody immutable principles of right and those which (like the immunity from liability for nonfeasance) are relative to transient stages of moral culture. It is one thing to limit civil liability for breach of statute by the requirements of fault and causation; but to restrict such liability to cases where a common law duty already exists would be to insulate the common law from a statutory source of ideas about duty which, because of its authoritative force and its greater responsiveness to changes in moral opinion, is (as Landis saw) potentially a prime catalyst for the development of the common law. Intuitively more sound, therefore, than either of these extreme positions is an intermediate

---

57 *Restatement (Second) of Torts*, 288B(1).
58 Landis, 'Statutes and the Sources of Law,' p. 10.

one that would sanction the judicial advancement of legislative policies even in areas of common-law immunity, yet subject to such limitations on liability as fault, forseeability, and proximate cause.

This essay has sought to provide a theoretical perspective within which this apparently eclectic solution appears as a coherent alternative. If the principles elaborated above were followed, the courts would be applying statutes to situations not expressly contemplated by the legislature, thereby furthering the policy underlying them. For not only would they be applying statutory standards of care to circumstances analogous to those for which they were explicitly designed, but they would often be using criminal statutes to create civil duties hitherto unrecognized by the common law. At the same time, however, the courts' promotion of legislative policies would be circumscribed by limitations on liability ensuring that individual defendants would not be sacrificed to social objectives.

Is the approach we have advocated consistent with the constitutional role of the judiciary in a democratic polity? To the extent that this approach favours the courts' use, without express authorization, of statutes to change the common law, it might seem to run afoul of democratic strictures against judicial law-making. However, this appearance is misleading. The kinds of circumstances under which we favour such judicial creativity are limited to only two: first, where the statute merely unfolds the implications of a basic human right already recognized by the common law; and second, where the statute fixes the standard of care appropriate in a certain type of situation. No argument is made here for the judicial imposition of civil liability as a means of deterring violations of statutes whose aim is the maximization of aggregate welfare, or which create new rights as distinct from effectuating antecedent ones. Accordingly, the approach advocated here is consistent with the theory of adjudication according to which judicial discretion is properly structured by considerations of principle rather than of policy.[59] Moreover, far from being inconsistent with its

---

[59] Dworkin, *Taking Rights Seriously* (1977).

legitimate role in a democracy, the judiciary's use of statutes to modify common-law standards of care is necessitated by that role. For the acceptance by the courts of statutory standards as authoritative is an acknowledgement both of legislative supremacy and of the legislature's superior claim to competence in formulating fixed, uniform, and precise standards of conduct.

*Yale Law School and Faculty of Law, University of Toronto*

JOSEPH M. STEINER

# PUTTING FAULT BACK INTO PRODUCTS LIABILITY: A MODEST RECONSTRUCTION OF TORT THEORY

ABSTRACT. This paper postulates that the proper function of tort law is to provide protection from, and redress of, non-consensual invasions of individual rights of person and property. It then proceeds to analyze and criticize, in that context, several theories of the law of unintentional torts including traditional English negligence law and the models of Posner, Fletcher and Epstein. That analysis proceeds in terms of the answers of each theory to a uniform set of questions which must be answered by any theory of the law of unintentional harms. The paper concludes that none of the theories examined is "rights-based" or, indeed, consistent with the existence of individual rights of person and property.

The paper goes on to elucidate a theory of liability which *is* rights-based. That theory turns out to be a variant of traditional English negligence law in which reasonable foreseeability of harm to legally recognized rights or interests is the sole criterion of liability, the burden of precautions on the agent of the harm being explicitly excluded from consideration.

Finally, the rights-based theory is applied to the area of products liability. It is demonstrated that this area of the law of unintentional harm does have the same moral foundations as the general law of negligence so that resort to the anomalous, and amoral, constructs of fictitious warranties, strict liability, enterprise liability and "the deep pocket" is neither appropriate nor necessary.

## 1. INTRODUCTION

A theory of tort law is concerned with finding an answer to the following multi-part question:

(i) Which victims[1] of

(ii) what sorts of harm

---

[1] I do not mean to prejudge the answers to any of the sub-parts of this question by use of the term "victim". I use it only as convenient shorthand for "a person suffering harm" with no inference as to whether the harm is or ought to be actionable.

(iii) arising in what circumstances
are to be compensated for the harm suffered
(iv) and by whom?
One would not, of course, expect the answers to the sub-questions to be mutually independent, but all must be answered for the theory to be complete.

The response of traditional English negligence law might be phrased this way:
(i) Persons to whom a duty of care is owed
are to be compensated for
(ii) harms to their persons or property or other interests recognized by law
(iii) caused by unreasonable conduct,
(iv) such compensation to be paid by the agent(s) who both owed the duty and whose conduct caused the harm.
This response raises as many or more questions than it answers. To whom is a duty of care owed by the agent and what is the scope of that duty? What is the standard against which conduct is to be measured for 'reasonableness'? What does it mean to say that the agent's conduct 'caused' the harm?

The meaning and function of 'duty of care' has always been problematic in Anglo-Canadian law. Fleming characterizes it as one of a number of devices "to prevent the incidence of liability from getting out of hand", and as "a brake upon the proclivity of juries to indulge their sympathies for accident victims without due regard for the wider implications of their findings in restricting freedom of action." This restraining function is shared with the concept of 'remoteness of damage',

> the prevailing pattern [being] to express in terms of 'duty' judicial policies of a more or less generalized nature, for example whether the plaintiff's *kind* of injury ... is compensable at all; leaving to 'remoteness of damage' the evaluation of more contingent and random features of each particular case.[2]

---

[2] John G. Fleming, *The Law of Torts* 4th ed. (Melbourne: The Law Book Company Limited, 1971), pp. 133–34.

Such a plastic notion of 'duty' is a far cry from the 'duty' which is the correlative of 'right',[3] and as such is inadequate to a conception of negligence law as an engine for the vindication of rights.

When we turn to the question of 'reasonableness' and the standard against which it is measured, the response of the common law is the standard of 'the ordinary reasonable person'. Assuming for the moment that what the ordinary reasonable person would do, see, know or realize in respect of an activity is determinable, there remains an ambiguity, reflected in the case law and explored more fully below, as to the stage of the activity at which the agent's conduct is to be evaluated. The choice of the stage, it will be demonstrated, can be crucial to the determination of whether or not particular conduct is negligent and actionable.

Finally, we come to the vexed question of causation. To say that an agent's conduct 'caused' the harm is to say, at least, that the conduct was a necessary condition of the occurrence of the harm.[4] But even a cursory reading of the cases reveals that the notion of causation which is a prerequisite to liability is much narrower. It is here that we find the notions of 'proximate cause' and 'remoteness of damage' being used as devices to limit the scope of both liability and recoverable damages. And again, the use of these devices is so flexible, if not idiosyncratic, as to preclude any clear connection between negligence law and the concept of rights.

Thus the response of traditional English negligence law to the multi-part question which must be answered is, at the very least, too loosely textured to provide clear guidance to the resolution of particular disputes. By the same token, it is incapable of defining or supporting a notion of rights to which there are correlative duties governing the manner in which activites are to be performed or, indeed, the conditions in which abstention from activi-

---

[3] W. N. Hohfeld, *Fundamental Legal Conceptions As Applied in Judicial Reasoning* (New Haven, Conn.: Yale University Press, 1923), chap. 1.

[4] I am ignoring the problems posed by multiple causes, whether concurrent or alternative. See Fleming, *Law of Torts*, pp. 171–74.

ties is required. At best the traditional formulation describes or defines certain interests which are worthy of protection, all other things being equal.

By this point in the discussion, I have, of course, displayed my bias as to the proper role of tort law. That role is the protection of individual rights of person and property against non-consensual invasions. I describe this position as a bias because, in some sense, it cannot be established as being 'correct' by logical deduction from more basic postulates. It is simply a corollary of a more general position as to the purpose of law as a social institution and the meaning of the 'rule of law'. This is not to say that no other conception of the proper function of tort law is possible. But, I would suggest, there has not been, as yet, any alternative formulation which, on analysis, can be derived from a postulate or postulates with the same quality of 'fundamentalness' and intuitive acceptability as the existence of and respect for individual rights of person and property.

Consider, for example, the pragmatic approach that the purpose of tort law, more particularly of negligence and nuisance law, is to adjust the inevitable frictions and collisions of life in society in a fair or equitable or reasonable manner. No grand (or grandiose) scheme here! But to what end are life's frictions and collisions to be adjusted? What are the hallmarks of fairness, equity or reasonableness? Is there to be some constancy in the way particular types of frictions are to be adjusted? If so, what are the principles which underlie such constancy? If not, what are the determinants of different treatment, and does the analysis of those determinants reveal consistent principles on the basis of which differentiation is justified?

An institution for resolving non-consensual interaction problems must comprise either a game of dice or a principled scheme for determination of whether there was a privilege to act in the manner complained of or a right to be free of the consequences of that act. All I suggest here is that there is something very compelling about the notion of tort law functioning to redress non-consensual deviations from the distribution of rights (and correlative duties) and privileges recognized or established[5] by law, i.e., tort law as corrective justice, and nothing very compelling in any alternative, systematic formulation.

Indeed, I think one can go a bit further. When a complainant claims from an agent compensation for the agent's interference with his person or property or other interest, only one of two responses can be appropriate. Either the agent should acknowledge the validity of the claim and make compensation, or the agent is entitled to reject the claim, with sympathy to be sure, as arising from the vicissitudes of life. Whether the first or the second response is appropriate must, I suggest, depend on whether the complainant was entitled to be free from the interference in question. Put differently, the question is whether the element of person, property or other interest interfered with was, in some relevant sense, owned by the complainant. In either formulation the issue is the same: did the complainant have a right not to be so interfered with? It is difficult to see how the complainant's claim can be made out if it is put lower, or otherwise, than as one of right.

In what follows I shall attempt to cast some alternatives to the traditional English common law formulation in the form of the answers they give to our basic multi-part question and to analyze them in that context. I shall then propose a further alternative which will be seen to be contained in, but, I hope, considerably more precise than, the traditional English view. Finally, I shall apply the proposed formulation to the sub-set of negligence (or accident) law known as products liability and attempt to demonstrate that it can account for, and provide a normative basis for, that branch of the law in a way that is consistent with negligence law and avoids the doctrinal anomalies inherent in the approaches known as 'strict liability' or 'enterprise liability'.

---

[5] I say "recognized or established" as some of the rights and privileges served, and duties enforced, by tort law, would be widely, if not universally, accepted as being natural, while others are purely conventional.

## 2. ECONOMIC ANALYSIS OF NEGLIGENCE LAW-POSNER[6]

Professor Posner would answer our multi-part question in this way:

(i) Persons harmed by the conduct of an agent
(ii) in respect of their persons, property or other interests (even if not antecedently recognized as interests protectable by law)
(iii) in circumstances in which the market value of the injury or loss to person, property or other interest exceeds the costs which would have had to be incurred by the agent to avoid the harm (whether by way of curtailment of his activity or adoption of preventive measures or both)

are to be compensated

(iv) by such agent.

It is readily apparent from this formulation, particularly items (ii) and (iii), that it allows of no rights in the sense of 'trumps'[7] or as forming "*barriers*[*s*] against collective judgments on overall maximization."[8] Fluctuations in the price of grain may one day render the railroad liable for the crops destroyed by fire caused by sparks thrown off by its locomotives and the next day decree that the farmer must bear an identical loss himself.

This evanescent notion of 'property' or 'rights' is a corollary of the principle which Posner advocates as the basis of negligence law, namely that assets, including rights in respect of person, property and other interests, are to be distributed so as to maxi-

---

[6] See: Richard A. Posner, 'A Theory of Negligence,' *Journal of Legal Studies* 1 (1972): 29; 'Strict Liability: A Comment,' *Journal of Legal Studies* 2 (1973): 205; *Economic Analysis of Law* (Boston: Little, Brown & Co., 1972), chap. 4.

[7] Ronald Dworkin, *Taking Rights Seriously* (Cambridge, Mass.: Harvard University Press, 1977), pp. xi, 82–90.

[8] Richard A. Epstein, 'Nuisance Law: Corrective Justice and Its Utilitarian Constraints,' *Journal of Legal Studies* 8 (1979): 68.

mize their market value. I do not mean to criticize this principle on the ground of circularity. While it is true that the price of assets is not, in general, invariant with respect to their distribution, it is nonetheless possible to frame Posner's principle in the form of a maximization problem which will, given the conditions generally assumed in microeconomic theory, have a determinate solution (possibly more than one). The question is why that solution is of any interest. It seems peculiar indeed that wealth or allocative efficiency, which are surely instrumental goals at best, should be treated as the determinants of distributive justice. It is equally peculiar that an economic theory based on the primacy of individual welfare, as conceived by each individual for himself or herself, should be pressed into service for the purpose of imposing a collective goal which subverts the very notion of individual rights.[9]

Nor can wealth maximization be rehabilitated by arguing, even if correctly, that it avoids the worst extremes of utilitarianism and that, given certain contingencies, it "accommodates ... the competing impulses of our moral nature."[10] Posner may be correct in asserting that ethical theories cannot be validated.[11] But this is so in the sense that, in justifying an ethical position by logical argument, we reach a point where we can simply postulate a basic principle or principles, but cannot deduce it or them from more basic principles. If there is disagreement at that point it may be that no further useful discussion can take place between the proponents of competing basic principles.[12] But until and unless we

---

[9] I have argued the logical incoherence of the Posner model more extensively elsewhere. See my 'Economics, Morality and the Law of Torts,' *University of Toronto Law Journal* 26 (1976): 229–39.

[10] Richard A. Posner, 'Utilitarianism, Economics and Legal Theory,' *Journal of Legal Studies* 8 (1979): 136.

[11] *Ibid.*, p. 110.

[12] Professor Hare has shown just how far the principle of universalizability can push moral argument between proponents of apparently irreconcilable positions. See R. M. Hare, *Freedom and Reason* (Oxford: Oxford University Press, 1963), and *The Language of Morals* (Oxford: Oxford University Press, 1952.

can comprehend the basic principles from which a purportedly moral prescription is derived, the prescription simply stands in a void attracting neither assent nor dissent, but simply blank stares.[13]

## 3. CORRECTIVE JUSTICE FORMULATIONS

### *(a) Fletcher's Paradigm of Reciprocity*

Professor Fletcher[14] describes the Posner view of negligence law as 'the paradigm of reasonableness' and allows that it has assumed the dominant position in modern times. He then sets out to erect and justify a competing view which he describes as 'the paradigm of reciprocity'.

The paradigm of reciprocity offers the following answer to our basic multi-part question:

(i) Persons harmed by the conduct of an agent
[(ii) in respect of unspecified interests,]
(iii) which conduct
(a) imposes on the victim a non-reciprocal risk, i.e., risk greater in degree and different in order from that created by the victim and imposed on the agent; and
(b) is unexcused as being done while labouring under compulsion or unavoidable ignorance,

are entitled to be compensated

(iv) by such agent.

The basic thrust of the paradigm of reciprocity is that friction or mutual interference is inherent in life in society, that losses therefrom cannot always be compensable else activity itself becomes impossible (or at least invites claims) and that something more

---

[13] For a more extensive critique of wealth maximization as a moral principle see: Ronald M. Dworkin, 'Is Wealth a Value,' *Journal of Legal Studies* 9 (1980): 191.

[14] George P. Fletcher, 'Fairness and Utility in Tort Theory,' *Harvard Law Review* 85 (1972): 537.

than the fact of friction and loss is needed to set the agent apart from the victim so that shifting the loss is appropriate. That something more is conduct which, by its nature, imposes risks in some sense greater than the risks which we all impose on each other in the normal course.

There are, I would suggest, a number of difficulties with this paradigm. First, the baseline, deviations from which both constitute and measure harm, is not addressed. The traditional English view appears to be premised on pre-existing rights of person and property or other legally protected interests. The Posner view, as we have seen, generates quasi-rights by comparing the effects on asset values of the assignment of the interest in dispute to one party or the other. Fletcher does not make it clear whether he presumes pre-existing rights, or simply defines and measures harm as the difference in the victim's position before and after the conduct in issue, any such difference being actionable if attributable to an activity generating non-reciprocal risk. In the latter case his theory, like Posner's, generates quasi-rights as a by-product, and those quasi-rights, to the extent that they purport to be in or to things, will be as ephemeral as Posner's. Such a theory cannot, I suggest, be described as one of corrective justice.

A second, perhaps more basic, difficulty is the indeterminacy of the paradigm as formulated. Are we concerned with the reciprocity or non-reciprocity of the risks generated by the activities in which the parties are actually engaged at the time of the loss? Or is the question whether or not the agent's activity is one that the victim engages in himself? Frequently? Sometimes? On occasion? Or must we inquire whether the agent's activity is one that is engaged in generally by individuals comprising the society in question? That the point of reference is crucial is clear from a consideration of an automobile/pedestrian accident. The automobile driver inevitably imposes on the pedestrian a risk of a higher degree and different order than that which the pedestrian imposes on him. Does it matter whether the pedestrian also drives cars? Do we inquire as to the proportion of individuals in the community who drive cars?

Despite this indeterminacy, however, there is something intuitively compelling in the notion that not all harms resulting from friction and mutual interference can be compensable in a functioning society and that there should, therefore, be something 'special' about the risk generated by the agent to justify shifting to him the loss in which the risk eventuated. We shall return to this consideration below.

Finally, Fletcher's treatment of excuses is problematic. Compulsion is not confined to situations in which the ostensible agent can deny that the conduct complained of was his act, as, for example, where someone has seized the agent's hand and caused it to strike the victim. Compulsion also comprehends the circumstance in which the agent generates non-reciprocal risk eventuating in harm to the victim in order to escape a grave risk to his own interests.[15] Allowing compulsion as an excuse, and therefore denying compensation, in this circumstance amounts to a denial of the victim's rights in the interest invaded or, at the least, to such redefinition or circumscription of the rights as to make them take on the evanescent quality of Posner's quasi-rights. Is it appropriate to inquire of the agent pleading compulsion in the second sense whether the grave risk which he sought to escape was imposed on him by a third party or resulted from his own conduct? It is difficult to see why the victim should bear the consequences of the agent's conduct in the latter case. I suggest that, from the victim's point of view, he is equally sacrificed to the agent's interests in the former situation.

Fletcher does not deal at any length with the excuse of unavoidable ignorance. Later in this paper I shall argue that this condition has moral and functional significance for the law of negligence, but as a denial of liability rather than an excuse.

---

[15] See Fletcher's treatment of *Vincent* v. *Lake Erie Transport*, 124 N.W. 221 (1910), and *Cordas* v. *Peerless Transportation Co.*, 27 N.Y.S.2d 198 (1941); 'Fairness and Utility,' pp. 546–47, 552–53. See also my comments, 'Economics,' pp. 249–50.

### *(b) Epstein's Theory of Strict Liability*

Professor Epstein has proposed an apparently radical alternative to the traditional and the economic formulations of accident law designed to avoid the conceptual inadequacies of the former and the ethical peculiarities of the latter.[16] He proposes a system of strict liability, allowing only restricted classes of defences. Liability attaches, at least *prima facie*, to the agent's conduct if it bears one of a specified set of causal relations to the victim's harm.

Epstein's structure can be described in the following answer to our basic multi-part question.

(i) Persons suffering harms caused by the conduct of an agent

[(ii) in respect of unspecified interests,]

(iii) which conduct consists in any of

(a) the application of force by the agent to the victim,
(b) the frightening by the agent of the victim,
(c) the compulsion by the agent of a third party to apply force to the victim, or
(d) the creation by the agent of dangerous conditions

unless,

(e) the agent's conduct itself stands in one of the causal relations (a) through (d) to conduct of the victim,
(f) the victim assumed the risk of harm of the class which he suffered, or
(g) in the case of injuries suffered on the agent's land, the victim was trespassing on the land,

are to be compensated

(iv) by such agent.

---

16 Richard A. Epstein, 'A Theory of Strict Liability,' *Journal of Legal Studies* 2 (1973): 151; 'Defences and Subsequent Pleas in a System of Strict Liability,' *Journal of Legal Studies* 3 (1974): 165.

This approach, if tenable, would seem to be most attactive as it appears to provide a mode of ascribing liability on the basis of nothing more than a physical description of the events in question. The theory, thus formulated, however, is hopelessly indeterminate. Note first that, at least in the two original papers where the system is expounded, Epstein does not indicate what sort of interests are protected, other than in casual references to 'person' or 'property'. He gives us no baseline whereby to recognize or measure harms. Nor can the baseline and measure of harm be supplied, as suggested in my analysis of Fletcher, by comparison of the difference in the victim's position before and after the conduct of which complaint is made. The reason for this is that, despite the apparent simplicity of the causal paradigms, neither the conduct nor the victim can be identified.

This conclusion is doubtless somewhat less than obvious. Let me elaborate. In Fletcher's model (ignoring for the present the questions I raised as to the identification of the risks to be compared) the ethical criterion of non-reciprocity of risk permits us to identify offending conduct. Having identified the offending conduct, identification of the victim and the harm is a matter of tracing causal relations in a purely physical sense. In the normal case, of course, the process would begin at the other end with a person claiming to be the victim of harm. To make out his case, he would have to identify non-reciprocal risk creating conduct on the part of an agent which was causally related in a purely physical sense to the change from his previous position.

Epstein's formulation provides no device for breaking into the web of causal conditions and relations. Consider his simplest paradigm, *A* hit *B*, or, for more concreteness, *A* hit *B*'s jaw with his fist. *B* says he has suffered harm caused by *A*'s blow to his chin. *A* responds that *B*'s harm was caused by *B*'s placing his jaw in the path of *A*'s fist, incidentally hurting *A*'s hand. If *A*'s defence sounds idiotic, it is only because of a widely shared ethical view that people ought not to hit other people, and not because of the physical description of the event. *A*'s defence is rejected because his fist movement is considered improper; of the various causal conditions giving rise to the contact between *A*'s fist and *B*'s jaw, *A*'s punch is the one that ought not to have been there. Thus the ascription of causative force to *A*'s punch and not to the location of *B*'s jaw at the relevant time is a normative judgment and not merely an inference from physical facts.

If the accuracy of this criticism is not seen in this simple example, consider a series of pleas beginning with the plaintiff's allegation in the form of one of the four causal paradigms followed by the defendant's defence that his conduct was caused, in the sense of one of the paradigms, by the plaintiff's conduct, the plaintiff replying in similar terms, and so on ad infinitum. One can only break this monotonous chain and make a statement as to direction of causation when one identifies an action on the part of one or other, that he ought not, on some wholly external criterion, to have done.

Epstein, in a more recent paper, has clearly acknowledged the fundamentally normative nature of causation in tort law. "Tort law ...", he tells us, "presupposes some prior independent method for defining and recognizing property rights in both the person and external objects."[17] Criticizing Coase's extension of the concept of joint causation to the conduct of the plaintiff and defendant in any negligence action, Epstein argues that:

> The weakness of the position is its failure to recognize that for legal purposes the question of causation can be resolved only after there is an acceptance of some initial distribution of rights. ...
>
> The clear distribution of rights is precisely what makes it possible to make a unique determination of what conduct is causally relevant and what is not.[18]

Conduct is causally relevant, and forms the basis for the attachment of liability, when it is a causal condition of the invasion of a legally recognized right or privilege or, alternatively, is not itself the exercise of a legally recognized right or privilege.

Once this position is accepted, however, the only difference between Epstein's position and that of traditional negligence law is

---

[17] Epstein, 'Nuisance Law,' p. 52.
[18] *Ibid.*, pp. 58–60.

the non-availability of the defence of reasonable care. This difference in the standard required of agents is certainly not without significance, but it does not represent a radically different point of departure.

## 4. CONCEPTS OF FAULT

All of the formulations of the answers to the basic question of tort law which we have examined involve notions of fault which are thought to justify the shifting of a loss from the victim to the agents. For Epstein, the fault lies in causing the invasion of a right or privilege of the victim *per se*. Faulty conduct for Fletcher consists in the creation of non-reciprocal risk. Posner's fault is the 'waste' of resources[19] comprising a loss whose market value exceeds the cost of preventive measures or activity curtailment adequate to avoid the loss.

These notions of fault, of course, can be no more compelling than the theories in which they are embedded. Thus Epstein's notion of fault is as indeterminate as his principle of causation. Fletcher's fault can be no better defined than 'reciprocity' of risk. Posner's concept of fault is well-defined, but bears no relationship to moral notions of fault if the domain of morality is seen as the universe of relations between individuals.

The traditional English negligence law concept of fault is failure to meet the standard of the ordinary reasonable person in one's conduct. I have commented above on the ambiguity of this standard. I suggest, however, that there exists a more precise notion of fault, which comprehends both intentional and unintentional torts, and which is capable of lending both descriptive and normative consistency to this area of law.

Tort law, I suggest, has fastened upon two quite independent aspects of conduct as alternative bases for fixing an agent with

---

[19] Whose resources? It would seem the answer is society's resources, giving Posner's notion of fault a peculiarly collectivist tone for a theory based on the individualistic model of neoclassical economics.

liability for a harm. The first aspect is the state of mind of the agent, by which I mean his intent or lack of intent to create the harm which eventuates or his indifference toward its eventuation. It is, of course, the case that tort law has attempted to objectify the analysis of the agent's state of mind, but the moral force and justification of the attachment of liability for conduct defective in this aspect is the assumption that such objective determination is a reliable indicator of the agent's subjective state of mind.

The second aspect of conduct which grounds liability in tort relates to the objective environment in which the conduct takes place as reflected in the *ex ante* probability of the harm resulting. This second dimension is continuous, unlike the first which is trichotomous. For purposes of analysis, however, it is adequate to confine our attention to three segments of the probability continuum, that over which the harm is, *ex ante*, substantially certain, that over which the harm is, *ex ante*, reasonably foreseeable, and that over which harm is, *ex ante*, not reasonably foreseeable.

Dividing each of these two aspects of defective conduct into three reference points, as I have done, yields nine possible combinations. Conduct intended to bring about the harm which eventuated is treated as an intentional tort regardless of the *ex ante* probability of the harm eventuating. The mental state of the agent and the occurrence of the harm are jointly sufficient to classify the conduct as intentionally tortious. Similar considerations apply to the conduct of an agent who is indifferent as to whether or not the harm eventuates. However, the notion of indifference I am using requires that the agent advert to the possibility of the harm. Thus if the *ex ante* probability is so low that the harm is not reasonably foreseeable, the agent could not be charged with being indifferent to the eventuation of the harm.

The resulting scheme divides the field of tortious conduct into four categories as follows:

*Ex Ante Probability of Harm Eventuating*

| *State of Mind of the Agent* | | Substantially Certain | Reasonably Foreseeable | Not Reasonably Foreseeable |
|---|---|---|---|---|
| | Intends to bring About the Harm | Intentional Tort | Intentional Tort | Intentional Tort |
| | Indifferent as to Whether Harm Eventuates | Recklessness | Recklessness | |
| | Does Not Intend to Bring About the Harm | Hazardous Activity | Carelessness | Non-Tortious Conduct |

My category of intentional tort essentially coincides with that of traditional tort law. The distinction between intentional tort and recklessness by reference to the state of mind of the agent, however, avoids the doctrinal anomalies of the presumption that a person 'intends' the natural and probable consequences of his acts and the notion of 'transferred intent',[20] and thus absorbs a portion of the field traditionally assigned to intentional tort. Recklessness also overlaps the conduct traditionally labelled as negligence, the balance of which is absorbed in the category of carelessness.

If there is any novelty at all in this reclassification of tortious conduct, it is in the category of hazardous activity. I will argue below that this tort comprehends the subset of accident law known as products liability, and does so in accordance with traditional fault principles and without need to resort to essentially unprincipled arguments for the application of strict liability to defective products. Before proceeding to that argument, however, it is necessary to consider the meaning and appropriateness of the 'reasonable foreseeability' formulation of the 'reasonable person' standard.

---

[20] See: *Restatement of Torts, Second*, ss. 8A and 13.

The criterion for distinguishing reasonable from unreasonable, and therefore actionable, conduct is, I suggest, a function of at most three variables. Those variables are the probability ($P$) of a particular type of harm resulting from a particular activity or manner of carrying on an activity, the magnitude of the loss ($L$) resulting from such a harm and the cost of burden ($B$) of avoiding the particular type of harm.[21] I suggest, further, that there are only four admissible classes of functional relationships between these variables and the threshhold of reasonableness, and they are as follows:

(i) Reasonableness is a function of $P$, $L$, and $B$ as, for example, the Learned Hand rule (also the Posner rule) that conduct fails to meet the standard if and only if $B < PL$.[22]

(ii) Reasonableness is a function of $P$ and $L$ only. An example would be a rule finding conduct negligent if and only if $PL > \bar{A}$, where $\bar{A}$ is a pre-determined constant.[23]

(iii) Reasonableness is a function of $P$ only, as where conduct is held to be unreasonable where $P > \bar{P}$, $\bar{P}$ being a pre-determined level of probability.[24]

(iv) Reasonableness is a function of $L$ only, for example a rule attaching liability where $L > \bar{L}$, $\bar{L}$ being a pre-determined magnitude of loss.[25]

---

[21] $B$ is assumed to be measurable in the same units as $L$, and to be the least burdensome combination of preventive measures and activity curtailment which will avoid the particular type of harm.

[22] *United States et al.* v. *Carroll Towing Co., Inc. et al*, 159 F.2d 169, 173 (2d Cir. 1947).

[23] This class of criterion is adopted by Lord Reid in *Bolton* v. *Stone*, [1951] A. C. 850 (H. L.) at 867.

[24] See the decision of Lord Porter in *Bolton* v. *Stone*, [1951] A. C. 850 (H. L.) at 858. See also Lord Reid at 868.

[25] Note that strict liability can be portrayed as a special case of this rule where $\bar{L} = 0$.

Not all of these classes of liability rules are consistent with the view of tort law as the protector of individual rights and privileges against non-consensual invasion. In particular, any criterion which is a function, in part, of $B$ is ruled out by a rights-based conception of tort law, for such a criterion must necessarily permit, indeed require, a case-by-case balancing of the 'rights' of the victim against the cost of preventive measures or curtailment to the agent or society.

Liability rules which are a function of $L$ only are, in a rather different fashion, inconsistent with the notion of tort law as the protector and enforcer of rights. The victim's right that the agent's conduct, which might prove invasive, meet a certain standard is correlative to the agent's duty so to conduct himself as not to cause an invasion. But if this duty is to be perceived as a moral directive on proper and improper conduct, then it must be a directive which is capable of being followed by ordinary humans. A rule that an agent must so conduct himself as not to cause losses exceeding a predetermined magnitude ($\bar{L}$) is, I suggest, not one that is capable of being followed. If an agent cannot *ex ante* conceive of a connection between his proposed conduct and the eventuation of harm of a particular type or magnitude to a victim, he cannot be called upon to alter his conduct so as to prevent that eventuality.[26]

Liability rules which are functions of $P$ and $L$ or of $P$ only are not, I submit, ruled out by the rights-based theory of torts or by the constraint implicit in the notion that 'ought implies can'. Such rules do not admit of trade-offs between 'rights' of the victim and interests of the agent. Nor do they necessarily lead to directives as to conduct which are incapable of fulfilment, though particular members of this set of functions may suffer from that defect.

If it be accepted that the role of tort law is to protect legally established rights and privileges from nonconsensual invasion, it

---

[26] Consider, in this light, *Palsgraf* v. *Long Island Railroad Co.*, 248 N.Y. 339; 162 N.E. 99 (1928).

follows that the standard of conduct should be set as high as is consistent with the 'ought implies can' constraint. It seems reasonable to assume that an individual's ability to perceive that a risk of harm is consequent upon his conduct is a function not only of the probability of harm, but also of its magnitude. The greater the magnitude of the harm, the lower the probability required to make it perceptible to the conscious mind and the more insistently one can require that the agent take the risk into account.[27] If this perception is accurate, then the liability rule should be a function of P and L. Such a liability rule is, I suggest, what we generally understand by the term "reasonable foreseeability".

It remains only to deal with the ambiguity in the traditional reasonable person standard as to the stage of the agent's activity at which the standard is to be applied. To this point the argument has been that the reasonable person standard should be interpreted as the test of reasonable foreseeability. The question of where or when that test is to be applied admits of two possible answers. Either it is applied to evaluate the agent's entire course of conduct from the point of choosing to engage in the activity and continuing through the carrying on of the activity. Or it is applied to evaluate the agent's conduct in carrying on the activity *given* the choice to engage in it. The difference, of course, is in the power of the standard to dictate that the agent refrain from the activity altogether. Put another way, the issue is whether the duty to refrain from causing reasonably foreseeable harms is unqualified, or is in some way mitigated by the nature of the activity in question. Once put this way, however, it becomes clear that the question has already been answered. For if some characteristic of the activity other than the probability and magnitude of consequent harm is to be taken into consideration, what can that characteristic be other than some element or elements entering into the determination of *B*? But, as we have shown, any liability rule which is, in part, a function of *B* is inconsistent with a rights-based theory of tort law.

---

[27] Consider your attitudes to the risk of walking down a crowded sidewalk and the risk of living near a nuclear power station.

There is one line of attack on this rights-based theory of tort law which should be dealt with before proceeding further. That criticism argues that the proposed fault criterion makes fault a function, in part, of the scale or level at which the activity in question is carried on, a feature of no moral significance. Suppose, for example, that we can conceive of an activity being carried on at a unit level, and that the probability of an accident resulting from each unit of activity is one in ten thousand. It follows that the expected number of accidents occurring when the activity is operated at a level of one thousand units is one tenth, while the expected number of accidents occurring when the activity is operated at a level of ten thousand units is one. Thus, though the mode of operation of the activity is identical in both cases, an accident might well be said not to be reasonably foreseeable at the lower level of activity while it is reasonably foreseeable, and therefore actionable, at the higher level.

This criticism is, I believe, misplaced, at least in the sense that it can be levelled against any theory of tort law with equal force. This is the case because the issue, properly understood, is not the scale of the activity, but the definition of the activity which is to be evaluated by standards of conduct mandated by tort law. The force of the criticism arises from the fact that there is an inevitable element of arbitrariness in the definition of the activity. Why do we confine our evaluation of an automobile driver's conduct to the last few seconds before the accident rather than examining his driving from the moment he started his engine that day, that week, that year or, indeed, since he first began driving? The answer, presumably, is that we are concerned only with that segment of the conduct that is causally related to the accident and that segment alone is the "activity" which is to be tested against tort standards.

The answer, of course, is not logically rigorous. Yet it seems reasonable to conclude that the conduct which is causally related to an automobile accident is that beginning a few seconds prior to the accident so far as the people actually involved in the accident are concerned. If, on the other hand, a malfunctioning brake caused or contributed to the accident, other conduct becomes significant. We may examine the conduct of the mechanic in the repair of the brake. That may be the end of the matter. But the inquiry may lead further as, for example, to the manufacture of the brake itself. And that inquiry may need to focus on manufacturing and design processes as the causally related conduct, processes affecting the production of thousands or millions of sets of brakes.

It is, I suggest, the shift in focus from "atoms" of activity to processes governing the mode in which an activity is carried on that imports the scale effect. If that is arbitrary, it is because the definition of the activity to be evaluated is arbitrary, but that element of arbitrariness is inescapable and equally applicable to any theory of tort law.

## 5. A MODEST REFORMULATION

We have now reached the point at which the theory of tort law which I have been attempting to elucidate can be cast into the form of an answer to our basic multi-part question. That answer is as follows:

(i) Persons harmed by the conduct of an agent

(ii) in respect of their persons, property or other interests recognized by law

(iii) in circumstances in which the conduct of the agent was:
(a) subjectively intended to create a situation of peril;
(b) substantially certain, *ex ante*, to cause the harm which occurred; or
(c) such that the harm which occurred was, *ex ante*, a reasonably foreseeable consequence,

are to be compensated

(iv) by such agent.

Comparing this formulation with that which I have ascribed to traditional English negligence law, it can be seen that the concept of 'duty' has disappeared, its function being absorbed by the criteria of substantial certainty or reasonable foreseeability of harm. This is hardly an innovation, dating back as it does at least to the decision of the House of Lords in *Donoghue* v. *Stevenson*:

> You must take reasonable care to avoid acts or omissions which you can reasonably foresee would be likely to injure your neighbour. Who, then, in law is my neighbour? The answer seems to be – persons who are so closely and directly affected by my act that I ought reasonably to have them in contemplation as being so affected when I am directing my mind to the acts or omissions which are called in question.[28]

This reformulation also reduces to manageable proportions the problems of causation which are inevitable when that concept performs a normative as well as a descriptive role. To say in this model that an agent's conduct 'caused' the harm is to say first, that the conduct is a cause of the harm in a physical sense, and second, that the conduct was intended to create peril or that the physical relationship between the conduct and the harm was sufficiently close that the harm was a substantially certain or reasonably foreseeable outcome of the chain of events commenced, or contributed to, by the conduct.

## 6. PRODUCTS LIABILITY

To test the usefulness of the suggested reformulation, I propose to apply it to the sub-category of accident law known as products liability. This is an area which has caused the common law courts, whether of the Commonwealth or the United States, a substantial amount of difficulty and has led to the development of doctrines and devices which sit uneasily with the rest of tort law and, indeed, with the whole notion of principled decision making.

In both the United Kingdom and the United States, the first obstacle to be overcome in developing a comprehensive law of defective products was the privity rule. Thus both English and American courts held that the manufacturers of products owed

---

[28] [1932] A.C. 562 (H.L.), per Lord Atkin at 580.

a contractual duty of care to their immediate purchasers (absent contractual provisions to the contrary) but no duty of care whatever to others.[29] Such a result is, of course, absurd. Why should the entitlement of a victim to compensation for a non-consensual invasion of his person or property depend on the existence or nature of a juridical relationship between the agent and a third party? While the expressed reasoning in such decisions is opaque, it is reasonably clear that the courts were using privity in this totally inapt fashion so as to avoid apparently open-ended liability, a possibility which seems to be a recurrent judicial nightmare. The nightmare can be avoided, however, by the application of the test of reasonable foreseeability.

The strict privity position was not long maintained, however, no doubt because of the shocking results it produced. Both British and American law began to develop classes of exceptions for 'inherently dangerous things'[30] or 'things imminently dangerous to life.'[31] The sharp distinction between these classes of things (e.g., poisons) and other products is also without principled basis. What is significant about these special classes of product is the notoriety of the risks entailed by their use if defective. Such notoriety, of course, leads directly to, indeed is the equivalent of, a very high level of foreseeability. But foreseeability is a continuous and not a discrete variable, so that the selection of these particular classes for special treatment was inescapably arbitrary.

The citadel of privity was breached first in the United States in the well-known case of *MacPherson* v. *Buick Motor Co.* But it is interesting to note that the result is achieved not so much by way of a direct attack on the use of privity in a context where it has no place, but by an expansion of the category of products exempted from the privity rule to all those as are "reasonably certain to place life and limb in peril when negligently made."[32]

---

[29] See: *Winterbottom* v. *Wright*, (1842), 10 M. & W. 109, 152 E.R. 402.
[30] *Longmeid* v. *Holliday*, (1851), 6 Ex. 761.
[31] *Thomas* v. *Winchester*, 6 N.Y. 397 (1852).
[32] 111 N.E. 1050, 1053 (1916).

This is essentially the language which I used earlier in defining the class of tort which I labelled 'hazardous activity'.

In England privity fell with the decision of the House of Lords in *Donoghue* v. *Stevenson*. Again the court pointed out the arbitrariness of the classification of certain products as inherently dangerous and the consequent creation of special rules for them.[33] Henceforth general negligence principles were to be applied to defective product claims as to any other accident claims. And, in the view of Lord Macmillan, those principles fell to be applied in the ordinary fashion without benefit of presumptions of negligence or the doctrine of *res ipsa loquitur*. "Negligence must be both averred and proved".[34]

Despite Lord Macmillan's injunction, products liability law turned very quickly in the direction of evidentiary and semantic devices so as to fasten liability on manufacturers in situations where no failure to take care could be identified. Thus where the manufacturer led evidence of a 'fool proof' quality control system, the existence of a defect *per se* led to the necessary inference that some employee was at fault.[35] Similar developments occurred in the United States.[36] The net effect is a 'Catch 22' approach whereby the stronger the evidence of the stringency of the manufacturer's quality control system, the more irresistible the inference of negligence consisting in some unspecified failure of that system.

Commonwealth jurisprudence in this area has not developed beyond the application of these devices clothed in the language of negligence law. No so in the United States. In *Escola* v. *Coca Cola Bottling Co. of Fresno*, Traynor J. announced the abandonment of

---

[33] [1932] A.C. 562, per Lord Atkin at 595.

[34] *Ibid.*, p. 622.

[35] *Grant* v. *Australian Knitting Mills Limited*, [1936] A.C. 85 (P.C.), per Lord Wright at 101. To similar effect in Canada, see: *Arendale* v. *Canada Bread Co. Ltd.*, [1941] 2 D.L.R. 41 (Ont. C.A.), per Gillanders, J.A. at 42; *Zeppa* v. *Coca-Cola Ltd.*, [1955] 5 D.L.R. 187 (Ont. C.A.); *Cohen* v. *Coca-Cola Ltd.*, [1967] S.C.R. 469.

[36] For example, the decision of Gibson C.J. in *Escola* v. *Coca Cola Bottling Co. of Fresno*, 150 P. 2d 436 (1944).

negligence rules and called for the imposition of absolute liability on the basis of an essentially fictional warranty deemed to flow from the manufacturer to the user of the product. The rationale for creation of this new basis for liability is a peculiar combination of factors including a superficial economic analysis of accident prevention, 'deep pocket' and loss-spreading considerations and enterprise liability:

Even if there is no negligence, however, public policy demands that responsibility be fixed wherever it will most effectively reduce the hazards to life and health inherent in defective products that reach the market. It is evident that the manufacturer can anticipate some hazards and guard against the recurrence of others as the public cannot. Those who suffer injury from defective products are unprepared to meet its consequences. The cost of an injury and the loss of time or health may be an overwhelming misfortune to the person injured, and a needless one, for the risk can be insured by the manufacturer and distributed among the public as a cost of doing business ... Against such a risk [of injury from defective products whether negligently manufactured or not] there should be general and constant protection and the manufacturer is best situated to afford such protection.[37]

It requires but little reflection to see that none of the grounds offered by Traynor J. for a uniform rule of shifting losses from defective products to manufacturers is consistent with a rights-based theory of torts. He begins with a quasi-utilitarian injunction to shift costs to the most efficient cost avoider, an injunction in no way based on any moral failing on the part of the latter. He goes on to justify the shift by reference to the manufacturer's wealth and its ability to shift loss and to insure, again characteristics in no way related to any moral notion of responsibility for the loss.[38]

This determination to achieve what is 'fair' in the court's eyes rather than what is 'just' by reference to a set of universalizable principles, came into full flower with the abandonment of the

---

[37] *Ibid.*, pp. 440–41.

[38] If these criteria have any validity, one wonders why they are applied on a class basis at a very minimal level of refinement. Why not apply the deep-pocket criterion on a case-by-case basis to all accidents?

fiction of warranty, and the concomitant loss of whatever contractual elements might have been called up in support of this brand of liability. This abandonment occurred in the case of *Greenman* v. *Yuba Power Products, Inc.* in which Traynor J. announced the arrival of strict liability for harms arising from defective products:

> The purpose of such liability is to ensure that the costs of injuries resulting from defective products are borne by the manufacturers that put such products on the market rather than by the injured persons who are powerless to protect themselves.[39]

I should perhaps make it clear at this point that I do not take issue with the results of either the Commonwealth or the American lines of cases so much as with the unprincipled fashion in which the results are reached. In the law, after all, principled reasoning is the only device for protecting rights. The failure in both jurisdictions, I suggest, arises from the same misconception of fault. In the Commonwealth cases, the misconception lurks in the background causing nagging unease. In the American cases it has been explicitly adopted.

The misconception, of course, lies in the consideration of the burden of preventing accidental harms as an element in the definition of reasonable conduct. The Learned Hand rule mandates consideration of that variable. The English cases are, to say the least, ambivalent. Lord Reid, in *Bolton* v. *Stone* explicitly rejects any consideration of such burden. Yet in *Morris* v. *West Hartlepool Steam Navigation Co. Ltd.* he pronounces a rule which is identical to the Learned Hand rule.[40]

The semantic tricks of the English and Canadian cases mask, I suggest, a perceived tension between the concurrent feelings that

---

39 377 P. 2d 897, 901 (1962).

40 [1956] A.C. 552 (H.L.) at 574. To similar effect, see Lord Reid's judgment in *The Wagon Mound (No. 2)*, [1967] A.C. 617 (P.C. – N.S.W.) at 642–643. I would point out however, that in these and other English cases where the burden of preventive measures is mentioned, the decision seems always to turn not on it, but on the magnitude of the risk.

the person injured by a defective product is innocent and should be compensated and that the modern manufacturer, with the latest production and quality control techniques in place, has done all that he can do to avoid defects. The tension in the American context is even greater because the Learned Hand rule requires a finding that such a conscientious, state-of-the-art manufacturer is not negligent.

In the light of the analysis of Part 4 of this paper, this tension is seen to be misplaced. The state-of-the-art manufacturer knows full well that he can anticipate with near certainty a reasonably well-defined frequency of defective products over a sufficiently long production run. Quality control techniques for large-scale production processes are almost invariably based on a statistical design incorporating a sample size which, from the manufacturer's point of view, optimizes the trade-off between sampling expense and frequency of defects. Thus the judge who infers negligence from the existence of a defect in a product produced under stringent quality control does not reach the wrong result, but his reasoning is faulty. Liability should attach not because the quality control process has broken down, but because it is known in advance that it will not detect all defects. It is that certainty, as an objective fact, which requires compensation to the victim, for to deny compensation is to sanction a preventable invasion of the victim's rights. How is the invasion preventable? By closing down the activity. This is not to say that the activity ought to be closed down or that merely potential victims should be entitled to have it enjoined. All that is suggested is that the enterprise is not licensed to seize the rights of individuals without compensation.

Before closing this discussion of products liability, I should point out that the analysis I offer may lead to different results from the American strict liability approach where the defect in question is one of design rather than execution. A defect in execution results from a failure of quality control and is identified as a deviation of the actual product from the design specifications. This is the type of defect we have already dealt with.

Defects of design are more problematic both as to definition and as to their attraction of liability. A relatively easy case is that of the manufacturer who consciously trades off safety against other desirable qualities (performance, ease of use, durability, cost) in the design of the product. This situation is quite similar to the defect in execution situation. The manufacturer is consciously choosing to create a certain degree of risk, which will translate into a certain frequency of accidents, as part of an optimizing process. Thus there is substantial certainty of harm resulting and liability should follow.[41]

More difficult, however, is the defect in design which is not the result of a conscious optimizing process, but simply the consequence of a failure to recognize that the incorporation or omission of some component or feature is capable of giving rise to harm. The analysis which I am proferring would require that such a defect be defined by the foreseeability of the harm. Thus, at first blush, it would seem that a system of strict liability would impose liability for some design defects while the proposed fault system would not.

In fact, I suggest, this question is incapable of being addressed for the notion of a defect in design is incoherent in a strict liability system. That incoherence arises from the fact that the concept of 'defect' necessarily involves an appeal to external standards, standards, moreover, which are known or knowable. But failure to meet standards which are known or knowable, when such standards serve the function of preventing harm, is 'fault' in the sense developed in this paper.

---

[41] This assertion, both with respect to this type of design defect and as to defects of execution, may need to be qualified to the extent that the functional relationship between probability and magnitude of loss which defines reasonable foreseeability reduces the foreseeability of the harm below the reasonable level. This could occur where the statistical design of the quality control system is such that the frequency of defects is small and the magnitude of harm, given a defect, is also small. In such a circumstance, a strict liability system might yield a different result.

## 7. SOME CONTINUING PROBLEMS

I have endeavoured in this paper to set out a moral, rights-based theory of tort law capable of distinguishing tortious from non-tortious behaviour on a principled and consistent basis. In the area of non-intentional, non-consensual conduct causing harm, I have argued that the test of reasonable foreseeability provides the appropriate criterion. Foreseeability has been argued to be a function of the *ex ante* probability of harm occurring as a result of the conduct in question in the given circumstances and of the magnitude of the loss should such harm occur.

I have argued that this reasonable foreseeability standard can provide doctrinal consistency absent in other theories of liability for unintentional harm, and that, properly understood, it can restore the notion of moral fault to areas of tort law from which such considerations seem to have disappeared. I do not pretend, however, to have solved all the theoretical problems of tort law and it is to some of those problem areas to which I now turn.

Part of the argument for the reasonable foreseeability standard involved invocation of the "ought implies can" principle of moral theory. Invocation of that principle, however, raises the long-standing problem in tort theory of objective as opposed to subjective standards. With few exceptions, tort liability for unintentional harm has been imposed for violation of objective standards. The criterion of reasonable foreseeability developed here is an objective standard. But if tort theory is a moral theory, how can it justly impose liability on persons incapable, perhaps by reason of infancy or mental illness, of the foresight on which the standard is premised? A rights-based theory is equally an obligations-based theory. And one cannot have a moral obligation to do that which one cannot do.

The notion that tort law functions to protect legally recognized rights and privileges raises certain questions with respect to the appropriate remedy for tortious conduct. In most cases of unintentional harm, the objectionable conduct is not continuing so that no question of injunctive relief, as opposed to or in addition to damages, arises. In cases of continuing harm, typically of the nuisance variety, the question of remedy may be all important.

If the victim has a right to non-interference in the circumstances, the agent has a correlative obligation not to interfere and an injunction merely enforces that obligation. Yet there are situations where most people would feel that the cost to the agent of an injunction is wholly out of proportion to the damage inflicted on the victim. Suppose that the victim can be fully compensated by an award of damages that is dwarfed by the cost to the agent of closing down or altering the offending activity so as to prevent the nuisance. If the victim is confined to his damages remedy, the court effectively confers on the agent a private, non-statutory power of expropriation. Yet to allow injunctive relief is to impose a penalty on the agent greatly in excess of that required to compensate the victim, a peculiar result for a system of corrective justice.

It may be, however, that the dilemma is falsely posed for, on further analysis, it is arguable that the victim cannot be fully compensated by any monetary award less than the cost to the agent of curtailing or altering his activity so as to prevent the harm. The reason is that the victim enjoys a monopoly on the legal right or interest which the agent's conduct invades. Unless an injunction is granted, the victim is denied the right to exploit his monopoly to its full extent by forcing the agent to purchase the right from him at the highest price which the agent can profitably pay. Seen this way, the problem is structurally similar to eminent domain situations and one may hope that principles developed in that area of law will be of assistance.

The eminent domain analysis may also shed some light on the last problem area to which I will refer, the notion of a "justifiable" invasion of a right. I am thinking here of situations in which the agent, without malice and for the sole purpose of protecting his own "legitimate" interests, acts in a fashion which causes foreseeable harm to the victim. The cases of *Vincent* v. *Lake Erie Transport* and *Cordas* v. *Peerless Transportation Co.*[42] are prototypical.

[42] See footnote 15.

I would suggest that the adjective "justifiable" in this context cannot sensibly refer to the actionability or otherwise of the conduct. Rather it refers to the appropriate remedy. To say that the conduct was justifiable is to say that the condition required to justify a compulsory taking were present. But the taking is a taking, an expropriation of the victim's right, and compensation must be paid. If that analysis is sound, *Vincent* is correctly decided while *Cordas* is wrong.

*Osler, Hoskin & Harcourt*
*Toronto, Canada*

THEODORE M. BENDITT

# LIABILITY FOR FAILING TO RESCUE

ABSTRACT. Should there be civil liability when a person who could easily and without risk rescue another fails to do so? It is argued that the failure to act does not cause the harm that follows, and that the misfeasance/nonfeasance distinction provides no basis for liability. In spite of this, it is maintained that there can sometimes be a duty to rescue, and even a right to be rescued, even in the absence of a voluntary undertaking or an explicit assumption of responsibility.

There are convincing arguments for some sort of legal recognition of a duty to rescue, but these arguments do not support tort liability. Nor is a case for tort liability made with the argument that a growth of tort law in this direction would be compatible with the values most centrally involved in the division between torts and contracts. Furthermore, there is a case against tort liability – namely, that the purpose of tort liability is to compensate, that there are certain sorts of situations in which compensation is apposite, and that failure to rescue does not fit into these categories. Criminal liability is the appropriate way for the law to recognize a duty to rescue.

## 1. LIABILITY FOR OMISSIONS: THE STATE OF THE LAW

Usually a person is legally liable, civilly or criminally, for what he has done or caused, not for what he has failed to do or allowed to happen. If, for example, I drive my car into yours, I am liable to pay you damages. If I am speeding illegally when I do this, I am liable both to pay damages and to a fine. If I assault you, I am liable to pay damages and to a jail sentence. But if I see you staggering down the street dripping blood, and I do not try to get you help, I am not liable either criminally or civilly. If I see you walking into danger and do not even call out a warning, I am not liable. Nor is a doctor required to come forward to aid someone who has collapsed, and in a recent case in Pennsylvania it was held that a person need not submit to a bone marrow transplant for the benefit of his cousin.

The philosophy underlying this legal position is sometimes said to be individualism, the idea that each person is responsible only for himself, except when he stands in a relationship, usually voluntary, with someone else which imposes on him an obligation to act for the benefit of the other. Thus, Judge Flaherty, in the bone marrow transplant case, said that "In our law, there's no duty to rescue someone or save someone's life. ... Our society is based on the right and the sanctity of the individual."[1] Saying that the underlying philosophy is anti-collectivist may (though it may not) just be another way of saying the same thing. For there are some who think (whether they are favorable or unfavorable to the idea) that principles involving the promotion of "the interests of the State as a whole" and "the collective good" support a legally enforceable duty to rescue.[2]

In many other countries the law regarding rescue differs from the prevailing American and Canadian law. In France, Germany, and Holland there are jail sentences as well as fines for failing to aid where there is no risk, and similar laws exist in most European countries. There is one state in the United States that also requires rescue. In 1973 Vermont passed a statute called the "Duty to Aid the Endangered Act," which provides a maximum fine of $100 for willfully violating the following:

> A person who knows that another is exposed to grave physical harm shall, to the extent that the same can be rendered without danger or peril to himself or without interference with important duties owed to others, give reasonable assistance to the exposed person unless that assistance or care is being provided by others.[3]

Despite the prevailing common law rule regarding rescue, however, over the years courts have found bases for imposing liability in a number of cases where harm to one individual was thought to be

---

[1] Quoted by Eric Mack in 'Bad Samaritanism and the Causation of Harm,' *Philosophy & Public Affairs* 9 (1980): 230.

[2] Ibid., p. 234 n. 15.

[3] VT. STAT. ANN. tit. 12, 519 (1973).

connected[4] with another individual's failure to act in such a way as to prevent it.[5] Holmes, in *The Common Law*, describes some of the early moves of this sort: "To charge a man for not acting, you must show that it was his duty to act. ... The ground of liability was that the defendant had started upon the undertaking, so that his negligent omission, which let in the damage, could be connected with his acts as a part of his dealing with the thing."[6] This line of thought, according to Holmes, supported the following cases of criminal and civil liability:

> Although a man has a perfect right to stand by and see his neighbor's property destroyed, or ... to watch his neighbor perish for want of his help, yet if he once intermeddles he no longer has the same freedom. ... The same reasoning applies to civil liability. A carpenter need not go to work upon another man's house at all, but if he accepts the other's confidence and intermeddles, he cannot stop at will and leave the roof open to the weather. ... The immediate occasion of the damage ... may have been a mere omission letting in the operation of natural forces. But if you connect it ... with the previous dealings, you have a course of action and conduct which, taken as a whole, has caused or occasioned the harm.[7]

A harder case, according to Holmes, would be one in which we try to make someone "answerable for not having interfered with the course of nature when he neither set it in motion nor opened the door for it to do harm," as in the case of "a farrier who receives a sick horse and omits proper precautions. ..."[8] Holmes speculates that the basis of liability in such cases may be that defendant's behavior "was probably assumed to have consisted of a combination of acts and neglects, which taken as a whole amounted to an

---

[4] I have deliberately chosen a vague term here, for the character of the connection between failure to act and harm, if there is one, is a central issue with respect to the duty to rescue.

[5] See, generally, William L. Prosser, *Handbook of the Law of Torts*, 4th ed. (Mineola, New York: West Publishing Co., 1971), pp. 338–50.

[6] Oliver Wendell Holmes, *The Common Law* (Boston: Little, Brown and Co., 1963), p. 145.

[7] Ibid., pp. 218, 219.

[8] Ibid., p. 219.

improper dealing with the thing."[9] But he also surmises that a promise made by a defendant may have had something to do with finding a duty to act, and that such cases later came to be dealt with by means of the emerging action of contract.

There are several other sorts of cases in which courts have found grounds for imposing liability for failures to act. Prosser reports that duties have been imposed where there is a relationship between plaintiff and defendant which is economically advantageous to the latter;[10] the thought is that the expected benefit justifies imposing a special duty. A related class of cases involves duties imposed on the owners and occupiers of land, on the theory that the enjoyment of land ownership carries with it certain burdens – especially, to use the land in such a way that others aren't harmed (for example, the attractive nuisance rule), which includes taking steps to prevent even naturally caused harms. Whereas the usual rule regarding natural conditions on one's property (such as falling rocks) that threaten harm to others is that there is no duty to inspect and make safe, the rule in urban areas seems to be changing, so that if, on one's property, there is a tree next to a city street, one must inspect it and take steps to prevent an unsafe tree from injuring passersby.

Of course, there is liability for failure to act when one has voluntarily undertaken to prevent exactly the harm that has occurred. A lifeguard is hired to act when a swimmer is in trouble, and so it has been easy to impose liability. Likewise if someone, though not a professional lifeguard, contracts to look after a child swimming, or merely agrees to do so as a favor. Some of Holmes's remarks, made earlier, apply in these cases of voluntary assumption of a duty.

Another sort of case involves a defendant who has negligently created a risk of harm to another, and then fails to rescue. "For example, if a man rapes a girl who because of grief jumps or falls into a river and drowns, he may be criminally responsible for her

---

[9] Ibid., p. 220.
[10] Prosser, *Handbook*, p. 339.

death if he could have saved her, but refrained from doing so."[11] And Prosser reports that there is civil liability in such cases. When it comes to an innocently caused risk of harm to plaintiff, it has been the rule that no duty to aid arises, but, Prosser says, citing cases from the 1960s, this is changing.[12] For example, it has been held that one who has hit a golf ball errantly has a duty to call out a warning.

One of the most important classes of cases in which there is a duty to aid is that in which there is a special relationship between two individuals. One who operates a ship has a duty to aid someone who has fallen overboard; a school has a duty to a pupil, an employer to an employee, a proprietor to a customer, a jailer to a prisoner, a husband to his wife and vice versa, and a parent to his or her child. In one case a host was held liable to a drunken guest whom he allowed to go out into a snowstorm rather than stay overnight; and in another case a young man who, along with a friend, had been involved in a fight was held liable for failing to get medical attention for the latter.

There is no doubt that the duty to aid has been extended a good bit over the years, and that the "I'm all right, Jack" individualism bravely pronounced by the occasional writer or judge holds sway in only a limited number of cases. Even this remnant, though, is under attack. Numerous articles have been written arguing for some sort of legal recognition of a duty to rescue, and one might get the impression that there must be something behind all of this intellectual effort – a social problem of some magnitude. But that does not seem to be the case, and one writer, at least, has expressed some doubt about it. "It may be that in fact it is not a major social problem except insofar as newspaper sensationalism has made it such. I do not know. If it should be a problem of newspaper sensationalism rather than a problem of increasing public

---

[11] Arnold H. Loewy, *Criminal Law in a Nutshell* (St. Paul: West Pub. Co., 1975), pp. 146–7, citing Jones v. State, 43 NE2d 1017 (Ind., 1942).
[12] Prosser, *Handbook*, p. 342.

callousness or confusion and fear, then we might do better to let the law alone."[13]

Nevertheless, the question of a generalized duty to rescue, one that extends to strangers, is important if only because of its ideological implications. As indicated earlier, some see it as an issue of individualism versus collectivism. Others see it as a mark of the tone of, or the underlying attitude in, society – the difference between a society in which people are called upon to help their fellows, and in which, after a time, they come to do so willingly and not only when coerced, and a society in which people are indifferent to the suffering of others.

## 2. THE QUESTION OF CAUSATION

It is a general principle of law, as well as of morality, that people are liable for the harm they cause. Many writers take the view that one person's failure to rescue can be regarded as a (and perhaps even *the*) cause of harm to another, so that there is no special problem about liability for such failures: it is seen as just another way of causing harm. Accordingly, the threshhold question with respect to such liability is whether non-action, including refraining, omitting, or whatever, can be regarded as causing the harm that befalls someone.

My view of the matter is that in a situation in which one person has not brought about another's predicament but could easily alleviate it and does not do so, the failure to act is not a cause of another person's harm. Despite this, I think and will later argue that there can be a duty to rescue even though one's failure to rescue does not cause the harm that befalls the victim. Nevertheless, since the view that such failures to act are causes of harm has so many partisans, I think it will be useful to look at some of the arguments.

---

[13] Herbert Fingarette, 'Some Moral Aspects of Good Samaritanship,' *The Good Samaritan and the Law*, ed. James M. Ratcliffe (Garden City: Doubleday, 1966), p. 223.

One argument for there being causation in such cases is that the failure to act is blameworthy and *therefore* the cause of the harm that occurs. Another way of putting this is to say that the assertion that a failure to act is a cause is a 'normative' assertion, attributing responsibility to the one who has failed to act.[14] This has been dubbed "the responsibility thesis" in a recent article by Eric Mack, who has given the following rather neat argument against it. Suppose Jones is in trouble in deep water, but I have no duty to try to rescue him (either because there is no general duty to rescue, or if there is, because of the risk to me). Suppose further that Jones yells to me: "If I'm not out in five minutes, I'll pay you to come get me," and I agree. Now on the responsibility thesis, if Jones dies within the five minutes, my failure to rescue is not a cause of his death, whereas if he lasts longer than five minutes and I fail to rescue (we will assume that an attempt to rescue would succeed) and he drowns, then my failure *is* a cause of his death. But, Mack argues, it would appear to the contrary that the causal situation is the same in the two cases. How, after all, could it be the case that my failure to rescue is a condition that is causally necessary to Jones's drowning after, but not prior to, the time when the agreement imposes an obligation on me?[15]

What, then, is the case for causation if we do not accept the responsibility thesis? It is simply that examples can be produced in which it seems plausible to attribute causation to some failure to act, sometimes buttressed by the suggestion that we really cannot explain away the appearance of causation. There are a number of examples that might be appealed to. A guard's failing to lock the door might be said to be the cause of the loss when a burglary occurs. A nurse's forgetting to give the medicine might be said to be the cause of the patient's death. A dog owner's not calling off his attacking dog might be said to be the cause of someone's injury.

---

[14] H. L. A. Hart and A. M. Honoré, *Causation in the Law* (Oxford: Clarendon Press, 1959), pp. 61–62 (italics in original).

[15] Mack, 'Bad Samaritanism,' p. 238. I have altered the example slightly.

> The pharmacist who fails to check his labels does something which, given someone's death, might be cited as its cause. My omitting to turn off the tap is a candidate for citation if the house floods. Likewise my withholding of aid may be the difference between someone's life and death. If F is floundering in the water, and I can help him, but do nothing, my withholding aid is a causal factor in his drowning.[16]

Some of these examples are mistakenly taken to be cases of omissions being causes, for in some of the examples the agent himself has acted in such a way as to create the problem, so that it is not his failing to prevent the harm that is its cause, but his prior action. If we assume that the pharmacist himself dispensed the mislabelled medicine, that it was the dog owner who let his dog loose, and I who opened the tap, then in each case it is an action, not an omission, of the agent that has caused the harm.

But while this reply does defuse some of the examples, it does not do much to blunt the force of the argument, for similar replies are not available in the cases of the guard who didn't lock up and the nurse who forgot to give the medicine. And the other examples can be resuscitated merely by assuming that the person who failed to act was not the same as the one who brought about "the initial phase of a causal process,"[17] or "positively created a dangerous condition which eventually resulted in death."[18]

The theory of causation that proponents see as underlying the examples is usually some variant of Hart and Honoré's account.[19] The idea is that if it is usual for certain things to occur, then on an occasion when the failure of one of those things to occur is

---

[16] John Kleinig, 'Good Samaritanism,' *Philosophy & Public Affairs* 5 (1976): 393. Kleinig regards the failure to aid not as *the cause* of harm, but as *a causal factor* in that "it allows an *already operative* peril (or harm) to continue." (Italics in original.) It is "harm-exacerbating" rather than "harm-initiating."

[17] Elazar Weinryb, 'Omissions and Responsibility,' *Philosophical Quarterly* **30** (1980): 6.

[18] Mack, 'Bad Samaritanism,' p. 242. Tenses have been changed.

[19] Hart and Honoré, *Causation in the Law*, pp. 35–37. See also John Harris, 'The Marxist Conception of Violence,' *Philosophy & Public Affairs* 3 (1974): 204 and passim.

followed by an unusual occurrence, the nonoccurrence of the former can be regarded as the cause of the latter. For example, if Jones regularly waters the flowers, but fails to do so on some occasion, and they die, his failure can be regarded as the cause of their dying. Of course, many other people also did not water them, but since they were not regular waterers of the flowers, their not doing so is not a cause of the flowers' dying.

I see two difficulties with this. First, suppose that it is usually the case that when the flowers look a bit wilted, and the gardener seems to have failed to water them, someone or other takes it upon himself to water them. This time, however, no one waters them, and they die. In a Hart-Honoré explanation of why they died, we would have to give as the cause not only the failure of the gardener to water them, but also the failure of anyone else to water them. But note that there is no particular omission that we are able to cite as cause. This seems to violate the notion that if an event is caused, then there is some identifiable occurrence which is its cause. The gardener's omission is an identifiable occurrence, at least insofar as it is attributable to a designatable individual. The failure of others to water, however, is not attributable to any specifiable individual, and so can hardly be reckoned a cause.

The second difficulty is this: if an attribution of causation is not merely a disguised attribution of moral or legal responsibility (the responsibility thesis), then it will be reasonable to ask why there should be liability for causing harm. Now whatever people take to be the basis for liability where one has caused harm in the usual sense – that is, where there is a "positive" act – it seems likely that a different reason would be given for imposing liability in a situation where an act that is usually performed has been omitted. The point is that saying in both cases that there is causation obscures the fact that there are (or at least may be) different reasons for ascribing responsibility. I rather doubt that the reason people think there should be liability in cases of omissions is that there is causation, and so struggling to bring such cases under the banner of causation only has the effect of begging the question of responsibility.

There is a final comment about negative causation that I think well worth making. Even though we sometimes explain an occurrence by pointing to someone's failure to do something that would have prevented it, it does not follow that the explanation is causal and that the failure to act is a cause of the occurrence. Erick Mack has put it well:

> That Jones' rescue activity would prevent the drowning does not show that, should the drowning occur, the absence of this activity by Jones would be among the factors bringing it about. The power to avert or not is not the power to cause whatever is not averted. The absence of averting activity is not among the conditions [causally] necessary for the non-averted outcome. This is because for it to be true of Jones that he averted Smith's demise, it must be true that conditions sufficient for that harm existed independently of Jones.[20]

The mistake made by negative causation theorists is in regarding Jones's failure to save Smith as one of the causally necessary conditions in Smith's drowning. It is true, of course, that had Jones not failed to rescue, Smith would not have drowned. But what follows is not that Jones's failure to rescue is a causally necessary condition of Smith's drowning, but that it is a necessary condition of Smith's drowning not being prevented. All of the causal antecedents of Smith's drowning were in place independent of Jones, and non-rescue, by Jones or anyone else, is not among them.

## 3. MISFEASANCE AND NONFEASANCE

Some writers think that the issue of legal liability for non-action is dealt with in part by means of the distinction between misfeasance and nonfeasance. These are terms often used in law in making an active/passive, or an action/non-action, distinction. Prosser characterizes it as a distinction between "active misconduct working positive injury to others" and "passive inaction or a failure to take steps to protect them from harm."[21] The basic idea, I take it,

---

20 Mack, 'Bad Samaritanism,' p. 259.
21 Prosser, *Handbook*, pp. 338–39.

is that whereas in nonfeasance a person does not act, in misfeasance a person does act, but improperly, either by doing something he is prohibited from doing, or doing something he is permitted to do, but negligently. The issue of a duty to rescue, expressed in these terms, is whether there can be legal liability for nonfeasance.

What interests us here is that the division between liability and nonliability is going to depend on how the misfeasance/nonfeasance distinction is made, and there are ways of characterizing it that put certain cases of nondoing into the misfeasance category, and so make them subject to liability. Professor Ernest Weinrib, in a recent article, suggests that while my failing to toss you an easily available rope when you are drowning is nonfeasance, my failing to apply my brakes in time to avoid driving my car onto your foot is not.[22] In each case there is a failure to act, and in each case I am a "but-for" cause of harm (but for my failure to act, you would not have been harmed). But in the second case I have played a part in the creation of the risk to you; had I not put you in that position, you would not be in need of my positive act of applying the brakes. Such a case is only "pseudo-nonfeasance"; it is really misfeasance. Notice, Weinrib says, that it is not my fault in creating the risk that makes it misfeasance, for suppose I drove my car onto your foot entirely without fault, and now the car needs to be moved off your foot. My failing to do so is not nonfeasance – it is pseudo-nonfeasance, because I have (albeit faultlessly) "participated in" the creation of the risk. As a result, while I am not liable for the damage between the time I drove onto your foot and the time when I could have removed the car from it, I am liable for damage incurred thereafter, should I fail to remove it.

I am not concerned at this point with Weinrib's conclusions about liability in the foregoing cases. My problem is that I am not sure I see the basis for categorizing the car-driven-on-the-foot cases as misfeasance. This is especially troublesome because Weinrib nowhere explains why merely participating in the creating of a

---

22 Ernest Weinrib, 'The Case for a Duty to Rescue,' *Yale Law Journal* **90**, (1980): 247–93, especially 251–58.

risk results in liability whereas merely failing to help doesn't, yet the consequence of calling the former a misfeasance and the latter a nonfeasance is exactly that.

Professor Weinrib's approach is reminiscent of Holmes, in the passages quoted earlier in this article. A man, Holmes says, has a right to stand by and watch his neighbor die, "yet if he once intermeddles he no longer has the same freedom." And when a carpenter fails to close the hole in the roof, "the immediate occasion of the damage ... may have been a mere omission. ... But if you connect it ... with the previous dealings, you have a course of action and conduct which, taken as a whole, has caused or occasioned the harm." Thus, Holmes, too, can be taken to be treating certain nondoings as pseudo-nonfeasances. For both Holmes and Professor Weinrib, once you've gotten involved (either, in Holmes's case, by undertaking some task, or, in Professor Weinrib's, by creating a risk of harm to someone) and then fail to take certain further steps, you are not merely not acting – rather, you are acting, but improperly.

The trouble with this sort of extension of the notion of misfeasance is that it does not illuminate, for to decide that something is a misfeasance rather than a nonfeasance is already to have drawn a conclusion about liability. How is it misfeasance for me to fail to remove my car from your foot, but nonfeasance for Jones, a bystander, so to fail, unless its being my car, or being driven by me, imposes a duty on me? For that is the only difference between Jones and me. And in the case of the carpenter, think of anything whatsoever that the carpenter does not do, the doing of which would have been a benefit to the owner of the building. Is his failure a misfeasance? Obviously we cannot tell until we know whether it is something the carpenter is supposed to do. In each case, to categorize as a misfeasance is to draw a conclusion. Calling the failure to remove the car a misfeasance does not explain why an innocent creator of a risk has a duty to alleviate that others do not have, nor does calling the failure of a carpenter to do certain things a misfeasance explain why those things are to be done.

The law does, however, impose civil liability in the sorts of cases

Holmes and Professor Weinrib describe – and rightly so, as they see it. But inasmuch as the category of misfeasance merely records but does not explain this, we are still in need of an explanation of why civil liability is appropriate.

## 4. MORAL DUTY TO RESCUE; RIGHT TO BE RESCUED

A young child is in trouble in a few feet of water, and you could easily rescue it with only a bit of inconvenience to yourself. Or, in Judith Thomson's striking example, she is sick unto death and only the cool hand of Henry Fonda on her fevered brow will save her. But fortunately Henry Fonda is in the room, and only needs to take a few steps to save her.[23] Do you or Henry Fonda have any moral duties?

Everyone would agree that it would be a good thing for you and for Henry Fonda to take the appropriate steps, and that each would be justly subject to censure for failing to do so. But some (including Thomson) would insist that neither of you have to offer aid, that both of you would have a right (be at liberty) not to aid. It is the "have to" that is in issue. For most people, including most moralists, there is a distinction between what a person must, morally speaking, do, and what it would be good for a person to do but which he doesn't have to do. This is often called a distinction between duty and supererogation – between what duty requires and what is "above and beyond" duty. For those who accept this distinction, the question is where exactly is the line to be drawn between what a person has to do and what is supererogatory.

There are some who say that there are only two situations in which a person must, morally speaking, do something – first, where one has voluntarily undertaken to do something, as by promising, and second, where one would be harming others unless one did (or refrained from doing) something. But in the absence of a voluntary undertaking it is, on this view, never required that

[23] Judith Thomson, 'A Defense of Abortion,' *Philosophy & Public Affairs* 1 (1971): 61.

one do something for the benefit of another. The moral ideal that most often underlies such views involves a conception of the self and human freedom, according to which, if others can demand certain behavior from us apart from our own undertakings, we are not fully free beings, and some would go so far as to say that others are part owners of us. Conceptions of human freedom have, to be sure, been used to reach just the opposite conclusion; but it is not to our purpose to pursue these lines of thought.

That this moral point of view is inadequate can easily be seen by considering special relationships, such as the relationships between parent and child, spouses, lovers, close friends, and others. Virtually everyone, I would expect, thinks that if your own child is drowning, you are morally required to try to rescue it. People might disagree about how much risk you are required to expose yourself to, so we'll suppose that the risk is almost nil. Furthermore, it seems to me that virtually everyone thinks that in rescuing the child you are not merely doing a particularly good thing that you don't have to do, but rather that you are required to do it. If there is someone who denies this, I cannot prove it, and this argument is not for him or her; but I am going to regard it as a datum.

Now someone, especially a partisan of the moral conception outlined above, might say that the reason one is morally required to try to save one's own child is that one is responsible for the child, and that one is responsible because one has assumed or taken responsibility for it. But, as Thomson has shown us, the notion of taking responsibility for another is tricky.[24] Certainly a person is responsible for someone if he explicitly assumes responsibility – but there are problems even here. If you are going out for the evening, and I say "I'll take care of your child," I have assumed responsibility. So far so good. I might assume only partial responsibility – I might say "but I won't be responsible for his doing his homework." Again, so far so good. I might even try to limit my responsibility further: "I'll give him dinner and

[24] Ibid., pp. 57–59, 64–65.

get him to bed on time, but if he hurts himself it's none of my affair." A purist about commitments might go along with this; others will have doubts. But everyone must be clear that one cannot do this with respect to one's own child. One cannot, on conceiving or having a child or at any other time, say "I'll feed and house this child, but will do nothing to insure its safety; if it is drowning, I assume no responsibility for doing anything about it." So if one is morally required to save his own child, it is not on account of an explicit assumption of responsibility. What voluntary undertaking, then, does the moral requirement rest on? One might be tempted to say that there are certain obligations that are part and parcel of the parent-child relationship, and that one undertakes these obligations by voluntarily entering into the relationship. But clearly this won't get us far, for our very question is just how such obligations get built in. Does the friend-friend relationship, or the relationship of mere acquaintances, carry with it an obligation to rescue, or an obligation to lend money, or to tell a lie when asked? The answers to these questions need the sort of moral appraisal that the voluntary undertaking view just can't provide.

The cases just mentioned are indeed problematic; the parent-child example we have been considering is not. Suppose now that a child to whom you have no special relationship is drowning, and you could save it at no risk to yourself. The foregoing argument shows that you cannot avoid a moral requirement to rescue merely by saying that haven't voluntarily assumed any responsibility for the child. So how is one to argue that where there is a special relationship there is a moral requirement, but absent such a relationship there is no requirement at all? My own sense of these things is that special relationships do make a moral difference, but not the difference between the presence and absence of a moral requirement. You may be required to take greater risks to save your own child, and if both your child and another child are drowning, you may be required to save yours first, and even to prefer yours if a choice must be made, but at least in the non-risk case you are morally required to rescue any child, absent circumstances that make a moral difference.

Indeed, I would also say that the child in the example has a right to be saved. I do not, however, maintain this on the ground that, as a matter of logic, where there is a requirement there is a corresponding right, for there are obligations, such as the obligation to stop at a red light, without corresponding rights.[25] Nor is it a matter of there being a determinate individual who is the object of the moral requirement, for that does not yet show that the duty is owed to that individual, such that the latter can claim rescue as his due. The case for there being a right is simply that to have a right is to be justified in insisting that someone behave in a certain way (either for one's benefit, or at one's behest), and that the same considerations that impose a requirement on you to save the child also justify the child in insisting on it.[26]

## 5. LEGAL RECOGNITION OF DUTY TO RESCUE

Even among those who agree that there is sometimes a moral requirement to rescue, some think it is "merely" a moral duty, the performance or non-performance of which is up to the individual, and that it is therefore not a matter that the law should be concerned with. Some people think that even though there is a moral duty, they should not be forced to fulfill it; it should be left up to them, at most under the pressure of informal moral sanctions, whether to conform to these moral demands. So, since we accept the presumption that legal coercion is not to be imposed unless an adequate justification is given, we must examine the case for legal recognition of the duty to rescue. And as we have just seen, it is not enough merely to show that there is sometimes

[25] See Joel Feinberg, 'Duties, Rights, and Claims,' *American Philosophical Quarterly* 3 (1966): 141–42.

[26] There can be cases where, though someone is required to act for your benefit, you are not justified in insisting on it. The idea of a right presented here is discussed at greater length in my book *Rights* (Totowa, New Jersey: Rowman and Littlefield, 1982.)

a moral requirement, for it is possible to accept this and still to deny that it should be enforced in any way.

In what way might the law recognize duties to rescue? The law could recognize the duty merely by encouraging rescue in a variety of ways – for example, by providing for compensation of rescuers for the costs and damages incurred in rescuing or attempting to rescue. Compensation could be paid by the public, or suits could be permitted to recover costs and damages from persons rescued, or sought to be rescued, or from their estates. Rescue could also be encouraged by rewarding those who attempt rescues. But there are also more direct ways of encouraging rescue. Criminal penalties could be imposed for failing to try to rescue in certain sorts of circumstances, or those failing to attempt rescues could be held liable to pay victims for the injuries (and perhaps other losses) attributable (in ways needing specification) to the failure to rescue.

There are two fairly familiar lines of argument for some sort of legal recognition of the duty to rescue, and in particular for requiring and not merely encouraging rescue. (We will not, at this point, worry about whether the requirement comes as part of tort law or criminal law, or both.) One is the utilitarian argument. In the classical version of the argument the claim is that despite the costs and other negative consequences of enforcing a duty to rescue, the greatest good overall would be promoted by some sort of legal requirement. One reply that is often made to this argument is that here, as elsewhere, utilitarianism proves too much, for by the same argument the enforcement of a great deal more beneficence would be justified. So a utilitarian must either accept the result that the law should enforce not only rescue but other beneficence as well, or else show that it is not the case that he is committed to forms of beneficence that go beyond fairly easy rescue. It seems likely that a utilitarian can make a reasonably good showing for his position, though one is always uneasy with arguments that rely on assessments of the long term consequences of adopting this or that rule and the reactions of a large number of people to them; there are just too many imponderables involved. On the other hand, if the utilitarian has at least a plausible case, some social and legal experimentation may be indicated, with revisions to be made if it does not work out as expected.

Another argument for a legal requirement of recue is that the law should enforce the shared morality of the community, including the widely held opinion that people should help others when they can, and especially when in a position to effect an easy rescue. Very often, of course, people resist appeals to the shared morality, which in recent debates have been offered in support of restrictions on prostitution, homosexuality, drug use, pornography, and the like – to so-called victimless crimes. Those who resist the appeal to widely shared moral convictions regarding these matters are very much concerned about individual liberty. Strangely, though, it seems that it is some of the same people who argue the individual liberty side with respect to pornography, etc., who also think the shared morality on rescue argues for some sort of legal requirement. Are these people being inconsistent? Probably not. For partisans of greater indivual liberty are not, usually, concerned with liberty itself, but largely with its contribution to people's lives.[27] Liberty promotes spontaneity, experimentation with ways of living one's life, and the like; so laws restricting what people can read, modes of sexuality, modes of consciousness, and other things that people regard as central to the character and quality of their lives are not to be readily accepted. But laws enforcing rescue, though they limit liberty, do not have consequences of this sort. Though the consequences of these laws may be serious for the occasional individual who is harmed trying to do his legal duty, on the whole the adverse consequences of enforced rescue for the character of people's lives would be quite minimal. So, assuming that there are advantages to enforcing the shared morality regarding rescue,[28] there is no serious problem about limiting liberty.

---

[27] I am here representing the views of those who value liberty for the sorts of reasons that John Stuart Mill recognized, and not Kantian reasons.

[28] See A. M. Honoré, 'Law, Morals, and Rescue,' in *The Good Samaritan and the Law*, ed. Ratcliffe, pp. 239, 240.

The foregoing arguments have some plausibility, and there is yet another which seems to me to have some plausibility. Earlier it was argued that sometimes there is not only a duty to rescue, but also a right to be rescued. It is usually taken to be part of the business of law to protect rights. Not all rights, however, are entitled to legal protection, for some are too trivial to call for that sort of apparatus and are best left to informal moral sanctions. But where important interests such as life and health are at stake, there are two grounds for legal intervention. First, it is obvious that important interests like these are already great concerns of the law; some would say that preventing harm is the most justified endeavor to which coercive law can be put. Second, independently of law, people quite justifiably protect their own rights, and it is another pre-eminently justified job of law to supplant the destructive attempts of individuals to protect their own rights and of their friends and relatives to vindicate them when they are violated.

## 6. HOW SHALL THE DUTY TO RESCUE BE RECOGNIZED?

It is often suggested that a person who fails in his legal duty to rescue (when the attempt to rescue would have succeeded) should have to compensate the victim for the injuries that would not have been incurred had the rescue been made. There are a number of practical difficulties with this idea, a couple of which will be mentioned here, but only briefly, for it is not my aim to discuss these problems.[29] One problem concerns the existence of numerous potential rescuers. One such person might claim that he can't be held liable because others also failed to rescue. This has been answered by suggesting that multiple non-rescuers be treated as joint tortfeasors are treated – plaintiff is entitled to one award, which he can get from any of the tortfeasors, who in turn is entitled to contribution from the others. But what should be done when one person has negligently created a risk of danger to another (the

---

[29] For some additional problems, see Anthony D'Amato, 'The "Bad Samaritan" Paradigm,' *Northwestern University Law Review* 70 (1975): 802–4.

victim) and a third person fails in his duty to rescue? Should all who are negligent with respect of the victim's injuries be treated as joint tortfeasors? But there may well be degrees of negligence involved. Perhaps the matter could be left to a jury, though the nature of the instructions to be given the jury seems to resurrect the problem. In the end it is unlikely that there are wholly satisfactory solutions to such problems, though if the courts were to be thrown this ball they would probably handle it tolerably well.

But now we get to the important question: What is the case for throwing this ball – tort liability for failure to rescue – to the courts? Classical utilitarian arguments do not make much of a case. The threat of having to compensate might lead some to rescue who would otherwise not do so. But compensation is not needed for this, for a sufficiently large fine will be just as effective. The case for compensation is no better on the enforcement-of-morals argument, for though there is a prevailing moral conviction in favor of a duty to rescue, there does not seem to be the same conviction that one who fails to rescue owes anything to the victim. The prevailing view seems to be that it is an attempt to rescue that is due – nothing less, but nothing more. We are outraged if a person stands by when he could help someone else at no risk to himself, but we are not outraged by the idea of his not compensating the victim. Notice, by way of contrast, that when one person intentionally or negligently harms another (by a "positive") act, we *are* outraged by a denial of any obligation to compensate. There are, to be sure, cases in which a failure to act does seem to call for compensation – for example, if a guard employed by a security firm fails to lock a clien't door, and there is a burglary. But it is interesting to observe that this is one of those cases which test distinctions between doings and nondoings – recall Holmes's suggestion that we are here dealing with a course of conduct, such that the failure to lock the door is a misfeasance rather than a nonfeasance. Furthermore, what is involved here is an explicit undertaking; locking doors is one of the things guards are supposed to do, and this is the basis of the demand for compensation.

The third argument to be considered for tort liability for failing to rescue arises in the course of a dialectic regarding the importance of liberty and the boundary between contract and tort. Richard Epstein has maintained that "the first task of the law of torts is to define the boundaries of individual liberty."[30] But, Epstein maintains, it is not possible, either in principle or in practice, to permit the recovery of damages for failure to rescue without compromising liberty. It is not possible in principle because there are other situations in which a legal duty backed up by tort liability would be equally supportable, such as giving money to charities serving the sick and needy, or requiring a surgeon to fly across the country to perform an operation. It is not possible in practice because any statement of the duty will have a reasonableness standard built into it, thus leaving it to the trier of fact to decide whether a defendant's behavior was reasonable and thereby undermining individual liberty, since people will not know in advance what they may and may not do. Once all of this is accepted, Epstein fears,

> it will no longer be possible to delineate the sphere of activities in which contracts (or charity) will be required in order to procure desired benefits and the sphere of activity in which those benefits can be procured as of right. Where tests of "reasonableness" – stated with such confidence, and applied with such difficulty – dominate the law of tort, it becomes impossible to tell where liberty ends and obligation begins; where contract ends and torts begins. In each case it will be possible for some judge or jury to decide that there was something else which the defendant should have done. ...[31]

Ernest Weinrib has recently answered Epstein in the following way: Epstein may be correct, Weinrib says, with respect to beneficence that goes beyond rescue in the narrowly circumscribed

---

[30] Richard A. Epstein, 'A Theory of Strict Liability,' *Journal of Legal Studies* **11** (1973): 203.

[31] Ibid., p. 199. Epstein is arguing not only against tort liability for failures to rescue, but against any tort liability that is not based on a strict notion of causation. Failing to rescue is, according to Epstein, just one case, though a stark one, where a defendant should not be held liable inasmuch as he hasn't caused any harm.

cases where plaintiff faces an emergency and there is no risk to defendant. But within this class of cases Epstein is not correct, and it is the underlying values of the common law itself which bring this out. There are certain sorts of situations, the argument goes, in which "contract values" are present – that is, where it is appropriate for, and the law wants to encourage, people to make private arrangements and engage in market transactions. But where such contract values are not present, coercion (i.e., tort liability) is appropriate. Thus, with respect to a police officer who was held liable for failing to warn drivers of a danger that he himself had not created, Weinrib says

> the court's holding required the policeman to confer a benefit on other drivers without permitting him to bargain for compensation. Because society's interest in upholding freedom of contract if present at all, is very attenuated, however, this coercion and the concomitant deprivation of the opportunity to contract are not serious.[32]

And in criticizing Bohlen's approach to the problem of the duty that family members owe each other, Weinrib says

> the contract-values analysis provides a much better justification for the family category. The common law has traditionally held that absent express evidence of intention to the contrary, family agreements are outside the realm of contract. ... The law thus deems some family relations never appropriate for market regulation. ...[33]

The point, Weinrib says, can be extended to rescue:

> The thread that runs through the apparently diverse cases of police officer and family member is the law's refusal to recognize persons in those roles as market agents and its consequent tolerance for the deprivation of liberty involved in coering them to act. When an endangered stranger can be rescued with ease, elements of the same pattern are present. If a potential rescuer struck a bargain with a drowning person before tossing him a rope, the agreement reached would be unenforceable as unconscionable or made under duress. ... [Where there is an] emergency, there are no contract values to be vindicated by the absence of a tort duty. It therefore seems that the imposi-

---

[32] Weinrib, 'Case for a Duty to Rescue,' p. 269.
[33] Ibid., p. 271.

tion of a duty to effect an easy rescue in an emergency would form a coherent part of a growing pattern in those doctrines that most fully embody the common law's notion of individual liberty.[34]

Now I agree that if the question is whether liberty in the form of market transactions is a value to be protected in rescue cases, the answer is that it is not. But this constitutes an argument for tort liability (though perhaps not exactly the argument Professor Weinrib intends) only if rescue must either be subject to tort duty or else relegated to the market. This is a false dichotomy, however, for it is surely possible neither to permit contracts nor to impose tort duty. Indeed, this is precisely what the position of the law has been in some of the cases Weinrib discusses as lacking contract values. The United States Supreme Court once held unenforceable a contract which rescuers extracted from some marooned whalers in the Arctic – but at the same time the law did not recognize any tort duty to rescue. (Were there such a duty, the contract would have failed for lack of consideration.)

However, the claim may simply be that tort liability for failure to rescue in certain cases is consistent with the values traditionally underlying tort and contract law and explaining the division between them. Perhaps this is so. But an argument is still needed to show why the absence of contract values argues for coherence with the coercion involved in tort liability, rather than coherence with cases in which neither a contract nor tort liability are recognized.

## 7. THE BASES OF COMPENSATION

So far we have looked at three arguments for tort liability for failing to rescue, and none have proven satisfactory. However beyond merely showing that these arguments are deficient, it seems to me that a more positive case can be made against providing for compensation for failures to rescue.

[34] Ibid., pp. 271–72.

Compensation seems to be called for in two classes of cases. First, compensation can be due as a return, a paying back, a restoration. This itself divides into two sorts of cases. One is the case in which there is unjust enrichment. The other is when something is owed in the nature of a reparation for causing a loss or preventing a gain. With regard to this second group of cases, two comments are in order. First, from the standpoint of the notion of compensation, it is not necessary that there be any sort of guilt involved in the causation of harm. Even one who innocently causes harm may be called upon to compensate – for example, when a golfer strikes another with a misdirected ball. The point here is not that there must be compensation for innocently caused harm (there may be reasons not to impose liability in such cases); it is only that there is something to compensate – i.e., the idea of compensation at least makes sense in such cases. The second comment is that compensation would make sense in cases where something that one owns, or is otherwise in charge of, causes damage that could have been prevented. Here I have in mind Professor Weinrib's car-on-the-foot case.[35] Compensation would be apposite for failing to remove the car not because I have participated in the creation of the risk, but because it is my car, and ownership or proper operation of a car includes taking reasonable steps to prevent its harming others, even if one is innocent with respect to the initiation of the harm-threatening situation. Similarly, if my boat is torn loose from its moorings and threatens your property, I must prevent its damaging your property if I can; ownership of property includes responsibility for what it does.

The common element in the two subclasses identified above – unjust enrichment and reparation – is that plaintiff has lost something he had (or at least a gain he should have had), and the point is to return him to the position he originally was in (or should have been in). The other class of cases in which compensation is called for is quite different, having to do with the idea of making good on a guarantee. As noted at the beginning of this article,

---

[35] See text following note 22.

courts have held that an employer can be liable for failing to rescue an employee, proprietors have been held liable to customers, a jailer to his prisoner, the operator of a vessel to one who has fallen overboard, and a host to his dinner guest. In other cases, a hospital has been held to have an obligation to its patients, a school toward its pupils, and a city has been held to owe protection to a witness who has been threatened in a criminal case. Obligations of spouses, and of parent and child, also fall within this group.

Courts and commentators have grouped these cases under the heading "special relationship." This category seems to me to be too broad, however, for there is no reason to think, at least initially, that every relationship, even every special relationship, is one in which one party, if not both, should be liable as a result of failing to help the other. Furthermore, merely identifying the category of special relationsips does not explain why there should be liability for failures to aid when such relationships exist.

What I suggest is that for some relationships and for some matters involving these relationships, it is plausible to regard one individual as a partial guarantor of another's welfare or well-being, such that if he fails to (at least try to) rescue he must make the victim whole. As a beginning, I suggest that one person is a guarantor of the welfare or well-being of another only when (1) there is a relationship established prior to the event in question, which is either (a) voluntary, or (b) familial, or (c) involves some professional or official capacity, and (2) the event in question is connected with[36] the relationship.

Some comments concerning the notion of a guarantee are in order here. The notion of a guarantee, if it is apposite, illuminates since it promises to make sense of the idea that compensation is owed, whereas the broader notion of a special relationship does not. But we must still face the question of what the underpinning

---

[36] This is, of course, a vague notion, and I make no attempt to spell it out. It is the sort of thing that is well left to jury determinations and case by case development.

of the guarantee is – otherwise we will only have provided a label for a group of situations which on other grounds we have determined to call for redress. The question is: when will it be plausible to regard one person, in the conditions listed above, as having become a guarantor of the welfare or well-being of another?

In some of the relationships we are considering there is an element of control by one individual over another or over the situation. A jailer, for example, has control over his prisoner, and a boat's captain has control over the boat. In other cases, and even in the same ones, there may be an element of expertise possessed by one individual – as, in the case of a hospital, or a boat's captain, or fellow mountain climbers. In yet other cases – especially where family members are involved – there is a long-term commitment to another's welfare and well-being. In special relationships where any of these – control, expertise, long-term commitment – are present, people rely on these things and expect the other party to the relationship to come forward on their behalf. This is not, however, to be taken as a reliance theory in the sense that there is liability *because* there is reliance, or even justified reliance. Rather, the point is simply that in these cases people naturally look to the other party to the relationship; they expect it, and regard it as something that they can rightly call upon.

The claim that in such cases one person is a partial guarantor of the welfare or well-being of another means simply that in the context of certain relationships the expectations described above are justified. And the justification, it seems to me, rests on this: where, in human relationships, one has status or position vis-a-vis another, then with respect to the matters that form the basis of that status or position, one has special responsibilities. In particular, one is committed to "living up to" that status or responsibility, which may include coming forward for the benefit of others with respect to certain eventualities arising out of the relationship.

The rationale for civil liability outlined here covers many of the sorts of cases in which courts have recently imposed such liability. The following case, however, is one that I find troublesome. The case of *Farwell* v. *Keaton*[37] involved two young men, Siegrist and Farwell, who, as a result of attempting to engage two girls in conversation on the street, were chased by the girls' friends. Siegrist escaped, but Farwell was severely beaten. Siegrist applied ice to Farwell's head, and the two then drove around to a number of drive-in restaurants. Farwell went to sleep in the back of the car. Later on, Siegrist, unable to rouse Farwell, left the car, with Farwell in it, at the home of Farwell's grandparents. The grandparents discovered him the next day and took him to this hospital, where he died. Farwell's grandparents sued for damages, and were successful. In the course of its opinion the court said: "Farwell and Siegrist were companions on a social venture. Implicit in such a common undertaking is the understanding that one will render assistance to the other when he is in peril if he can do so without endangering himself."[38] I doubt, however, that the rationale for compensation outlined previously reaches this case. For I do not see that in friendship there is the control or expertise that is requisite to creating status or position of one person vis-a-vis another, and thus I do not see a case for a guarantee. This does not mean, however, that there could never be a partial guarantee where the relationship involved friendship. Each case must be examined and a judgment made, and it may be that one has to push a bit (maybe too much) to find a basis for requiring compensation. However that may be, it seems to me that absent the sort of guarantee discussed here, there is no ground for requiring compensation. For compensation, if not in the nature of a return, a paying back, is in the nature of making good on a guarantee. So while I believe that a stranger can have a duty to rescue me in some circumstances, and even that I may have a right to his rescuing me, it does not seem to me that the stranger's duty to rescue fits either of these indicia of compensability.

But this does not mean that the law should be silent with respect to the duty to rescue. There is a case, as we have seen, for legal

---

[37] Farwell v. Keaton, 396 Mich 281, 240 N.W.2d 217, 222 (1975).
[38] 240 N.W.2d at 222.

recognition of this duty, and though compensation is inappropriate, criminal liability is not. A statute of the Vermont type, set out at the beginning of this article, recognizes the duty to rescue, and the right to be rescued, in a clear and straightforward way. The penalty provided in the Vermont statute is certainly minimal, and may be too small to make a sufficient difference in people's behavior. I do not speculate here as to what the penalty should be, though at the least stronger penalties would be appropriate where a failure to rescue is motivated by actual malice.[39]

*University of Alabama in Birmingham*

---

[39] For a different sort of argument in favor of criminal but not civil liability, based on the application of a role reversal criterion, see D'Amato, 'The "Bad Samaritan" Paradigm,' pp. 804–9 and 810–12.

S. C. COVAL AND J. C. SMITH

# RIGHTS, GOALS, AND HARD CASES

ABSTRACT. Rights have two properties which *prima facie* appear to be inconsistent. The first is that they are conditional in the sense that on some occasions it is always justifiable for someone to act in a way which appears to be inconsistent with someone else's rights, such as when the defence of necessity applies. The second is that rights are indefeasible in the sense that they are not subject to being defeated or outweighed by utilitarian or policy considerations. If we view rules and the rights which they establish as being subject to a *ceteris paribus* clause, the form of which generates out the exceptions, the conditionality of rights becomes reconcilable with their non-defeasibility. Such a view of rules and rights would entail that the goals of the law and their orderings be considered as a part of the law. When so viewed, propositions about goals and their orderings become legitimate premises for legal reasoning, furnishing solutions to hard cases in the law of torts, without resort to balancing of interests or judicial discretion.

## 1.

The function of the law of torts is the enforcement of rights through awards of compensation for damages suffered as the result of another person's breach of the duty which is the correlative of the right. All rights which a person has in regard to any of his interests, except those relating to contractual rights, fall within the ambit of torts. We know of no theoretical reason why even wrongs which constitute only a breach of a contractual duty should be excluded from torts. The reasons are likely to be of a practical nature.

Since tort law deals exclusively with rights and duties, and nearly all the various kinds of rights fall within the parameters of the law of torts, the concept of a right and its function in the legal decision process is of great significance to tort law. Theoretical problems or disputes relating to the concept of a right will be therefore particularly relevant to the law of torts, and in turn, problems raised in the context of tort law, and the methods by which they can be resolved, will be of special interest to rights theorists. We propose to take an important theoretical issue regarding the properties of rights, and propose a solution which, if viable, would have important implications for how hard cases are decided in the law of torts. The implications of the solution would be that the goals of the law and their orderings are to be considered as a part of the law, and propositions concerning their ordering and existence can be legitimate premises in legal reasoning, particularly in regard to hard cases. If this solution is acceptable, the goals or values protected by the law of torts become a matter of great importance in understanding and applying the law of torts.

We assume that a breach of a plaintiff's rights is a necessary condition for a remedy through a civil cause of action. We also assume that, if the rights-obligation language of traditional judge-made law is to be taken seriously, courts have no power to create rights by judicial fiat. The defendant's wrongful act must be a breach of a duty owed to the plaintiff by the defendant not to commit the act.[1] In theory at least, such duties are not to be created retroactively. The duty and its correlative right must be in existence at the time of the act complained of before a right to a remedy arises. The Court is not entitled to create the right and then find liability for its breach before the right even could be said to exist. It does not follow from this that courts have no power to create new causes of action. It means only that new causes of action must be derived from existing legal principles. Thus Mr. Justice Wright, in *Wilkinson* v. *Downton*,[2] deduced the new tort of intentionally causing nervous shock, from the principle that an intentional causing of physical harm without lawful justification constitutes grounds for a civil cause of action.

If all the above is true, we may have hard cases, but we cannot

---

[1] For a discussion of the rationale of compensation and the difference in the theoretical foundations of compensation and punishment see George Fletcher, 'Punishment and Compensation,' *Creighton Law Review* 14 (1981): 691.

[2] [1897] 2 Q.B. 57 at p. 58.

have impossible cases. While we might not need to go as far as Dworkin in assuming there is one and only one right answer,[3] we must at least assume that of any two postulated alternative answers leading to different legal results, one must always be a better answer than the other. Dworkin correctly saw that strong judicial discretion is inconsistent with a theory of rights.[4]

Equally, if the language of rights is to be taken seriously, two propositions about rights must be accepted. The first is that rights are not absolute, and the second is that rights are indefeasible. It is evident that rights are not absolute from the fact that on some occasions it is always justifiable to act in a way which is inconsistent with someone's rights, such as when acting in self-defence or the defence of others, or when two rights come into conflict and both cannot be served in a particular situation, such as when the right of freedom of speech comes into conflict with national safety and curbs must be placed on the free flow of information in order to protect state security.

It is evident from the very nature of rights themselves that rights are not defeasible. That is, rights are not subject to being defeated by utilitarian considerations, or outweighed by policies, goals or the interest of other persons. It is the indefeasibility of rights, in that rights cannot be outweighed by other considerations, that accounts for the incompatibility of rights theories with utilitarianism or various balancing of interests doctrines of legal decision-making. Equally it is the indefeasibility of rights which makes rights theory incompatible with judicial discretion.

One recurring problem in rights theories, however, is to reconcile the conditional nature of rights with their indefeasibility.[5] Various philosophical attempts have been made, but they invariably turn

---

[3] Ronald Dworkin, *Taking Rights Seriously* (Cambridge: Mass.: Harvard University Press 1977).

[4] Ronald Dworkin, *Taking Rights Seriously*, pp. 31–39 and 68–71.

[5] This problem is discussed, for example, (although not in the terms used in this paper) by *George Fletcher, 'The Right to Life,' Georgia Law Review* 13 (1979): 1371, and in Judith J. Thomson, 'Some Rumination on Rights,' *Arizona Law Review* 19 (1977): 45.

out to be inconsistent with the indefeasibility of rights. We cannot say that in certain circumstances one right overrides another right, as this would make the second right defeasible. A doctrine of prima facie rights is philosophically unsatisfactory. Something is either a right or it is not. We can only say that in certain circumstances what is purported to be a right is in fact not a right. A doctrine of forfeiture of rights is unsatisfactory because the forfeiture of a right is a form of defeasibility, and it applies only to a limited set of cases, such as the case of causing injury to an attacker in self-defence.

Neither can there be such a thing as a justifiable infringement or violation of a legal right if rights are not defeasible. If an act or inaction is justified, it cannot be in breach of a right. Rights are either rights to do or not do, or rights that something is to be done, or something is not to be done. Rights to do or not do entail obligations of noninterference. If an act of interference is justified, then there can be no obligation to refrain from doing it. The right to do is not protected against such an act; consequently, the act does not constitute a breach of the right. Equally if an act is justified, there can be no obligation to not do it, and thus there can be no correlative right that it not be done. Therefore the act cannot be in breach of a right that it not be done. A justified killing in self-defence would not constitute either a violation or a breach of a right to life, as a right to life, like all rights, is not absolute.

The thesis that rights are conditional entails that no matter how basic, important, or fundamental a right is, particular circumstances can always arise that may fall within the general description of the right, and yet the right cannot be said to exist. The thesis of the nondefeasibility of rights entails that if the plaintiff claims he has a right that the defendant not do act *C* under a particular set of circumstances, and the defendant claims that he has the right to do *C* under those circumstances, and the court holds for the plaintiff and the decision is upheld on final appeal, not only is it the case that the defendant does not have the right to do *C* under those circumstances, but it must be the case that he did not have the right to do *C* at the time he did it.

Rights are indefeasible in the way in which truth may be said to be indefeasible. If we discover that a proposition is true when we believed it to be false, we say that it was always true, and when we discover a proposition to be false which we had believed to be true, we hold that is was always false. The same drive towards objectivity through indefeasibility seems to be present in the concept of rights.

There is one way in which the indefeasibility of rights can be reconciled with their conditionality. That way is to qualify the general description of the right so that the circumstances when the right does not exist do not fall within the parameters of the description of the right. One method of qualifying the general description would be to define the right in such a way so that all the circumstances when the right does not exist are listed. These circumstances, however, are so varied and numerous that they often would not be thought of until they happen, so one could never get workable and complete definitions. If, however, one could describe the exception-generating mechanism, a catalogue of exceptions would not be necessary.

An adequate theory of rights requires that conflicting claims of right be decided in terms of exceptions rather than in terms of defeasibility. A theory of rights, therefore, requires an exception-generating mechanism which will allow us to reconcile the fact that rights are not absolute with the fact that they are not defeasible. The absence of such a mechanism in Dworkin's theory of rights is one of its primary weaknesses.

The problem of reconciling the conditionality of rights with their indefeasibility is not unique to rights alone, but a parallel can be found in regard to nearly all rules or rule-governed practices. The problem arises whenever a rule or practice is applied to situations which fall under or within its description, but when in the unique circumstances of the particular case its application would result in irrational results or would result in consequences in conflict with the point or goal of the rule or practice. The dilemma arises in the context of rights because appealing to rights is a kind of social practice, and there is a close interrelationship between rights and rules in that rights can be derived from rules, and rules from rights.

If rights have an exception-generating mechanism it will be rule-governed, and if there is such a mechanism it will likely reflect a mechanism common to most rule-governed practices, if we are correct in assuming that the problem exists for rights because of the connection between rights and rules.

An adequate theory of rights, therefore, will require an adequate theory of rules. Such a theory should not only resolve the apparent incompatibility of the conditionality and indefeasibility of rights, but should also shed light on the relationship of rights and rules.

An analysis of what such a structure might look like has been offered elsewhere by the authors.[6] There we argue that the structure of a rule can be shown by the following schema, where *R* stands for rule, *C* conduct, *b* the goal of the rule, and the arrow $\rightarrow$ shows causal relationship:

$R \rightarrow C \rightarrow b$, unless

(I) $\sim(R \rightarrow C)$, or

(II) $\sim(C \rightarrow b)$, or

(III) $C \rightarrow b$, but also the loss of a positive value greater than the positive value of *b*, or the gain of a negative value greater than the positive value of *b*.

We will shorten (III) to "*b* and something worse than *b*," asking the reader to keep in mind that the shortened version means (III) as set out above. According to this schema a rule is to be compiled with (I) unless under the particular circumstances rules cannot affect behaviour as in infancy or some forms of insanity, or (2) unless following the rule will not achieve the goal or point of the rule, or (3) where although the goal of the rule will be achieved if the rule is followed, a more important positive value is lost or a negative result is achieved which is greater than not achieving the goal, as in the cases of necessity in the law. If 1, 2, or 3 occur, we have a defence, all of which constitutes an exception to the rule. Thus the form of the rule generates its exceptions. In other

[6] S. C. Coval and J. C. Smith, 'The Causal Theory of Law,' *Cambridge Law Journal* 36 (1977): 110.

words, we incorporate into our description of a rule the conditions, in the form of a ceteris paribus clause.

The facts of *Grosvenor Park Shopping Centre* v. *Waloshin*,[7] and *Harrison* v. *Carswell*,[8] a paradigm example of a hard case, can be used to illustrate how the exception-generating structure of rules not only provides an answer in hard cases, but reconciles the conditional nature of rights with their indefeasibility. In these two cases an injunction was sought against striking employees who were picketing in front of the shop where they were employed. Unlike the normal case of picketing where the pickets are located on the public sideway or roadway, the pickets in these two cases were on private property since the shop was located in the middle of a shopping centre. Under the existing rules of law the picketing would be illegal as it would constitute a trespass. Unless such picketing were permissible, however, the striking employees would have no economic sanction in their collective bargaining. We thus have a conflict between the owner's right of property and the employee's right to picket. In the *Grosvenor* case the Court held that when the owner invited the public onto the premises, he gave up the right to exclusive possession, and therefore could not maintain a trespass action. In denying an important right of property, the Court acted contrary to the principle of the indefeasibility of rights, giving us a classic example of a hard case making bad law. In *Harrison* v. *Carswell* the Supreme Court of Canada overruled the *Grosvenor* case, and in doing so deprived the employees of their right to picket, and thus treating the right of property as more or less absolute.

In the majority judgment of Mr. Justice Dickerson, the Court indirectly reaffirmed the principle of the indefeasibility of rights by rejecting the doctrine of balancing of interests and affirming the importance of certainty and stability of expectations for the law. In his dissenting judgment, the Chief Justice indirectly reaffirmed the principle of the conditional nature of rights when he

---

[7] (1964) 46 D.L.R. (2d) 750.
[8] [1976] 2 S.C.R. p. 200.

stated that the loss of the right to picket far outweighed the minor infringement on the right of property, which would follow if the picketing were allowed.

Under our analysis the form of the rule generates the exception as a case of *b* and something worse than *b*. That this is such a case is confirmed by the reversal by legislation of the effects of the decision of *Harrison* v. *Carswell.*[9]

It could be argued that in deciding whether we have a case of a result which is worse than the goal of the rule, or protecting the interest of the right, we inevitably must resort to balancing interests, and thus the indefeasibility of rights will be denied. If the judgment as to which is the most important is a subjective one, the criticism will be valid. If, however, the ordering can be shown to be entailed in the existing law itself, the judgment will be objective, and the criticism, therefore, not valid. If rules and rights are subject by their very nature to the ceteris paribus clause, and the ordering is already contained within the law, the exception is not a post facto limitation on the right, but was entailed within the right, even though we may not have been aware of its existence because of not having made the necessary calculation or actually not having drawn the necessary inferences until an actual specific dispute had arisen.

Exactly this method of judicial reasoning was followed in the American case of *Schwartz-Torrance Investment Corporation* v. *Bakery and Confectionery Worker's Union, Local 31*,[10] the facts of which were similar to the *Grosvenor* case and *Harrison* v. *Carswell.* While in that case the Court spoke of itself as "balancing interests," it in fact inferred the ordering of goals from the law itself. The Court inferred that the goals of the law of collective bargaining took priority over the goals of the law of private property in the particular circumstances of the case because:

1. The Legislature has expressly declared that the public policy of Califor-

---

[9] Petty Trespass Act, R.S.M. 1970, c. P50, s. 5 as am. S.M. 1976, c. 71, s. 2.
[10] 394 P. 2d 921.

nia favors concerted activities of employees for the purpose of collective bargaining or other mutual aid or protection.[11]

2. The Legislature in dealing with trespasses [amendments to the criminal trespass law] ... has specifically subordinated the rights of the property owner to those of persons engaging in lawful labor activities.[12]
3. The policy of the state as expressed in the Labor Code accords with that embodied in federal legislation.[13]
4. Picketing ... involves an exercise of the constitutionally protected right of freedom of speech.[14]
5. The countervailing interest which plaintiff endeavors to vindicate emanates from the exclusive possession and enjoyment of private property ... Plaintiff suffers no significant harm in the deprivation of absolute power to prohibit peaceful picketing upon property to which it has invited the entire public.[15]

The Court, in conclusion, said

We conclude that the picketing in the present case cannot be adjudged in the terms of absolute property rights; it must be considered as part of the law of labor relations, and a balance cast between the opposing interests of the union and the lessor of the shopping center. The prohibition of the picketing would in substance deprive the union of the opportunity to conduct its picketing at the most effective point of persuasion: the place of the involved business. The interest of the union thus rests upon the solid substance of public policy and constitutional right; the interest of the plaintiff lies in the shadow cast by a property right worn thin by public usage.[16]

The *Schwartz-Torrance* decision gives us neither a hard case as in *Harrison* v. *Carswell*, nor bad law as in the *Grosvenor* case; rather, an exception to the general law of trespass was inferred from the law itself. Thus the principle of the indefeasibility of rights was not infringed as it was in the *Grosvenor* case, nor was the principle of the conditional nature of rights infringed as it was in *Harrison* v. *Carswell*.

---

11 Supra, note 10 at p. 922.
12 Id..
13 Id..
14 Id. at p. 923.
15 Id. at p. 924.
16 Id. at p. 926.

## 2.

Our analysis of the structure of rules and method of resolving the apparent inconsistency of the principle of the indefeasibility of rights with the principle of the conditional nature of rights assumes that we can infer from the law a set of goals and their interrelated orderings under specified sets of conditions. This set of ordered goals can be viewed as a matrix. We can tell whether a particular result is worse than *b* by determining its place in the goal matrix of the law. This can be done by seeing how those results and *b* are ordered in other areas of the law or by tracing the causal relations to a pair of goals having a fairly stable ordering. This task only becomes difficult when we are not certain of the cause-effect relations.

We can see that this is in fact the case by examining any particular area of the law. Our collective bargaining example focused on an area of the matrix concerning goals relating to the use and enjoyment of private property. The use and enjoyment of private property is an instrumental goal causally related to some very important and fundamental higher ordered goals such as privacy and shelter. But in the dispute in question, the use and enjoyment of private property was related to the goals of making profit through running a business enterprise, while the goal of communicating to the public through picketing, in the context of a labour dispute, is causally related to carrying out effective collective bargaining, which in turn is related to the earning of a living by individuals collectively selling their labour. The labour legislation of most jurisdictions furnishes many examples of the goals of collective bargaining dominating private property where only business interests are at stake.[17] And where courts have prohibited picketing on private property, legislation making such picketing

[17] s. 87, Labour Code of British Columbia R.S.C. 1973 (second session) chapt. 122.

lawful has often shortly followed.[18] Where, on the other hand, the freedom to communicate through picketing is sought for other purposes, such as supporting labour disputes in which the picketers themselves are not directly involved, there is no clear ordering of goals such that the application of the traditional rules relating to trespass gives us a case of *b* and something worse than *b*.

The rights of ownership or property in land reflect the dominance of the goals achievable through land use over other conflicting goals, while the limitations reflect the domination of other more important goals over those relating to the use of land. The limitations on the occupier of land in regard to protecting his property, for example, that traps may not be set for trespassers,[19] reflect the dominance of the goals of physical safety over the exclusivity of the use of private property. If a court reverses that ordering, we would consider it wrong in law. Our opinion that a particular case is wrongly decided is generally based on the recognition that the decision orders two goals in relationship to each other contrary to the way those goals are generally ordered in the law. Consider Lord Reid's statement in *Herrington* v. *British Railways Board*[20] that the decision of the same Court in *Robert Addie and Sons (Colliers) Ltd.* v. *Dumbreck*[21] settled the law in both England and Scotland in regard to the liability of occupiers of land for injuries to trespassers and, at the same time, that the case was wrongly decided.[22] It cannot be said that the *Addie* case was wrongly decided because it was inconsistent with other authorities because, until it was overruled in the *Herrington* case, by the same Court, the *Addie* case was the final authority on the

---

18 Zeller's (Western) Ltd. v. Retail Clerks Union, Local 1518 (1962), 36 D.L.R. (2d) 581 (B.C.C.A.); Zeller's (Western) Ltd. v. Retail Clerks Union, Local 1518 (1963), 42 D.L.R. (2d) 583 (B.C.C.A.); Section 85 Labour Code of British Columbia R.S.B.C. 1973 (second session) chapt. 122. Petty Trespass Act R.S.M. 1970, cP50, s. 5 as am. S.M. 1976, c71, 52.

19 Bird v. Holbrook (1828) 4 Bing. 628.

20 [1972] A.C. 877.

21 [1929] A.C. 358.

22 Supra note 20 at pp. 893 and 898.

subject. The only possible grounds for saying that it was wrong (in law) is the fact that by holding the position that an occupier owes no duty of care to a potential trespasser, the goals of the freedom of use of property by the owner are given priority over the goal of prevention of physical harm to persons, while throughout the rest of the law the goal of prevention of harm to persons takes priority over the interests of the property holder.

The law of nuisance reflects the ordering of goals arising from conflict between incompatible uses of land. The following case furnishes a typical example. The owners of summer cottages on a river brought an action against a company which was discharging effluent waste into the river in the operation of their kraft paper mill with the result that the fish died and the water had a foul odour and taste. The dispute pitted the plaintiff's interest in clean water and pleasant surroundings (goal $b^1$) against the defendant's interests in economically and efficiently running their plant (goal $b^2$). The precedents generally ordered $b^1$ over $b^2$, and the Court followed them and granted an injunction, the effect of which would have been to close down the mill.[23] The trial decision was upheld in the Ontario Court of Appeal[24] and in the Supreme Court of Canada.[25]

However, because the result of the injunction would have been the loss of jobs of an entire community which relied on the mill for employment, the Ontario Legislature promptly passed an act which specifically exempted the defendant company from the effects of the injunction.[26] The ordering of goals reflected in the general rules relating to the rights of Riparian owners and the law of nuisance is $b^1$ over $b^2$ which we denote as $b^1/b^2$. Where, however, the effect of achieving $b^1$ led to a major loss of employment of a community, we have a case of $b^1$ and something worse than $b^1$, $\sim b^3$. We shall symbolize employment in the community by

---

23 Mckie v. The K.V.P. Co. [1948] 3 D.L.R. 201.

24 [1949] 1 D.L.R. 39.

25 [1949] 4 D.L.R. 497.

26 The K.V.P. Company Limited Act, Ontario, Statutes 1950, Chapter 33.

$b^3$ and the correlative evil, loss of employment in the community, as $\sim b^3$. (In general we assume that any *desideratum* will have a correlative evil, which we will symbolize with the tilda sign.) The ordering of goals now represented by the Law of Ontario is $b^1/b^2$ except where $b^3$ is at stake, in which case $b^2/b^1$ since $b^3/b^1$.

The proper ordering of these three goals vis-à-vis each other had been anticipated a number of years earlier by the Ontario Court of Appeal when it refused to give an injunction against a tobacco factory in an action for nuisance for creating an obnoxious odour, where the effect of the injunction would be to close the factory and place 200 men out of work. The Court stated:[27]

> In the case at bar there is obviously the greatest disparity between the advantage to the plaintiff to be gained by the granting of an injunction and the inconvenience and disadvantage which the defendant and others would suffer in consequence thereof. The plaintiff has been subject to some special discomfort, though it may be a question how great the discomfort is; presumably his property has been diminished in value, at least to some extent; but for all this he can be compensated in money. On the other hand the defendant's factory, employing it is said some 200 men, has been equipped with every known device for preventing the escape of fumes and smell; it is impossible to avoid the discomfort caused to the plaintiff without stopping the operation of the factory altogether; to grant an injunction prohibiting the present nuisance would mean the closing of the plant, resulting not merely in loss to the defendant but in unemployment disastrous to a small community. It is not as if the defendant has acted in some arbitrary manner, invading with its operations a residential district; it is carrying on one of the normal industries of the district. Unfortunately it has caused the plaintiff some injury; for this there should be a remedy; but the remedy, to avoid gross injustice, must be not an injunction but damages.

Here we have a paradigm example of a Court recognizing a case of $b$ and something worse than $b$. If the injury is to human health, however, then an injunction would be the appropriate remedy because physical well-being outranks almost every other goal in the law.

---

[27] Bottom v. Ontario Leaf Tobacco Co., [1935] 2 D.L.R. 699 (Ont. C.A.) at p. 704.

The matrix-like structure of goals relating to land use can be found in other areas of the law. We can infer, for example, from the existence of the law of torts that certain values such as physical well-being take precedence over freedom of action. We can infer from the existence of the law of defamation that protection of reputation takes priority over freedom of communication. We can infer from the fact that truth is a complete defence to an action in defamation that truth is more important than protection of reputation. We can infer from the defence of absolute privilege, whereby utterances in particular circumstances give rise to no liability even though they are false and defamatory, that freedom of communication is essential for certain activities such as adjudication in courts of law or law-making in legislatures, and that in these circumstances freedom of communication is more important then reputation. This is because it is instrumental to achieving goals such as truth, which is higher in the stable ordering than is reputation or the goals to which reputation might be an instrument. We can infer from the defence of qualified privilege that in regard to many relationships such as that of employer-employee, or in regard to the activities of various associations such as clubs, businesses, or municipal councils, while freedom of communication is more important than protection of reputation, complete or unlimited freedom is not necessary for the proper functioning of the relationship or activities. Communications which are not relevant or which extend to a wider audience than is necessary are not protected. Thus, the ordering of the goals of freedom of communication and protection of reputation reverses back and forth according to the priority of other goals to which they are causally related.

Just as each cause of action reflects an ordering of goals, each defence to that cause of action reflects a reversal of the ordering under the conditions which give rise to the defence because those conditions bring into play further goals of a higher priority. We can infer from the existence of the tort of trespass to land that a set of goals related to the privacy possible through exclusive access to a space is given a higher priority by the law, than complete freedom of movement. If, however, the public highway is blocked and physical well-being is at stake, the defence of necessity will apply. Thus freedom of movement takes priority over privacy of space when life or health is in jeopardy.[28] The existence of the torts of assault, battery, and false imprisonment attest to the priority of the goals of protection of physical well-being and liberty over the range of goals sought by activity which would consitute the torts. Wherever the defence of justification functions, however, other goals, such as law enforcement and the apprehension of criminals, are given an even higher priority. The fact that no court would ever find a rescuer of a would-be suicide liable for an assault in preventing the self-destruction of the plaintiff, reflects the fact that the law places a higher priority on the preservation of life than on the right not to be caused minor harm or freedom of choice.[29]

## 3.

One might ask at this point how the goal of a rule is ascertained. A good deal of discussion is to be found in case law regarding the purposes or goals of particular legal rules. Often statutes contain in their preambles or elsewhere the purposes of the legislation. Even without such express statements, however, the goals of the law and their orderings can be indirectly inferred. The patterns of inference would be little different than those we normally use to infer the purpose of people's actions. We have a general background of experience by which we know that certain kinds of actions achieve certain kinds of results. When we see people intentionally doing those kinds of actions we can infer that the results which generally would follow are desired by the actor. It seems to us that the patterns of inference by which we decide purpose and preference can be as clearly defined as those which we use elsewhere in judicial reasoning. Once it is made clear to drafters of

---

28 Dwyer v. Staunton, [1947] 4 D.L.R. 393.

29 F. Bates, 'Consenting to the Necessary, *Australian Law Journal* 46 (1972):73.

legislation that rules cannot function properly without goals, the problem of ascertaining the goal of a rule should be enormously diminished.

There may be legal cases or statutes where it is not possible to ascertain with any degree of certainty a particular set of goals and their ordering. These would be few, however, as given time, the law generally eliminates useless or counterproductive precedents by the action of higher courts overruling them, distinguishing them, or merely ignoring them. Otiose legislation will eventually be repealed or simply no longer applied. Our thesis does not require that we can always infer from the law a set of goals and their orderings which will always generate a correct answer. We will have made out a case for our analysis if we can show that it is possible in general to ascertain legal goals and their ordering, and that we get better decision-making in terms of stability of expectations, certainty, consistency, and justice, if we use as premises of legal arguments, the goals of the law and their ordering rather than a subjective form of balancing of interests or an appeal to public policy or morality.

A further argument for our thesis that we can infer legal goals and their ordering from the law is the fact that judges do carry out patterns of judicial reasoning of this nature.

Courts have long recognized that there is a marked distinction between general notions of public good, expediency, or welfare, and the goals of the law. Some confusion has arisen because the term public policy has been used to refer to both. The courts have been extremely reluctant to use the former as premises in judicial reasoning since it leads to uncertainty, while no such problem is found with the latter. Concerning public policy, Mr. Baron Parke wrote the following in *Egerton* v. *Brownlowe*:[30]

> This is a vague and unsatisfactory term, and calculated to lead to uncertainty and error, when applied to the decision of legal rights; it is capable of being understood in different senses; it may, and does, in its ordinary sense, mean "political expedience," or that which is best for the common good of the community; and in that sense there may be every variety of opinion, accord-

[30] 10 E.R. 359 at 408.

> ing to education, habits, talents, and dispositions of each person, who is to decide whether an act is against public policy or not. To allow this to be a ground of judicial decision, would lead to the greatest uncertainty and confusion. It is the province of the statesman, and not the lawyer, to discuss, and of the legislature to determine, what is the best for the public good, and to provide for it by proper enactments. It is the province of the judge to expound the law only; the written from the statutes: the unwritten or common law from the decisions of our predecessors and of our existing courts, from text-writers of acknowledged authority, and upon the principles to be clearly deduced from them by sound reason and just inference; not to speculate upon what is the best, in his opinion, for the advantage of the community. ... The term "public policy" may indeed be used only in the sense of the policy of the law, and in that sense it forms a just ground of judicial decision.

Mr. Justice Cresswell made the same distinction when he stated: "I presume we are not asked our opinions as to public policy, but as to the law; and I apprehend that when in our law-books of reports we find the expression it is used somewhat inaccurately instead of 'the policy of the law.'"[31] Mr. Baron Alderson in the same case states, "if by public policy is meant the object and policy of a particular law, then I readily accept it as a rule" but public policy in the sense of "prevailing opinion, from time to time, of wise men" would "introduce an ever-shifting principle of decision, and no case hereafter could be ever determined upon precedents, if it was to be adopted."[32] Well over a hundred years later in *Warwick* v. *Townsend & Sons*, following the same pattern of decision-making, Lord Diplock asserts that when a judge is "confronted by the choice whether or not to extend by analogy to circumstances in which it has not previously been applied a principle to which has been applied in previous cases where the circumstances although different had some features in common with those of the case which he has to decide," they ought to examine the goals and policies of the law. He writes:[33]

---

31 Id. at p. 394.

32 Id. at p. 402.

33 [1979] 3 W.L.R. 68 at p. 75. See also Parry v. Cleaver [1970] A.C. 1 at p. 19; Hill v. C.A. Parsons & Co. Ltd. [1971] 3 All E.R. 1345 at p. 1355; and Harry v. Kreutzinger, 95 D.L.R. (3d) 231 at p. 241–2.

Where over a period of years there can be discerned a steady trend in legislation which reflects the view of successive Parliaments as to what the public interest demands in a particular field of law, development of the common law in that part of the same field which has been left to it ought to proceed upon a parallel rather than a diverging course.

## 4.

In any case where the dispute reflects a conflict between the interest of the plaintiff and a different interest of the defendant, the decision concluding the dispute will represent an ordering of those two or more sets of interest vis-à-vis each other under other circumstances like those of the particular case. Such a decision furnishes us not only with a rule regarding the particular legal issues at stake, but with a precedent regarding the ordering of the two goals. Any piece of legislation which in any way prescribes or prohibits certain kinds of behaviour and which, in so doing, furthers one interest at the expense of another, also reflects an ordering of goals under particular conditions. Precedents and legislation, therefore, are not just a source of rules; they also furnish us with a complex set of orderings by which we can tell if we have a case of $b$ and something worse than $b$. Nearly every legal principle embodies a generalization about the priority of one set of goals over another, and every statement of legal policy attests to the primacy of certain goals over others with which they may come into competition. Just as each precedent or statutory rule reflects an ordering of goals, each exception to the rule reflects a reversal of the ordering under the conditions which give rise to the exception, because those conditions bring into play further goals of a higher priority.

To see how this works in detail, let us assume that the plaintiff's case entails that $b^1$ should dominate $b^2$, and that the court finds for the plaintiff. We may derive from this precedent, the rule "Do $C$ in order to achieve goal $b^1$ ceteris paribus," and an ordering of $b^1$ over $b^2$. And if under particular conditions $x$, the doing of $C$ will give us $b^1$ and a $\sim b^3$, and if under conditions like $x$, judicial decisions or legislation have ordered $b^3$ over $b^1$, then $b^1$ and a

$\sim h^3$ will be a case of *h* and something worse than *h*. Whenever conditions *x* arise, the law should generate an exception to the rule. So the rule can now be restated as "Do *C*, except under conditions *x*, in order to achieve $h^1$." The rule and its exception now give us the following orderings $h^1/h^2$ except where $\sim h^3$, or $h^1/h^2$ except under conditions *x*, where $h^2/h^1$.

Conditions *x* furnish the causal link to a $\sim h^3$. And it is thus the presence of *x* which distinguishes a case which falls under the exception from one which falls under the more general rule. In this way, the rules of the law are causally related and reconciled. It is these causal ties which make the law function systematically. Each rule is linked in causal chains to the higher ordered shared goals. The exceptions to the rule limit its function to only those occasions where the causal links to accepted goals continue to function.

Each individual conflict ideally is resolved consistent with the ongoing processes of social life. The matrix of the law thus is the accumulation of wisdom from generations of experience in coping with social conflict. This communal wisdom, which is reflected in the goal orderings of the legal matrix, is a sounder basis of decision than a private individual weighing of values by a single judge could ever be.

The implications of the ordering of two goals in a particular decision or statute may be carried over to cover new cases requiring an ordering of the same two goals (all else being equal), if those goals bear the same causal relations to the other goals of the matrix. This allows us to use legislation and cases having different facts as precedents where there are similar goals at stake. Our stock of possible premises is thus enlarged because the breadth of cases and legislation is extended.

If there is a new factor present which was not present in the earlier case and which bears a causal connection to a more important goal such that achieving the goal reflected by the precedent would result in the loss of the more important goal, then the earlier case will not serve as a precedent.

Hard cases are hard because they do not fall clearly within any particular rule, or because there are competing applicable precedents available for both sides. However, when the precedents are viewed as including their goals, a reason can be found for assigning a hard case to a particular precedent. The decision is still reached in a rule-governed rather than an ad hoc way because the exceptions to the rules are generated in a rule-governed manner.

If the common law position alone is considered, the Court of Appeal decision in *Boston* v. *Bagshaw*[34] would be an example of such a hard case. In that case the defendant auctioneers sold three pigs to a man who gave his name as "Boston of Rugeley" and left with the pigs without paying for them. The auctioneers requested the police to put the matter on a television program called "Police 5," devoted to seeking the help of the public in obtaining information on, or the whereabouts of, criminals. The broadcast took place, and the plaintiff, a farmer in Rugeley by the name of Boston, brought an action in libel.

The Court found the common law position to have been altered by Sections 7 and 9(2) of the Defamation Act, 1952.[35] Item 12 in the schedule gives a qualified privilege to

> A copy or fair and accurate report or summary of any notice or other matters issued for the information of the public by or on behalf of any government department, officer, of state, local authority or chief officer of police.

In a common law jurisdiction without such legislation, this would be a hard case as there are no decisions directly on point. Generally, privileges are not extended to situations involving communication to a broader sector of the public except in the case of fair and accurate reports of the proceedings of court, parliamentary, or other similar specified bodies. There is, in other words, no common law precedent for a qualified privilege in a situation where publication is to the public in general. There is, however, no case which expressly denies the possibility of such a case arising, and a

---

34 [1966] 1 W.L.R. 1126 (C.A.).
35 (15 & 16 Geo. 6 & 1 Eliz. 2, C. 66).

simple report of a matter by a citizen to the police is covered by a privilege.[36]

To resolve such a case in a jurisdiction which does not have a statutory qualified privilege, we first identify the relevant legal goals:

$b^1$ – encouraging citizens to aid in law enforcement.
($b^1$ can be derived from the various privileges against actions in assault, battery or false imprisonment which are provided citizens who aid in law enforcement)

$b^2$ – the protection of the reputation of the citizens
($b^2$ can be derived from the law of defamation).

The issue can be stated as whether $b^1$ is to prevail over $b^2$ or $b^2$ over $b^1$ in the circumstances of this case. The qualified privilege of a person who merely makes a report to the police, while it places $b^1$ over $b^2$, does not do so in circumstances such as these, since the damage to $b^2$ is much greater than usual, as it involves publication to the general public. The tort of malicious prosecution shows us that $b^1$ is an important goal of the law because the defences are so wide. The presence of malice, a lack of reasonable and probable cause, the threat or possibility of imprisonment, and termination of the proceedings in the plaintiff's favour are all necessary conditions for success; the absence of any one is sufficient to defeat the action.

We know that $b^2$, protecting a person's reputation, can come into conflict with $b^1$, encouraging citizens to aid in law enforcement, since any report of a crime is defamatory of the person alleged to have committed it. (The goal of encouraging citizens to aid in law enforcement would be eroded if an action in defamation, which requires only the presence of malice to defeat the qualified privilege, could succeed where an action in malicious prosecution would fail because of the absence of any of the necessary conditions of that tort.) We know further that the law of malicious prosecution exludes an action of defamation under all

---

36 Wing Lee v. Jones [1954] 1 D.L.R. 520 (Man Queen's Bench).

conditions.[37] That is, where a plaintiff loses an action of malicious prosecution because of the absence of one of the necessary conditions for the tort, he cannot then turn around and rely on an action of defamation which is not subject to the same limiting defenses.

From the tort of malicious prosecution we can derive an ordering of goals $b^1$ and $b^2$, which will help us solve hard cases in defamation. The form of a rule, $R \rightarrow C \rightarrow b$ unless b and something worse than $b$, generates the exception. The general rule is that a publication to the public at large is not covered by qualified privilege. The rule is subject to a few statutory and common law exceptions where the achieving of the protection of reputation interferes with more important goals. This case would be an additional exception. The relevant provisions of the United Kingdoms Defamation Act[38] furnish a direct precedent for ordering $b^1$ over $b^2$ and could be so used if a similar case arose in a different jurisdiction not having this legislation.

The following hard case opposes the right to do what one wishes with his own body against the goal of the law to preserve life. It is a hard case because there is no precedent directly on point. Our hypothetical test case is as follows. A member of the Jehovah Witness sect who is to undergo an operation for removal of a part of an ulcerated stomach specifically directs the doctor not to give him a blood transfusion, even at the risk of death. The doctor answers by stating that the operation is straightforward and a blood transfusion will not be necessary. During the operation, the patient haemorrhages as a result of unforeseen complications. The doctor then administers a blood transfusion to the unconscious patient to preserve his life. The patient later sues the doctor for a surgical battery.

---

[37] Howard v. Thompson, 21 Wend. 319; Halberstadt v. New York Life Insurance Co. 194 N.Y. Rep. 1 at 8. F.V. Harper, 'Malicious Prosecution, False Imprisonment and Defamation,' *Texas Law Review* **15** (1937): 157 at 169.

[38] (15 & 16 Geo. 6 & Eliz. 2, C. 66).

Counsel for the plaintiff cites cases where doctors have been found liable for removing, without consent, organs which have been discovered to be diseased, during the course of the operation. In these cases, however, life was not at stake. These cases indicate the existence of the right but tell us little of its limits.

The principal case upon which the counsel for the plaintiff relies, however, is *Mulloy* v. *Hop Sang*.[39] The defendant's hand was badly injured in a car accident, and he was taken to the nearest hospital where the plaintiff surgeon examined him. During the examination the defendant told the plaintiff to "fix up" his hand but specifically instructed him not to amputate as he wished his own doctor in his own city about sixty miles away to make that decision. The plaintiff surgeon concluded that amputation was inevitable, and decided to amputate while the defendant was still anaesthetized to avoid the risk of blood poisoning. The defendant refused to pay the bill and in response to the plaintiff's suit countersued for a medical battery. The Court dismissed the suit for payment and found liability for a medical battery even though "the operation was necessary and performed in a highly satisfactory manner" because consent had been specifically denied.

Counsel for the defendant could cite *Leigh* v. *Gladstone*[40] where a fasting suffragette prisoner was forcibly fed. The action for a battery was dismissed by the jury on their being directed that the forced feeding was necessary to preserve the prisoner's life. This case would carry little weight under the circumstances of the present case because of the argument that the rights of prisoners are not the same as those of other citizens.

The strongest case for the defendant would be *Marshall* v. *Curry*[41], where the plaintiff sued for a medical battery because the defendant surgeon had removed a testicle during a hernia operation. The defendant succeeded in establishing that since the testicle was diseased, its removal was necessary for the preservation of the

---

39 [1935] 1 W.W.R. 714 (Alta. Supreme Court, Appellate Division).

40 (1909) 26 T.L.R. 139.

41 [1933] 3 D.L.R. 260 (NSSC).

plaintiff's life. The Court rejected dealing with the case in terms of the fiction of an implied consent, but instead held that in case of an emergency which could not be anticipated and in which life is at stake, it is the duty of the doctor to "act in order to save the life or preserve the health of the patient."[42]

Our hypothetical hard case falls neatly between the two precedents of *Mulloy* v. *Hop Sang* and *Marshall* v. *Curry*. It is like *Mulloy* v. *Hop Sang* in that there was an express denial of consent, but unlike *Mulloy* v. *Hop Sang* in that life was at stake. In the latter respect, it is like *Marshall* v. *Curry*, but it is unlike *Marshall* v. *Curry* in that there was an express denial of consent.

If the case were to be decided on the basis of the balancing of interest, it would be difficult to predict the outcome. And when we put the above hypothetical case to a group of seventy judges in a seminar situation and asked them to give a hypothetical decision on the basis of balancing the interest, they split about evenly.

If we seek precedents elsewhere in the law where these goals (freedom to do as one wishes with one's body and preservation of life) have come into conflict, we will likely find some fairly consistent patterns of ordering. We know that the law does not force people to take medical treatment to preserve their health or lives, nor does it require people to take wise precautionary measures to keep well. Yet the law carefully regulates the practice of medicine and prohibits many kinds of harmful or valueless forms of treatment, thus severely limiting choice. However, the law does not force people to take medical treatment, even to preserve their lives, because carrying out the degree of supervision required to make such a law effective would seriously erode the right to control one's body for both well and sick alike, and the price of enforcement would be horrendous. It would be a case of *b* and something worse than *b*. Regulating the practice of medicine and controlling the sale and distribution of drugs, however, is a relatively easy matter.

All the various safety legislation which require people to take

---

42 Id. at p. 275.

precautions to preserve their own lives, such as the compulsory wearing of helmets by motor cyclists and the compulsory wearing of seat belts, show the priority of the preservation of life over that of freedom to do what one wishes with one's own body. Drug laws and laws governing other forms of victimless crimes, decisions of Courts in ordering blood transfusions,[43] laws regulating the practice of medicine, and laws which make the aiding of a suicide a crime all reflect the same ordering. Hypothetical cases in which the doctrine of necessity would apply (e.g., where a defendant assaults a plaintiff in order to prevent a suicide) would also probably reflect the law's placing the preservation of life above that of the right to do what one wishes with one's own body.[44]

A goal of the law is to encourage rescuers and people to take life-supporting or life-saving actions. The law apparently values the preservation of life over freedom of choice except where such an ordering requires costly, freedom-destroying regulation and supervision. The law does this not just because life is an important value, but because the cost to society of poor health and of the care of people who are rendered unable to manage their own lives is extremely high.

In our hypothetical case, the freedom of choice is related to religious belief. Would this causal link be sufficient to reverse the normal ordering of $b^1$ over $b^2$? Apparently not. Although the law gives a very high priority to freedom of belief, it also places all kinds of restrictions on religious practices. These limitations support rather than contradict the ordering of $b^1$ over $b^2$. In addition, an ordering of $b^1$ over $b^2$ in the case at hand would not seriously erode $b^2$ since the preservation of life makes continuing choices possible.

In the application of precedent the hypothetical case would fall under *Marshall* v. *Curry* rather than *Mulloy* v. *Hop Sang* because the fact that preservation of life was at stake is the more relevant fact.

---

43 Application of Georgetown College, (1964) 331 F. 2d 1000.
44 Supra note 29.

Whenever one ordering of a pair of goals will maximize only one goal at the extreme expense of another, while the converse ordering will maximize one goal, and produce only a minimal interference with the other, the latter is generally preferable. Even though the interest which we have in deciding what happens to our own bodies ($b^1$) takes precedence over the doctor's freedom to exercise judgment to achieve the best results for the health of the patient ($b^2$) (except where preservation of life is concerned), the law will order $b^2/b^1$ when that will give us $b^2$ plus little interference with $b^1$ and when $b^1/b^2$ would give us $b^1$ and a $\sim b^2$.

Cases when a person is charged with the consensual mercy killing of a spouse, or when a child is charged with the killing of a parent, when poison is administered at the request of a person who has a terminal illness and is suffering terrible pain also raise questions regarding the ordering of the two goals, the preservation of life and the freedom to do what one wishes with one's body. The Court would likely deal with such a case by convicting and then ameliorating the penalty. A better way, one which would not bring uncertainty or hypocrisy into the law, would be to bring such cases under the doctrine of necessity as a case of $b$ and something worse than $b$. They would thus be exceptions to the law of homicide. It is clear that if the goal of preservation of life is maintained in such cases, the right to control one's body would be seriously eroded. On the other hand, if the person is allowed the right to choose the termination of his life, the goal of the preservation of life is not seriously affected because the illness is terminal, and life brings little benefit. Agency has already been substantially diminished by the illness.

## 5.

Transitivity would allow us to extend our precedents even further. The principle of transitivity provides that any relation which holds between $x$ and $y$, and between $y$ and $z$, holds also between $x$ and $z$, i.e., for $x$, $y$, and $z$, and any relation $R$, if $xRy$ and $yRz$ then $xRz$. Using the relationship "more important than" in terms of the goal matrix, we know that if $b^1/b^2$ and $b^2/b^3$ then $b^1/b^3$.

If Precedent 1 gives us $b^1/b^2$

and Precedent 2 gives us $b^2/b^3$

then in a case requiring a choice between either $b^1/b^3$ and $b^3/b^1$ the law will choose $b^1/b^3$, other things being equal. If we can assume relevantly similar conditions, transitivity would allow us to go beyond any particular statute or precedent to new cases and to produce premises and make connections which are purely inferential.[45]

---

[45] Georg. H. Von Wright in *The Logic of Preference* (Edinburgh: Edinburgh University Press, 1963) at p. 21 gives *asymmetry* and *transitivity* as the formal properties of the relation of preference. He points out, however, at p. 22 that, "The transitivity of the relation of preference is not entirely uncontroversial. It is possible to imagine situations which may appear to be counterinstances to the transitivity of preference." Wright would, however, explain counter examples to transitivity in terms of a distinction between what he terms 'intrinsic' and 'extrinsic' preferences, or as a change in preference (see pp. 13–15). If *A* is chosen over *B*, and *B* is chosen over *C*, *C* might still be chosen over *A* if a reason for a preference was present in a choice as between *A* and *C* which would not be relevant in a choice as between *A* and *B* or between *B* and *C*. The choice between *A* and *C* would be an extrinsic preference and therefore not a counterexample to strict transitivity. It could be argued that the use of transitivity in a legal context is limited in that it might not be possible to be aware of all the reasons for a particular preference, or to know that conditions are relevantly the same for each of the three choices. For a discussion of some of the problems of the use of transitivity in making choices, see Bruce Chapman, 'Individual Rights and Collective Rationality: Some Implications for Economic Analysis of Law' in *Hofstra Law Review* 10 (1982): 455. If, however, there are unique factors present in the third choice of the trio of choices making up a transitivity argument, that are not present in the first two choices, and which would lead to an 'extrinsic' preference or furnish reasons for a different choice, those factors would still be argued in terms of the goals of the law and their orderings, and the cause-effect relationships to other goals of the system. The issue then becomes whether we will get better decisions in a hard case by assuming

We will again take a hypothetical medical situation as a test case. A defendant psychiatrist knows that his mentally ill patient suffers from the delusion that he has discovered a rich body of gold-bearing ore. He knows that the plaintiff, who is ignorant of the patient's mental illness, believes the story and plans to invest a substantial sum with him that will inevitably be lost. He knows also that if he were to warn the plaintiff, the relationship between himself and the patient would be terminated and the patient would decline any further psychiatric help. The defendant decides not to warn the plaintiff, who makes the investment, loses his money, and on discovering the defendant's knowledge, sues for damages for failing to warn him. The plaintiff's case is based on *Tarasoff* v. *The Regents of the University of California*[46] where a psychiatrist was held liable for failing to warn a third party when he knew that his mentally ill patient would likely cause that party harm. The difference between the *Tarasoff* case and our hypothetical case is that in *Tarasoff*, the danger was of physical injury, while in our hypothetical case the danger is financial loss. The defendant relies on the case of *Furness* v. *Fitchett*[47] where a doctor was held liable for giving a written statement to a husband describing the mental illness of his wife when he knew that the wife believed she was not mentally ill, that the continuation of that belief was important for her mental health and continuing treatment, and that the wife would likely discover the fact of her mental illness since the statement was to be used in litigation between the husband and wife related to their divorce.

The issue in our case is whether the goals achieved through confidentiality, $b^1$, are to predominate over the prevention of economic loss, $b^3$. This is a hard case because it is not directly governed by

---

if we can find no reasons for an extrinsic preference that the relevant characteristics are the same for the three choices, or whether we assume that the relevant characteristics can seldom be the same, even if we are unaware of the differences, and that using discretion in such hard cases would give us "better" judgments than the use of transitivity. We think the former to be the case.

46 529 P. 2d 553.

47 [1958] N.Z.L.R. 396.

either the *Tarasoff* case, which tells us only that $b^1$ is subordinate to the prevention of physical harm, nor by the *Furniss* v. *Fitchett* case, which tells us that $b^1$ prevails over the interest of the husband in gathering information for his pending litigation.

We know that a duty of confidentiality is a limit on freedom of communication, which we will identify as $b^2$. We know that $b^1/b^2$ because the law has recognized a duty of confidentiality in the doctor-patient relationship for example, *Furniss* v. *Fitchett* and *AB* v. *CD*.[48] We know that where there is a danger of physical harm we have a case of $b^1$ and something worse than $b^1$; therefore the order is reversed to $b^2/b^1$. Our case raises the issue of whether economic loss is a case of $b^1$ and something worse than $b^1$. We know, also, that the law gives freedom of communication a higher priority than the prevention of economic loss (*Derry* v. *Peek*[49]), since it does not recognize any liability for economic loss resulting from a negligent misstatement. (An exception is found in the *Hedly Byrne* v. *Heller*[50] case.)

So we have:

1. $b^1/b^2$ (*Furniss* v. *Fitchett*, and *AB* v. *CD*)
2. $b^2/b^3$ (*Derry* v. *Peek*)

Therefore: $b^1/b^3$.

So, there is no liability for the failure to warn because such a warning would be a breach of the duty of confidentiality.

The distinction between social policy and the policy or goals of the law, the ordering of those goals in terms of decisions in cases of conflict of interest, and the view of rules and rights subject to a ceteris paribus clause gives us a teleological theory of law which maintains the values of certainty and stability of expectations which are the rationale of legal positivism. It thus avoids the disjunctive choices of traditional theories as between bad law and hard cases, or justice and certainty. It furnishes an analytical structure applicable not only to legal rules and rights,

---

48 1853 15 Dunlop (Ct. of Sess.) 976.

49 (1889) 14 App. Cas. 337.

50 [1964] A.C. 465.

but to most social practices. It permits a rights theory of law to function consistent with the best values of positivism, and it furnishes one kind of resolution to the apparent contradiction between the indefeasibility and conditionality of rights. Finally, it furnishes a relationship between rules, justifying us in viewing the law as a system.

In legal philosophy the critical question is not whether a theory is true, because in law, theory does not just attempt to mirror reality; rather, the law also structures reality to follow theory. In this sense, law becomes what we believe it to be. The question raised by this paper, therefore, is best put by asking whether we would get a higher degree of certainty, consistency, and stability of expectations in the law, and at the same time more just decisions, if we were to use propositions about the goals of the law and their orderings as premises in judicial reasoning, rather than reverting to a subjective balancing of interests, appealing to a nebulous public policy, or merely applying the rules irrespective of the consequences.

While we would not claim that the goals of the law and their ordering will generate a correct answer to every hard case, we would maintain that as a minimum our view would have the salutory effect of producing a greater focus on the goals of laws and their interrelations, a subject which we ignore at the cost of exactly those things which laws are meant to further.

*University of British Columbia*

# INDEX